JOHN BERRIEN LINDSLEY

PAINTED BY CORNELIUS HANKINS FROM A STEEL ENGRAVING. THE PORTRAIT IS AT GEORGE PEABODY COLLEGE FOR TEACHERS, NASHVILLE, TENNESSEE

John Berrien Lindsley

Educator, Physician, Social Philosopher

By

JOHN EDWIN WINDROW

Chapel Hill
The University of North Carolina Press
1938

COPYRIGHT, 1938, BY
THE UNIVERSITY OF NORTH CAROLINA PRESS

To
LOUISE GRUNDY LINDSLEY

daughter of John Berrien Lindsley, whose care in preserving the manuscripts of her family and whose generous cooperation made possible this work and its publication

PREFACE

THE NASHVILLE Academy of Medicine assembled on the evening of December 16, 1897, in memorial service to a distinguished member, John Berrien Lindsley. The following statement, taken from the resolutions read on that evening, epitomizes the life of the man whose story is herein presented: "*Resolved,* That his long and worthy life as a scholar, teacher, medical journalist, historian, hygienist, minister, and philanthropist . . . has been unusually blessed and unselfishly useful."

This estimate of Dr. Lindsley by his colleagues was well warranted. He was indeed one of the South's most useful and versatile men. His intelligent and courageous efforts led to many social reforms. He founded the medical school of the University of Nashville, and thus contributed notably to the medical profession. He pioneered in the field of public education, and his efforts led to the founding of George Peabody College for Teachers. He labored in the interest of public health, and contributed vitally to the foundation of Tennessee's health program of today.

He was a thoughtful student and writer. A partial bibliography found in the annual reports of the American Historical Association for the years 1889-92 lists the titles of twenty-nine papers written by him. He compiled and edited the *Military Annals of Tennessee,* a volume of one thousand pages which was published in 1886. He wrote numerous manuscripts, which were included in reports or left unpublished.

In 1849, the year of a memorable cholera epidemic in the South, Dr. Lindsley began writing a diary, which he kept rather consistently for almost twenty years. During the South's darkest decade, he wrote penetratingly, usually philosophically, of the social, political, and economic conditions around him. The preservation of these diaries and other papers by his daughter, Louise G. Lindsley, made possible these pages.

Philip Lindsley, the father of John Berrien, is well known in educational literature as an educator and a student of the classics. The three volumes on his life published by the Lippincott Company as early as 1866 insure the permanency of his record. His son, John Berrien, whose contribution to society equaled or exceeded that of his father, lives only through the writings of his own pen. The purpose of this volume is to give a measure of recognition to one who in his day contributed so vitally to the public welfare.

Dr. Lindsley lived in a period of stark reality and tragedy. He saw the University of Nashville, over which his father had presided for twenty-five years, close because of epidemics and financial stress. The periodic visitation of cholera and yellow fever to Nashville and the South are vividly described by him in his several diaries. He saw friends and relatives suffer and die as a result of these scourges.

He saw the system of Negro slavery flourish and collapse, and watched the social structure of the region, which he and his family had helped to build, disintegrate around him. He knew the bitterness of a divided allegiance within his own family circle. His favorite brother-in-law, Randall McGavock, a colonel in the Confederate army, gave his life for the Southern cause on a hot hillside near Raymond, Mississippi. His brother Van, whose sympathies were with the North, supported the Union. The University of Nashville, over which Dr. Lindsley presided as chancellor, never recovered from the shock of war. Confronted by the grim realism of a tragic era, Dr. Lindsley maintained a poise which comes only from a deep and abiding philosophy.

The author is indebted to a number of friends and acquaintances for valuable assistance in the preparation of this volume. More help has been received than he has space adequately to relate. He wishes to acknowledge his indebtedness to Miss Louise G. Lindsley for making available to him the files, unpublished manuscripts, letters, and other private papers of the family. He owes a special debt of gratitude to Professor A. L. Crabb, whose encouragement and advice were invaluable during the progress of the study. He is obligated to Professor Charles E. Little, Professor Fremont P. Wirth, and Professor Frank Owsley for helpful suggestions on certain parts of the manuscript. Particularly does he desire to acknowledge the kindness of Bessie Bray Harris, who assisted in preparing the manuscript for publication. He is grateful for the service given by members of the library staff of Peabody College, the University of Pennsylvania Medical School, the University of Tennessee, the University of the South, Cumberland University, the Tennessee State Library, and the Library of the Tennessee Historical Society.

J. E. WINDROW

Nashville, Tennessee
July 1, 1938

CONTENTS

CHAPTER	PAGE
PREFACE	vii
I. PRELIMINARY YEARS	1
II. CHANCELLOR OF THE UNIVERSITY OF NASHVILLE	22
III. DURING THE CIVIL WAR	60
IV. PIONEER IN PUBLIC EDUCATION	84
V. CHAMPION FOR PUBLIC HEALTH	113

APPENDICES

    A. Chronological Outline of Lindsley's Life 164

    B. Lindsley's Writings 167

    C. Letters from William Walker 178

    D. Miscellaneous Correspondence 193

    E. Resolutions and Letters of Condolence on the Death of John Berrien Lindsley 203

    F. Record of Readings 1842-1863 Found in Dr. Lindsley's Diary 209

BIBLIOGRAPHY 229

INDEX 233

ILLUSTRATIONS

J. Berrien Lindsley .... *Frontispiece*

Facing page

Philip Lindsley 22

Professor Gerard Troost 32

University of Nashville—Medical Department 42

University of Nashville—Literary and Military Department 60

William Walker 84

JOHN BERRIEN LINDSLEY

CHAPTER I

PRELIMINARY YEARS

JOHN BERRIEN LINDSLEY was born in Princeton, New Jersey, October 24, 1822. He lived into the seventy-sixth year of a useful life, and died at his residence in Nashville, December 7, 1897. He was descended from the Lindsleys who were among the first settlers at Morristown, New Jersey, and the Lawrences who settled at Hell Gate, Long Island, in 1660. His ancestors on both sides emigrated to America following the downfall of the Cromwell party, to whose cause they were firm adherents.[1] He was named for his mother's grandfather, John Berrien, who died on April 22, 1772, while serving as chief justice of the Supreme Court of New Jersey.[2] His ancestry includes a number of families distinguished in American life. The Berriens, the Lawrences, the Condicts, and the Lindsleys are important names in the social, intellectual, and political development of our country.

The Berrien family, much respected for its integrity and moral worth, is understood to have been of French Huguenot origin. We find the Berriens first on Long Island in the vicinity of New York. Whether they came direct from France or from England or Holland is not definitely known. The distinguished Judge John Berrien, great-grandfather of John Berrien Lindsley, removed in early life from Long Island to Rocky Hill, or Rockingham, near Princeton, New Jersey. Judge Berrien's old home, occupied at the time of the Revolutionary War by his widow and children, was selected for the headquarters of George Washington and was used by Washington from August 24, 1783, until November 10 of the same year.[3] It was evidently while there

---

[1] *Southern Practitioner*, XX (1898), 35.
[2] Philip Lindsley, MS Diary, in the possession of Miss Louise G. Lindsley, of Nashville, Tennessee.   [3] *Ibid*.

that Washington wrote his farewell address to the army, which is dated "November 2, 1783, Rocky Hill near Princeton."[4] The Berrien home was bought in 1896 by the Washington Headquarters Association of Rocky Hill, which had been organized to restore and maintain it.[5] Judge Berrien was a trustee of Princeton University (then the College of New Jersey).

His son, John Berrien II, was a major during the Revolutionary War and was wounded at the battle of Monmouth. He later moved to Georgia, where a son, John McPherson Berrien, was born. This son graduated from Princeton in 1795 at the age of fifteen and became prominent in the political life of Georgia. In 1829 Jackson appointed him Attorney General in his Cabinet.[6] He resigned this position on account of the famous "Peggy O'Neil affair," Mrs. Berrien having declined to call on Mrs. Eaton.[7] In 1840 he returned to Washington as United States senator from Georgia and remained there until 1852. It is said that he was a brilliant and able man. John McPherson Berrien's father and John Berrien Lindsley's maternal grandmother were brother and sister.[8]

John Berrien Lindsley's maternal grandfather, Nathaniel Lawrence, was born on July 11, 1761, into a family of wealth and culture. "In 1776 he entered Princeton where he was admitted to the freshman class, half advanced." When classes were discontinued and the students dismissed because of the war, Nathaniel Lawrence joined the army as a lieutenant in a North Carolina regiment.[9] He was captured and held prisoner for about two years. Being exchanged, he became a captain in an independent corps, probably with the New York troops. He was present when General Washington took final leave of the officers of

[4] Fred L. Holmes, *George Washington Travelled This Way*, p. 165.
[5] The Lindsley Papers, in the possession of Miss Louise G. Lindsley, of Nashville, Tennessee. These papers consist of journals, diaries, private correspondence, unpublished manuscripts, addresses, and newspaper and magazine articles. Duplicate copies of most of the collection are found in the vault of Peabody College Library.
[6] James Parton, *Life of Andrew Jackson*, III, 288.
[7] *Ibid.*, pp. 302-357.
[8] Philip Lindsley, MS Diary. [9] *Ibid.*

the disbanded army in New York City on December 4, 1783. His own letter, which may be found among the Lindsley Papers, gives "a most affecting and graphic description of that truly sublime and deeply pathetic interview and farewell scene." Because of his service in the army, North Carolina granted him warrants for two tracts of land of 2,560 acres each.

Nathaniel Lawrence was granted the A.B. degree in the graduating class of 1783 at Princeton. The college records pay high tribute to him, both as a gallant officer (he is referred to as "Captain") and as an accomplished scholar. After graduating from Princeton, he studied law with a Judge Egbert Benson and soon attained eminence at the bar. He succeeded Aaron Burr as attorney general of the state of New York.[10] On April 14, 1787, he married Elizabeth Berrien, daughter of Judge John Berrien of Rockingham.[11] One child was born of this union, a daughter, Margaret, who married Philip Lindsley and became the mother of John Berrien Lindsley.

John Berrien Lindsley's paternal grandfather, Isaac Lindsley, married Phebe Condict on January 19, 1785.

It is understood that the Condict family came over from England and settled in New Jersey about the time that the Lindsleys came to this country. Tradition says they crossed the Atlantic in the same ship. Members of this family in Essex County, New Jersey, spell the name "Condit," but those in Morris County preserve the original English spelling, "Condict." The name in both forms occurs frequently in the catalogues of graduates of the College of New Jersey (Princeton). The clergy of this family have been for the most part pastors of Presbyterian, Dutch Reformed, or Congregational churches. It is said that the family were all Whigs during the Revolutionary War, several of them rather prominent. Among the latter were Colonel Ebenezer Condict, John Berrien Lindsley's great-grandfather, and Silas Condict, the brother of Ebenezer, both of Morris County, New Jersey. From Philip Lindsley's diary we read:

[10] The Lindsley Papers.   [11] Philip Lindsley, MS Diary.

The American army under Washington had their winter quarters at Morristown & vicinity, on two different occasions. The first time was in January 1777, immediately after the battles of Trenton & Princeton. The second was during the winter of 1779-80. The Pennsylvania line was also stationed here in the succeeding winter.

The Camp ground extended from Morristown to Mendham—along the south side of a range of lofty hills (there called mountains) within a mile of my grandfather Condict's then residence, & upon a portion of his farm. In the camp at or near Mendham (with his regiment in winter quarters) he died of the small-pox then raging among the troops, on the 2nd of April 1777, aged 40. His tomb is in the burying ground adjoining the Presbyterian Church in Mendham. He was born Feb. 23, 1736.

Silas Condict (my mother's uncle) his brother was a member of the State Convention, or, so called Provincial Congress, in 1774-5-6. He was a member of the Continental Congress from 1777 to 1789.

Dr. John Condict was a patriot soldier & surgeon during the struggles of his country for freedom; a member of the N. J. legislature, and a representative & senator in the Congress of the United States for thirty years in succession. (He was a cousin of Ebenezer and Silas.)

My father, Isaac Lindsley, and Phebe Condict were married Jan. 19th, 1785, by the Rev. Timothy Johnes D.D. of Morristown, N. J. Phebe Condict was the daughter of Col. Ebenezer Condict.

My mother often saw General Washington while the army had their winter quarters at Morristown and vicinity, and she retains a distinct recollection of his appearance, manners, etc. He occasionally visited at her mother's house, where was quartered General Gist, of the Maryland line. He sometimes dined there. He often amused himself with her as a playful child—spoke kind words to her about her father, whom he highly esteemed, and whose recent death (by small-pox in camp) he deeply deplored. She became greatly attached to him. His benevolent, affectionate, pleasant manner won her confidence, and caused her to forget the warrior in the friend.

She mentioned numerous little events and incidents characteristic of the good man—such as a child nine or ten years old would be likely to notice and to be impressed with. She was present in the old Presbyterian Church at Morristown, when General Washington partook of the Lord's Supper with the Rev. Dr. Timothy Johnes and his people, as narrated by Dr. Hosack in his life of De Witt Clinton (see also Barber and Howe's Historical Collections of New Jersey, p. 388).

She described to me, with minute particularity and accuracy, the localities, seats, tables, persons present and officiating—differing much from present modes and forms, but corresponding exactly with the usages of that day, and of the early period within my own memory.

She remarked that she had never seen a good—that is, a correct—likeness of Washington. Perhaps her opinion would have been different, had she ever beheld the general at the head of his troops or on the battle-field. The portraits are all too grave, solemn, warlike, to accord with the smiling, cheerful, benignant countenance of the social guest and orphan's friend—as she had known and loved him.[12]

The Lindsleys, who were among the earliest settlers of the New Haven colony, emigrated from a place not far southwest of London and settled at Bransford, Connecticut, prior to 1640. The tradition is that Colonel Francis Lindsley, with one or two brothers, left England during the latter part of the reign of Charles II on account of religious persecution, and that they were among the first colonists and proprietors of Morris County, New Jersey.[13]

The early Lindsley family was distinguished for its preachers and teachers. A number became college presidents, and we find Philip Lindsley stating in one of his journals that "about a dozen clergymen of our family have been known to me in my time."

Philip Lindsley, the father of John Berrien Lindsley, was one of the most influential men in the intellectual development of Tennessee and the Southwest. Sought by many institutions for presidential leadership, recognized as a scholar of profound learning, he at last yielded to the entreaties of the University of Nashville to become its chancellor, though he was at the time (1824) acting president of Princeton and had been invited to become president. He resigned his position at Princeton on September 28, 1824, and on October 15 set out for Nashville with his family—Mrs. Lindsley and four children. When the Lindsley family arrived in Nashville on December 24, 1824, John Berrien was exactly two years and two months old.

The other children born at Princeton were: Adrian Van Sin-

[12] Also in Le Roy J. Halsey, *The Works of Philip Lindsley*, III, 61.
[13] Dr. M. B. DeWitt, *Biographical Sketch of Dr. John Berrien Lindsley*.

deren, born September 8, 1814; Nathaniel Lawrence, born September 11, 1816; a son, born August 20, 1818, who died September 12, 1818; and Margaret Lawrence, born August 28, 1819. Eliza Berrien was born March 23, 1825, in Nashville and a son, Philip, who died in early childhood, was born there June 27, 1835.

There are few references to the life of John Berrien Lindsley prior to his entering the University of Nashville at the age of fourteen. Mr. M. C. Venable of North Carolina related in later life that his class at Princeton had presented congratulations to Philip Lindsley upon the important occasion of the birth of John Berrien on October 24, 1822, whereupon they had been released from recitation that day. From Philip Lindsley's diary we learn that John Berrien was baptized on May 18, 1823, in the chapel of Princeton University by the Rev. Dr. Samuel Miller. Scattered through the family diaries and correspondence we find evidence that he was at an early age a very studious and observing lad, fond of outdoor life and especially interested in nature study. Swimming, boating, hiking, bowling, and horseback riding were among his favorite sports. He became when a boy a student of conchology and to the end of his life remained interested in the subject. In Volume I of "Thoughts and Hints," a journal kept by Dr. Lindsley, under date of August 27, 1862, we read:

When a boy, four books were devoured by me with perfect avidity, on account of the intensely interesting narratives they contained. The Book of Revelation, the *Arabian Nights' Entertainments, Pilgrim's Progress,* and *Robinson Crusoe.* My earliest recollections of books are of these. Warm, bright, glowing, varied, ethereal, charming, magnificent, fairy scenes, pictures and images they brought up before the mental vision never equalled in all my reading since, and only parallelled by the rich and unchangingly glorious wonders of the material creation; which indeed furnish to the eye and the mind a perpetual feast of nectar and sweets.

The well-organized life led by John Berrien Lindsley in later years indicates a carefully planned and well-ordered development during this early formative period. That this was a sheltered

PRELIMINARY YEARS 7

period for him and for his brothers and sisters is indicated in the tribute paid by their father to their mother at the time of her death on December 5, 1845:

In her youthful days, in the city of New York and elsewhere, she had seen enough of fashionable life to be able to estimate at its face value the whole circle of its vanities and enchantments. She studiously and resolutely avoided every approach to its insidious and un-Christian dominion. She kept her children from its allurements. She neither read, nor permitted them to read, novels, romances, or any books calculated to dissipate the mind or to weaken the moral and religious principles which she daily inculcated and uniformly exemplified in her conduct. None of them ever learned even to dance. . . . Nor were they suffered to look into a ball room or theatre. . . . Thus consistent and devoted she ever lived. She would never allow a child to go where it would be unseemly for her and me to go also. This was her rule: Whatever is lawful for Christian parents is lawful for their children. Whatever is forbidden to the former ought never to be allowed or conceded to the latter. She did not admit the usual excuse or apology that children not being members of the church may innocently participate in the customary pleasures and amusements of youth, though the professing parent must keep aloof from them. Shall an inexperienced child—son or daughter—be exposed to dangers, temptations, allurements, associations, indulgences, frivolities, and "wickedness in high places" to which the Christian father and mother would not dare to expose themselves?[14]

On March 27, 1844, John Berrien Lindsley received from Paris a letter written by William Walker, an extract from which suggests Dr. Lindsley's early penchant for nature study:

I almost envy you the life you lead at Nashville; and though we do not walk bodily together, my mind figuratively wanders with you over the green grass and midst the high trees. And how plainly every thing comes before me! Now we are on the cliffs of the Cumberland, just below the reservoir; you have a long tin mustard box in your hand, and every now and then a luckless snail is thrown into it. . . .[15]

The early education of John Berrien Lindsley was received for the most part under the instruction of his father and mother and

[14] Philip Lindsley, MS Diary.   [15] Appendix C, p. 186.

Mrs. Henry Middleton Rutledge. Mrs. Rutledge, who seems to have steered him through the processes of reading, writing, and arithmetic, lived on a place adjoining that of the Lindsleys. She was the daughter of Arthur Middleton, a signer of the Declaration of Independence, and was a woman of education and culture who spoke the modern languages fluently, played with some artistry upon the Italian harp, and was prominently identified with the religious life of Nashville.[16] John Berrien Lindsley was fortunate to come under the influence of this rare personality during these early years.

The training received by John Berrien at home was so thorough that he was able to finish a four-year university course in three years. He entered the University of Nashville at the age of fourteen, and graduated three years later, October, 1839, with the A.B. degree.[17] Two years more and he received from the same institution the A.M. degree. On June 4, 1841, he entered the office of Dr. William G. Dickinson, under whose direction he began the study of medicine. On October 26 of the same year he left Nashville to attend a course of lectures in the medical school at Louisville, Kentucky. He returned to Nashville in March, 1842, and on October 18 of the same year he left again for the University of Pennsylvania where, in March, 1843, he received the M.D. degree.[18] William Walker, of Nicaraguan fame, was one of his classmates,[19] and the friendship here formed remained unbroken until that twenty-first day of September, 1860, when Dr. Lindsley made the following entry in his diary: "My friend, William Walker, reported to have been shot by the Honduran Government." The report was confirmed a few days later. William Walker was shot on the morning of September 12, 1860.[20]

[16] A. L. Crabb, "Henry Middleton Rutledge," *Peabody Reflector and Alumni News*, VI (1933), 44.
[17] *Bulletin of the University of Nashville*, 1839.
[18] Letter received by the writer from Dr. William Pepper, dean of the medical school, University of Pennsylvania, dated March 5, 1935.
[19] DeWitt, *op. cit.*
[20] This diary is in the possession of Miss Louise G. Lindsley of Nashville, Tennessee.

PRELIMINARY YEARS 9

While a student at the University of Nashville, John Berrien studied under his brother, N. L. Lindsley, who instructed him in freshman subjects and sophomore mathematics. He studied languages under Professor L. J. Halsey in his sophomore year, and under Professor Abednego Stephens in his junior year. In his senior year he studied mathematics under Professor Abram Litton. Under his father he studied senior rhetoric, logic, economy, international law, moral philosophy, evidences of nature, and religion; under Dr. Gerard Troost, chemistry, geology, mineralogy; under Professor Nathaniel Cross, a preliminary course in medicine.[21]

A journal and notebook rather carefully kept while a student at the University of Pennsylvania in 1842-43 give an insight into the interests of those days. We find in this journal rather copious notes on courses taken under Dr. William Gibson, professor of surgery. At the conclusion of one particular course, which included fifty-three lectures, the distinguished professor delivered the following valedictory to his students:

We must now, gentlemen, bring our course to a close. I thank you for the attention with which you have listened to me. During the present winter I have given you an account of the organic man; last winter I spoke of the animal man. The organic man and the animal man are distinct beings; the latter has been ingrafted on the former. I have endeavored to place you on the tide of knowledge at present setting toward us. Keep on that tide for if you remain stationary you will certainly be submerged. I have given you an account of what the microscope and organic chemistry are doing for physiology. They are destined to renovate it. For the last forty years medicine has been too material; we have been too much engaged in examining matter; we have not searched for the laws of the forces which control this matter. A change is now taking place. I can only recommend you to continue the study of physiology; it is the key to pathology. Study it also with religious views, for it is thus we see the hand of God. In human art it is not the hasty strokes of the hammer which perform the works most to be admired. It is by diligent touches that these are accomplished. So in nature, it is the minute which is most wonderful. Again I say, go forth filled with love and zeal for your profes-

[21] The Lindsley Papers.

sion. You can not all be great; you can all be good. A good physician will receive the blessings of a generation yet unborn. That such may be your luck is my earnest prayer.

The following excerpt from a letter written by Dr. Lindsley on Saturday, April 8, 1843, from New York, to his brother, A. V. S. Lindsley, in Nashville, gives some important facts and is not without interest:

DEAR VAN,

Being rather tired of rambling about, and feeling quite lonesome now that William Walker has bid me a long farewell, I concluded that nothing would more effectually dissipate my solitary feelings than dropping a few lines to you.

To be sure I have very little to write that can be interesting to you, but that makes no difference because I can just go ahead as though my nonsense were sound sense. And what more important subject can I select for an epistle than EGO, therefore I propose to give you some account of what I have been about during the past week, which would doubtless have been better spent in bringing me somewhat nearer to you than I am now.

However, not to consume too much time in useless prefaces, let me proceed at once to my important business; and that you may better understand my movements I will give a sort of journal of the past week.

Friday, March 31st, was the day of Commencement of the Medical Department of the Univ. of Penn. Of course your humble servant had no right to participate in the transactions of that day, not having studied, by 14 months, long enough to entitle him to the degree. Nevertheless he had the honor of hearing a few Latin words muttered at him, in most ungraceful style. Thus you see nothing is lost by telling the truth; for though I told Dr. Horner at the beginning of the term, how long I had studied, and though he told me that I could by no means graduate before 1844, yet, nevertheless, notwithstanding, it was found expedient to forget what I had said and to let me through like the rest of them.[22]

This important business being finished, and the no less important business of dinner being attended to, I took my plunder in my hand, and proceeded to the foot of Walnut St., which is the point of de-

---

[22] Dr. Lindsley studied medicine with Dr. William G. Dickinson of Nashville and attended the Louisville Medical College before going to Philadelphia, where he passed an excellent examination.

parture for New York; for crossing the Delaware, you take the cars at Camden on the opposite side.

. . . .

Do not forget to tell Mr. Walker that I saw William safe on board the Emerald (bound for Havre), that he is comfortably fixed, and in good health and spirits. I have a letter for him from William.

Give my love to all the folks on the hill and remember me, etc., etc., etc. When I stop through Philadelphia, I expect to draw on you for 50$, which will be under ordinary circumstances more than enough to bring me home. You need not expect me before the first of May.

As ever, your affectionate brother,

BERRIEN

After graduating from the school of medicine at the University of Pennsylvania on March 31, 1843, John Berrien Lindsley returned to Nashville and, concurrent with his study of geology under Dr. Troost, there must have come to him an urge to harmonize the spiritual and the material in his nature, for he now turned his attention to the ministry.[28] There were many influences in his life which led him in this direction. First, his whole life had been lived in the atmosphere of a theologian. Then there was the Presbyterian influence of Princeton which had permeated his childhood, and the mystic communion with nature through long days spent in the open. It is certain, too, that whatever inclination he had toward the study of theology was encouraged while he was a student at the University of Pennsylvania, especially by his major professor, Dr. Gibson.

William Walker, writing to Dr. Lindsley from Paris on November 14, 1843, said:

The information contained in your letter regarding yourself was different from what I expected. From what you said last winter I thought it very probable that you would fix yourself near Lebanon and practice medicine during the last summer. You seem, however, to have given up all idea of practicing the healing art. . . . I really think that there is more need of preachers than of physicians in the western country. Besides, the turn of your mind, the education which

[28] Charles E. Little, "John Berrien Lindsley, A.B., M.D., D.D.," *American Historical Magazine*, III (1898), 34.

you have received, the principles which you have imbibed, the circumstances which surround you, all tend to lead you into the theological rather than the medical profession.[24]

There is convincing evidence that Dr. Lindsley considered serving in the foreign field, for on November 19, 1844, he received this letter from William Walker:

You must be quite learned in Theology by this time; in a year and a half of study a man may do a vast deal. I hope you have given up your idea of becoming a missionary, and purpose taking up your abode in some civilized part of the world where a fellow can have a chance of seeing you every now and then. Ah! John, it is a hard thing to live in the world without our natural friends—those whom birth has given us. So, I hope you have fallen, or will fall, in love with some young lady near Nashville and get married; and I hope like a true *cara sposa*, she will govern you completely and not let you emigrate into any outlandish region where you will have no companions but gibbering savages or half-civilized pagans.[25]

In later years Dr. Lindsley stated emphatically that if there was one defect in the curriculum of medical education more prominent than all others it was a neglect of the subject of theology. "Man is too much treated of as a mere material mechanism, and the mysterious but mighty influence of his passions, affections, and intellectual powers upon his physical nature too little understood or recognized."[26] Regardless of the forces that influenced his decision, the study of theology was quite in keeping with the life purpose of John Berrien Lindsley.

We find him, therefore, on December 2, 1843, presenting himself as a candidate for the ministry under the care of the Nashville Presbytery. On April 10, 1845, he was licensed to preach, and on October 25 of that year he began preaching as stated supply to the Hermitage Church, where he served for eight months.[27] That he was present at the bedside of Andrew Jackson when the latter died on June 8, 1845, is attested by the following

---

[24] Appendix C, pp. 184-85. [25] *Ibid.*, p. 189.
[26] *A Brochure on the Life and Character of Robert M. Porter*, p. 11.
[27] Little, *loc. cit.*

PRELIMINARY YEARS 13

paragraph written by Philip Lindsley in the minute book of the University of Nashville of that year:

1845 June 8th Sunday   6 O'clock P.M.
Died at his residence, The Hermitage, General Andrew Jackson, late president of the U. S. and a trustee of the University. Perfectly calm, self possessed, resigned and happy in his last moments. My son John Berrien Lindsley was with him a few hours before and at his death. He was born March 15th, 1767; lived 78 years and nearly three months. Was buried on Tuesday, June 10th at 11 o'clock A.M., or rather his funeral commenced at that hour. The University attended in mourning.

Dr. Lindsley was assigned to the Smyrna Church of Rutherford County on June 6, 1846, and served as pastor there for about six months. On October 13 of that year he was ordained as an evangelist in the First Presbyterian Church of Nashville. The sermon on that day was delivered by Dr. R. L. Lapsley and the charge was given by Dr. J. T. Edgar.

Dr. Lindsley's name as a minister first appears in the minutes of the General Assembly of the Presbyterian Church, U. S. A., in 1846. It is listed in the proceedings of this assembly thereafter each year until 1869, with the exception of two years, 1863 and 1864, when he was absent. In 1874 we find him listed as a minister of the Cumberland Presbyterian Church in the minutes of the General Assembly of this church. The transfer of his membership and activities to the Cumberland Presbyterian Church is explained by the Rev. M. B. DeWitt in a letter dated March 11, 1898, from Hopkinsville, Kentucky. Dr. DeWitt said:

In the issues of the Civil War his convictions of duty led him [Dr. Lindsley] to a careful questioning of his ecclesiastical relations, and having been a Presbyterian always and an ordained minister in the old unbroken body anterior to the great strife, he felt that his position was and must be embarrassing to remain in connection with the Northern Assembly, and so considering the circumstances in all their bearings, he decided to unite with the Cumberland Presbyterian church which had not been divided by the fratricidal conflict.[28]

[26] *Op. cit.*

We find Dr. Lindsley, beginning in 1874, listed in the minutes of the General Assembly of the Cumberland Presbyterian Church as a minister of the Nashville Presbytery until 1884. In 1884 he transferred his membership, with a group of other Nashville men, to the Lebanon Presbytery, where it remained until his death. Dr. DeWitt was called to the editorship of books and papers of the Cumberland Presbyterian Board of Publications in the summer of 1872. Knowing the literary ability of Dr. Lindsley, Dr. DeWitt sought and obtained his promise to contribute articles to the *Theological Medium,* the quarterly review of this church. In referring to Dr. Lindsley's contributions to the publication, Dr. DeWitt says:

He gathered wherever he went throughout the state and doubtless other states materials in the form of old books, papers, letters, manuscripts, and by conversation with old people and well-read persons. He systematized, culled, enlarged, harmonized, and arranged, in order of time, whatever he saw fit to publish, and at length edited and prepared with care eighteen articles of sixteen or eighteen pages each of octavo size, which I had the great satisfaction, as editor of the quarterly review, of publishing in eighteen successive numbers, requiring four years and a half to finish the series. I am assured that in time to come the future historians of the rise, progress, and work of the Cumberland Presbyterian church will need and seek for valuable data on which to pursue their labors, and they will turn with pleasure and ample reward of research to the pages of Dr. Lindsley's excellent courses of study in *Sources and Sketches of Cumberland Presbyterian History.*[29]

As early as 1838 John Berrien Lindsley's many-sidedness began to manifest itself in the concurrent undertakings which in such marked degree characterized his later life.[30] It was during this year that he became a private pupil of Gerard Troost, who was an eminent scientist on the faculty of the University of Nashville, and a pioneer in the advancement of American science. Dr. Lindsley's interest in science increased during several years of study with Dr. Troost, and he continued late in life an active student of geology. In 1848 he was invited by Dr.

[29] *Ibid.*   [30] Little, *loc. cit.*

PRELIMINARY YEARS

Troost to accompany him on an extensive geological tour which included many of the northern and eastern states. This tour was begun on June 7, 1848, and included St. Louis, Chicago, Mackinac, Detroit, Buffalo, Niagara Falls, Rochester, Ithaca, the Catskill Mountains, Albany, Saratoga, Lake George, Ticonderoga, Amherst, Boston, Salem, Plymouth, Burlington, Montreal, Quebec, Mount Washington, Portland, Newport, New Haven, New York, Newark, Philadelphia, Baltimore, Washington, Pittsburgh, Louisville, and Bowling Green.[31] When Dr. Troost died in 1850 his geological collection was committed to the care of John Berrien Lindsley. This collection was sold in 1874 to the Library Association of Louisville, Kentucky, for approximately twenty thousand dollars, about one third of its intrinsic value. Dr. Lindsley made repeated efforts to secure sufficient funds to enable him to retain the collection for one of the Tennessee universities, but the money never became available.[32] So active was Dr. Lindsley as a geologist that at least one contemporary of Dr. Troost expected him to succeed the distinguished scientist as professor of geology at the University of Nashville. This is indicated in the following letter:

AMHERST, MASS., Sept. 20, 1850

DR. J. B. LINDSLEY,

MY DEAR SIR, Your favor of the 7th was received on the 18th. It will afford me great pleasure to continue our exchanges.

Anthony has sent me a few shells from his region; out of Ohio I have no Western correspondent.

Murmeister's *Manual of Entomology* is the best for the generalities; cost about $5.00; 1 vol. octa.; I use the English translation "with additions by the author," published in London, 1836. Shuckard was the translator. Then for Classification you want Westwood's *Introduction to the Classification of Insects,* also published in London, 2 vol's octa., cost about $12.00. For details of genera and species, a library is necessary.

I will take pleasure in sending you, when you have made another "sending" as you propose, the shells, etc., which you desire.

[31] John Berrien Lindsley, MS Diary.
[32] John Trotwood Moore, *Tennessee, the Volunteer State,* II, 166.

Contrary to my expectations I find extreme difficulty in getting leave of absence during term time. I am extremely desirous to accept your kind invitation, but can have no definite plan now. It is a long way from this corner to the centre of the Union.

Do you take the place of Professor Troost?

Sincerely yours,

C. B. ADAMS[33]

Dr. Lindsley's many diaries and private journals are filled with material indicating a sustained interest in the study of theology and of natural science. He made field trips far and near and always returned with copious notes on his observations. From one of his several diaries, dated 1849, we take the following account of "a little missionary and geological excursion."

He left Nashville on Monday, July 23, at half-past two in the afternoon. At eight o'clock that evening he had reached Dr. Gooch's home, nineteen miles from Nashville in the Smyrna community, where he was hospitably entertained. He left Dr. Gooch's home at half-past nine the next morning, after opening Mr. Buell's school with prayer and a few remarks, and reached Dr. Yandell's at half-past twelve, just as a heavy shower commenced its deluge and just as the family were about to sit down to a good dinner. He spent the night with Dr. Yandell, and the next morning took a swim in Stone's River and wrote in his diary that Dr. Yandell's farm included three hundred acres of land valued at thirty dollars an acre and had two houses on it. He left Dr. Yandell's, five miles from Murfreesboro, at ten o'clock, and his next stop was at the home of Major Houston, seventeen miles on the Shelbyville Turnpike. After a good night's rest at Major Houston's, and a few hours spent in Shelbyville, he joined Dr. Ogden at eleven o'clock and they continued their journey eleven miles on a muddy road to Mr. Dryden's, where they "preached to about thirty or forty people in a new church."

Saturday, July 28, was spent at Petersburg camp ground, where a great meeting was being held by the Sons of Temperance.

[33] The Lindsley Papers.

PRELIMINARY YEARS 17

At least fifteen hundred people were present and Dr. Lindsley observed that most of them were well dressed and that altogether they constituted an intelligent-looking assembly. Dr. Ogden preached for nearly two hours in the morning from the text, "Be temperate in all things." The barbecue was then "attended to, and wheat and corn bread, ham, shoat, and lamb were served in plenty." After dinner, John M. Bright spoke for about an hour and a half. At four o'clock the meeting closed, as it had opened, with prayer. We are told that excellent order was observed by the people, who were very attentive, especially to Dr. Ogden's sermon. The next day Dr. Ogden preached for an hour and a half at the Unity Church and distributed some literature.

On Monday, July 30, as they journeyed by buggy to Fayetteville, about eight miles distant, a heavy rain set in and continued all afternoon. After crossing Elk's Ferry, just beyond the town, they ascended Pea Ridge, which Dr. Lindsley indicated was the same as Tyree's Ridge, a carboniferous formation. His description of the country as they neared Huntsville, Alabama, after having passed the mountain, indicates a limestone country, "level, fertile, fine cotton and corn fields." The heavy rain made the road muddy enough. They dined at Harper's, twenty-three miles from Huntsville, and passed the night at Strong's Tavern, at a cost of seventy-five cents each. On August 1 they rode over the turnpike through beautiful farm country and past handsome residences to the Bell Tavern in Huntsville. They called on Dr. Newman and secured directions about a noted locality for Pentremites, called by Christy the "Garden of Pentremites." The following entries from Dr. Lindsley's diary will indicate how persistent he was in seeking this "garden":

August 1. After an early breakfast rode to Huntsville, 6 miles, 4 of it turnpike. Beautiful farms and quite a number of handsome residences. Took a room at the Bell Tavern. Called on Drs. Newman and Robinson, got directions about a noted locality for Pentremites, called by Christy the "Garden of Pentremites." Started for it and failed to find it. Rode to the summit of the mountain in the Big

Cove Road, 3 miles from Huntsville. Very fine and extensive prospect. These are the Cumberland Mountains, not quite so high as at Bon Air.

After dinner Dr. Robinson sent his little son with me to show me the Garden of Pentremites, but though we almost reached the spot we failed in finding it as the little boy could not remember the route. So I returned a second time disappointed after another ride of 7 miles. No sooner got to Dr. Robinson's office than he mounted his horse and in 35 minutes we were at the "Garden," 2½ miles from Huntsville. The Pentremites are found in great abundance near the summit of the hill. There are other localities in these mountains where they occur in equal abundance. In an hour collected 280 (pyriformis, globose, florealis). Dr. Robinson gave me 380, only a portion of his gathering in the same time.

August 2, Thursday. Rained heavily in the forenoon. After dinner rode all through the town, and then to the "Pentremite Garden." In two hours myself and two country men (Williams) to whom I gave 50 cents, gathered 2,200 Pentremites.

August 3. Went to the 2nd toll gate on the Madison Turnpike, 8 miles from Huntsville on the Tennessee River. Soon as I got there a heavy shower came up. After this was over started for a hill to the left, nearby where fine encrinites are found. Another heavy shower forced me back. After dinner made another start for a hill on the right; again driven by the rain. When this was over it was time to return to Huntsville. Made an arrangement to exchange minerals with Dr. Newman for encrinites.

One cannot study the life of John Berrien Lindsley without being greatly impressed by the amount and variety of his labors and the dignity and ability with which he accomplished them. A brief sketch at this time will indicate the scope of his activities and will suggest the pages which are to follow.

In addition to his ecclesiastical work, Dr. Lindsley devoted much time during the five years, 1845-50, to the study of natural science. He traveled during eight months of the year 1848 in the northern states on a geological tour. In 1850 he organized the medical department of the University of Nashville; he served on the faculty as professor of chemistry and pharmacy from 1850 to 1873. In 1852, and again in 1859, he went abroad for instruc-

PRELIMINARY YEARS

tion in European institutions.[34] He was elected chancellor of the University of Nashville in 1855, and under his management this institution perhaps entered upon the most successful period of its existence. In 1867 he organized Montgomery Bell Academy in Nashville,[35] and during this same year he made the contacts that later resulted in the establishment of Peabody Normal College. In 1870 he assisted in the organization of the College of Pharmacy, of which he was professor of materia medica throughout its existence. In 1876 he was elected city health officer, in which capacity he served for four years.[36] As a practical sanitarian he rendered able service during the cholera epidemics of 1849, 1854, 1866, and 1879. In 1877 he was elected secretary and executive officer of the State Board of Health of Tennessee. He was president of this board during the year 1884. He was in charge of the health work in Tennessee during the yellow fever plague which swept over the South in 1878. In 1880 he was elected professor of sanitary science and state preventive medicine in the medical department of the University of Tennessee.[37]

Dr. Lindsley was a member of the medical society of the state of Tennessee as early as 1843. The new constitution adopted by this society in 1876 "was largely the work of his hand."[38] He was a member of the American Medical Association in 1851; of the American Association for the Advancement of Science (of which he was one of the founders) in 1848;[39] of the American Academy of Medicine; of the Royal Historical Society, England; of the Numismatic and Antiquarian Society

---

[34] DeWitt, *op. cit.*
[35] Minutes of the University of Nashville, 1867.
[36] Minutes of the Nashville City Board of Health, 1876.
[37] DeWitt, *op. cit.*
[38] *Centennial History of the Tennessee Medical Association*, p. 73.
[39] In conformity with a resolution of the Association of American Geologists and Naturalists at its Boston meeting in 1847, that body agreed to resolve itself into the American Association for the Advancement of Science, the first meeting under the new organization to be held in Philadelphia in 1848. John Berrien Lindsley's name appears as one of the charter members of this small group.—*Proceedings of the First Meeting of the American Association for the Advancement of Science*, September, 1848.
  At the time of the twenty-sixth annual meeting of this association in Nashville in 1877, Dr. Lindsley was in charge of all local committees.—MS Diary, 1877; also *Daily American* (Nashville), August 29, 1877.

of Philadelphia; a charter member of the Tennessee Historical Society (when this society was reorganized in 1849, Dr. Lindsley's name appeared first on the list of those who indicated a desire to become members);[40] a member of the National Prison Association; of the National Conference of Charities and Corrections; of the American Public Health Association (being treasurer of this organization, 1879-91); secretary of the State Board of Education;[41] superintendent of the Nashville public schools, 1866, and member of the City Board of Education;[42] and president of the Tennessee State Teachers' Association.[43] In 1856 Princeton University conferred upon Dr. Lindsley the honorary D.D. degree.

By special request Dr. Lindsley was placed in charge of the numerous Confederate hospitals in Nashville previous to occupation of the city by Union forces in 1862, and he was highly commended by the Federal surgeons for the condition in which these hospitals were found.[44] Dr. Lindsley perhaps made a more intensive study of sanitary science and medical education than any of his contemporaries.[45]

The annual reports of the American Historical Association for the years 1889 and 1892 contain a bibliography embracing the titles of twenty-nine papers, historical, educational, and sociological, from his pen.[46] He edited the *Confederate Military Annals of Tennessee,* a volume of nine hundred pages published in 1886. He also collected material for an encyclopedia of Tennessee history, but this was never published.[47] He made valuable

[40] Minutes of the Tennessee Historical Society, 1849.
[41] DeWitt, *op. cit.;* also Minutes of the Tennessee State Board of Education, 1875-1887.
[42] Minutes of the Nashville City Board of Education, 1866.
[43] L. S. Merriam, *Higher Education in Tennessee,* p. 54.
[44] John Berrien Lindsley, MS Diary.
[45] Minutes of the Nashville City Board of Education, 1866.
[46] *Annual Report of the American Historical Association,* 1892, pp. 265-66.
[47] Many references have been made to the encyclopedia of Tennessee history as having been published. There is ample evidence that it was near completion. With reference to this Dr. Lindsley said in his diary of 1878: "Estimate four months' work on Tennessee Annals needed. Yet 300 pp., say, long primer, equals 600 pages manuscript. At three hours per day six pages of manuscript can be written. Hence 100 days will be needed. Have planned the work now, and it is half executed at least."

contributions to the history of the Cumberland Presbyterian Church; was associate editor of the *National Encyclopedia of American Biography*, 1891-95;[48] edited the second and third reports of the Nashville Board of Health, 1877-79; the *Second Quadrennial Report of the Tennessee State Board of Health*, 1880-84; and thirteen volumes of the *State Board of Health Bulletin*, 1885-97.[49] Several of his pamphlets were widely circulated, especially *A Brochure on the Life of Robert M. Porter*, 1856; *African Colonization and Christian Missions*, 1873; *On Prison Discipline and Penal Legislation*, 1874; *On Medical Colleges*, 1858; *Our Ruin: Its Cause and Cure*, 1868; and *The History of the Law School of Cumberland University at Lebanon*, 1876.[50]

Dr. Lindsley was married in 1857 to Sarah McGavock, daughter of Jacob McGavock and Louisa Grundy, granddaughter of Felix Grundy, eminent jurist and statesman of Tennessee. Six children were born of this union: Jacob McGavock; Louise Grundy; Annie Dickinson; Margaret Lawrence (the late Mrs. Percy Warner of Nashville); Mary McGavock (Mrs. Robert C. Kent of Pulaski County, Virginia); and Randall McGavock, who died in infancy.

Any one of the various phases of the life of John Berrien Lindsley would seem to warrant his permanency. As founder of the medical school of the University of Nashville, and in turn as dean and chancellor, he contributed vitally and valuably to the cause of organized medicine in the South and Southwest. He was one of Tennessee's pioneer partisans in behalf of public education, and his efforts to secure an equity in educational opportunity led to the founding of Peabody College. His activity in the cause of public health laid the foundation for the public health program of today in the state of Tennessee.

Then follows this outline: "Annals of the State of Tennessee, compiled from official and other sources. From 1795-1878, (a) Political Annals; (b) Industrial and Commercial Annals; (c) Religious, Educational, Literary, and Scientific Annals; (d) Miscellaneous Annals; (e) Military Annals."

[48] DeWitt, *op. cit.*
[49] *Report of the Tennessee State Board of Health*, 1890-94.
[50] DeWitt, *op. cit.*

CHAPTER II

CHANCELLOR OF THE UNIVERSITY OF NASHVILLE

WHEN JOHN BERRIEN LINDSLEY assumed the chancellorship of the University of Nashville in 1855, succeeding his distinguished father, who had presided over its destiny for more than twenty-five years, this institution had already to its credit a notable record of educational service.

The origin of the University of Nashville lay deep in the history of Davidson Academy, which was incorporated by the General Assembly of North Carolina on December 29, 1785. In the preamble of the act creating Davidson Academy, we read this significant statement: "It is the indispensable duty of every legislature to consult the happiness of a rising generation and fit them for an honorable discharge of the social duties of life." This same thought, restated by a great philanthropist, was to become the watchword of another institution: "Education: a debt due from present to future generations."[1]

Davidson Academy was originally located at the Spring Hill meetinghouse about six miles east of Nashville on what is now the Gallatin Pike. When the Board of Trustees met for the first time, on August 19, 1786, Thomas Craighead, a graduate of Princeton, was elected president. For more than twenty years this eminent scholar presided over the cradle of the University of Nashville. Andrew Jackson and James Robertson were two of the most active members of the Board of Trustees during the early years and supervised the construction of the new building when the location of the school was changed.[2]

The alluring prospect of government aid for educational purposes led the trustees of Davidson Academy into an expansion

[1] Phebe A. Hanaford, *The Life of George Peabody*, p. 82.
[2] Merriam, *op. cit.*, pp. 21 f.

THIS PORTRAIT OF PHILIP LINDSLEY, PAINTED BY DURY, HUNG IN THE HOME OF JOHN BERRIEN LINDSLEY, HIS SON, FOR MANY YEARS. PRESENTED TO PRINCETON UNIVERSITY BY JOHN BERRIEN'S DAUGHTER, LOUISE G. LINDSLEY, OF NASHVILLE, TENNESSEE

program in 1806. A petition made to the legislature was granted, and on September 11, 1806, Davidson Academy became Cumberland College.[3] Thomas Craighead continued as president of the institution until 1809, when he was succeeded by Dr. James Priestly, a prominent graduate of Liberty Hall. It has been said that these two men gave to the early institution the nonsectarian stamp which was later so strongly impressed upon it by the Lindsleys.

The administration of Dr. Priestly began in 1810, to be interrupted in 1816 when the institution was closed for lack of funds. Associated with Dr. Priestly during these years was the scholarly William Hume, who was later known as "the good man of Nashville." After four years of suspended activity, Cumberland College reopened in 1820 with Dr. Priestly again its president. When James Priestly died, on February 6, 1821, the plans of the Board of Trustees for a great college were for the second time thwarted and the educational outlook was gloomy.

Then came the brightest period in the history of the institution—the administration of the Lindsleys.[4]

The members of the Board of Trustees bestirred themselves and launched a financial campaign in 1822 which enabled them to enlarge the main building on the campus and to erect two new buildings. The expectation of securing additional funds from the sale of government land stimulated their efforts. With hopes now high for adequate means, Philip Lindsley, president-elect of Princeton University, was called to the presidency of Cumberland College. He refused the offer, but was again called the following year. Again he refused. He was called a third time, on May 12, 1824, when he accepted. Philip Lindsley in his lifetime was offered the presidency of several colleges and universities. Among them were Transylvania University, the University of Alabama, Ohio University, the University of Pennsylvania,

[3] *Laws of the University of Nashville*, p. 30.
[4] W. K. Bowling, *Historical Address to the Graduating Class of 1868, University of Nashville*, p. 9.

Dickinson College, the College of Louisiana, and Princeton. The hardest to reject, no doubt, was the invitation which came to him in 1823 from Princeton, his alma mater.[5]

Philip Lindsley perhaps would not have come to Nashville "but for the assurance given that Cumberland College had a foundation of at least one hundred thousand dollars, the donation of the mother state through the National Congress and guaranteed by the General Assembly of the State of Tennessee."[6]

There were, however, other determining factors. Educationally, much was expected from this fast-growing western country. The westward movement was rapidly filling the Mississippi Valley and this vast region was at the time without an adequate institution of higher learning. It was Philip Lindsley's purpose to build a university which would be to the Southwest what Yale, Harvard, and Princeton were to the North and East. He had every reason to believe that the people would support such an institution with patriotic pride. There is no doubt that he dreamed of building an Oxford at Nashville. In a baccalaureate address delivered in 1829, he said, "In casting my eye over the map of Tennessee, it struck me from the first that this was precisely the place destined by Providence for a great university, if ever such an institution were to exist."[7]

Dr. Philip Lindsley outlined his plan for this great university in his inaugural address, January 12, 1825:

> We hope to see the day, or that our successors will see it, when in Cumberland College, or in the University of Nashville, shall be found such an array of able professors, such libraries and apparatus, such cabinets of curiosities and of natural history, such botanical gardens, astronomical observatories, and chemical laboratories as shall ensure to the student every advantage which the oldest and noblest European institution can boast. So that no branch of experimental or physical, of moral or political science, or of ancient or modern languages and literature shall be neglected. Let us aim at perfection, however slowly we may advance towards the goal of our wishes.[8]

---

[5] Merriam, *op. cit.*, p. 26.
[6] *Ibid.*
[7] Halsey, *op. cit.*, I, 167.
[8] *Ibid.*, p. 54.

Throughout his administration he kept constantly before the people this picture of the ideal university.

Cumberland College became the University of Nashville by legislative enactment on November 27, 1826. Two reasons were given for changing the name of the institution at this time: first, the new name was more in harmony with the broader field of usefulness planned for the college; and second, it seemed necessary to distinguish it from a college of the same name in Kentucky.[9]

Philip Lindsley gathered around him a notable faculty during his administration. Among the more prominent professors serving between 1824 and 1850 were:

George W. McGehee, mathematics and natural philosophy; elected 1824, resigned 1827.
George T. Bowen, chemistry; elected 1826, died 1828.
Nathaniel Cross, A.M., ancient languages; elected 1826, resigned 1831; reelected 1838, resigned 1850.
James Hamilton, A.M., mathematics and natural philosophy; elected 1827, resigned 1829; reelected 1831, resigned 1835; reelected 1838, died 1849.
Gerard Troost, M.D., chemistry, mineralogy, and geology; elected 1828, died 1850.
John Thomson, A.M., mathematics and natural philosophy; elected 1830, resigned 1831.
Consider Parish, ancient languages; elected 1831, resigned 1833.
Nicholas S. Parmantier, French language and literature; elected 1832, died 1835.
Abednego Stephens, A.M., ancient languages; elected 1835, resigned 1838.
Abram Litton, A.M., mathematics and natural philosophy; elected 1835, resigned 1838.
Alexander S. Villeplait, A.M., modern languages; elected 1838, resigned 1842.
Alexander P. Stewart, A.M., mathematics and natural philosophy; elected 1849, resigned 1850.

The following men served as tutors, generally for short terms: George Martin, Harvey Lindsley, Alfred A. Sowers, Abednego

[9] Merriam, *op. cit.*, p. 31.

Stephens, George Ely, Le Roy J. Halsey, N. Lawrence Lindsley, James A. Watson, Carlos G. Smith, George P. Massey, Jacob Harris Patton, Alfred William Douglass, John A. McEwen, Elbridge G. Pearl, James M. Coltart, Joseph W. Lapsley, William Rothrock.[10]

The enrollment of the University of Nashville during Philip Lindsley's administration was never large. The total number of students who matriculated during this period, excluding duplicates, did not exceed 1,059, as the following table[11] will indicate. No preparatory school or department was ever a part of the university during his incumbency. While the number of students was small, they were all regular college students—not preparatory students. Only 432 received degrees from the university during this period. Speaking to the citizens of Nashville in 1837, Philip Lindsley said:

> Whether a Preparatory Department should be connected with our University, has been doubted. If it should be resolved on, I have no hesitation in giving a decided preference to the system of Geneva, already adverted to.*
>
> *For various weighty reasons I have hitherto objected to any such connexion. Of course, in comparison with other Western colleges, our catalogue of students may frequently appear diminutive. In all of them, the preparatory department, or college grammar school, furnishes a large proportion of the names which are periodically published in their catalogues of students. The four or five excellent classical seminaries in the town of Nashville, with many others throughout the State, constitute in fact the preparatory department of the University; which is organized, in all respects, agreeably to the plan which long experience at the East has sanctioned as the most eligible. With this explanation, our number of students, attached as they all are to the four college classes, will be found superior to that of the same order in most Western institutions. This number, for several years past, has generally averaged from 100 to 125—not merely on our books, but actually present.[12]

---

[10] Taken from *Catalogue of the Officers and Graduates of the University of Nashville*, 1850.   [11] *Ibid.*

[12] Halsey, *op. cit.*, I, 369.

UNIVERSITY OF NASHVILLE
NUMBER OF STUDENTS DURING EACH SESSION, 1824-1849

Year	Students	Year	Students
Winter 1824-25	35	Summer 1837	103
Summer 1825	51	Winter 1837-38	88
Winter 1825-26	69	Summer 1838	72
Summer 1826	74	Winter 1838-39	78
Winter 1826-27	81	Summer 1839	100
Summer 1827	92	Winter 1839-40	82
Winter 1827-28	78	Summer 1840	76
Summer 1828	66	Winter 1840-41	76
Winter 1828-29	51	Summer 1841	81
Summer 1829	45	Winter 1841-42	93
Winter 1829-30	58	Summer 1842	84
Summer 1830	73	Winter 1842-43	81
Winter 1830-31	90	Summer 1843	76
Summer 1831	97	Winter 1843-44	72
Winter 1831-32	77	Summer 1844	85
Summer 1832	64	Winter 1844-45	82
Winter 1832-33	57	Summer 1845	78
Summer 1833	72	Winter 1845-46	67
Winter 1833-34	79	Summer 1846	74
Summer 1834	83	Winter 1846-47	73
Winter 1834-35	105	Summer 1847	75
Summer 1835	99	Winter 1847-48	72
Winter 1835-36	111	Summer 1848	66
Summer 1836	126	Winter 1848-49	60
Winter 1836-37	121	Summer 1849	52

Although the number of graduates was relatively small, the quality was unusually high. It is easy to believe that the University of Nashville stood second to no college of that day in the achievements of its alumni. Says Phelan, "It was remarked that at one time there were twenty-eight members of the United States House of Representatives who had graduated at that institution."[13]

High standards of scholarship no doubt reduced the enrollment. In an article on Robert Massengill Porter, who graduated from the university in 1841, Dr. A. L. Crabb refers to the quality of work done by the institution in the following appropriate phraseology:

A century ago the University of Nashville had nothing to offer the anemic-minded. Either one could take it or he could not; and if he could not, the enrollment of the University went down and the quality went up. President Philip Lindsley, Dr. Gerard Troost, Professors Nathaniel Cross and James Hamilton, for all their scholarship,

[13] Merriam, *op. cit.*, p. 28.

did not know how to formulate a policy that trafficked with mediocrity.[14]

Philip Lindsley no doubt would have come nearer to the realization of his ideal university had he not been continually hampered by lack of funds. The institution was constantly borrowing money on the security of individual trustees, and this sort of thing could not go on forever. Private subscription, investments in real estate, and tuition fees constituted the main financial support. The help that was expected from the General Assembly never came.

In 1848-49 the tuition fees amounted to only $3,220. This represented a serious condition. Private and denominational colleges with invitingly lower standards had been multiplying rapidly. Competition was keen; rugged institutional individualism was rampant. In 1824 there had been no colleges within two hundred miles of Nashville; in 1847 Philip Lindsley himself tells us there were nine within fifty miles of Nashville:

In 1847, in the twenty-third year of his presidency, Philip Lindsley said: "When this college was revived in 1824 there were no similar institutions in operation within two hundred miles. There were none in Alabama, Mississippi, Louisiana, Arkansas, or in Middle or West Tennessee. There are now thirty or more within that range, and nine within fifty miles of Nashville. These all claim to be our superiors, and at least the equal of old Harvard. Of course, we cannot expect to command a large range of what is miscalled patronage. I have now before me a list of twenty colleges in Tennessee alone. Several of these belong exclusively to individuals and are bought and sold in the open market like any other sort of private property. They are authorized to confer all university degrees at pleasure. This is probably a new thing under the sun, but Solomon's geography did not comprehend America."[15]

Among the colleges in Middle Tennessee were Franklin College, Wirt College, Irving College, Clinton College, Jackson College, Burritt College, Ravenscroft College, Giles College, Lawrence

---

[14] "Lines to an Alumnus," *Peabody Reflector and Alumni News*, VII (1934), 55.
[15] Bowling, *op. cit.*, p. 10.

College, Union University, Cumberland University, and Masonic University.

The competition thus established made inevitable inroads on the enrollment of the University of Nashville. And then, in 1849, came an epidemic of Asiatic cholera, which prevailed in Nashville to such an extent that many students left the university and others were prevented from coming. Diminished resources made it impossible to continue operation much longer. In May, 1850, Philip Lindsley was called to the chair of ecclesiastical polity and biblical archaeology in the New Albany Theological Seminary in Indiana. He accepted the call and thus brought to an end his official relation with the University of Nashville. John Berrien, his son, succeeded him. With what faith and effectiveness this son labored during the next twenty years, a summary of his administration will determine.

The Board of Trustees passed a resolution on September 14, 1850, to close the university for the time being, setting January 1, 1852, as a possible date for reopening. The reasons given for suspension were: first, that the faculty had been broken up by resignation and death; second, that the enrollment was small, due to epidemics, and the income of the university was not sufficient to carry on the operating expenses; and third, that it would be very difficult to continue class work while the old buildings were being torn down and the new ones were being erected.[16]

The following appraisals of the scholarly man who piloted the University of Nashville through the vicissitudes of a quarter of a century are deemed worthy of republication:

It was chiefly through his baccalaureate addresses that Dr. Lindsley reached and influenced the world that lay without the college walls. These addresses were delivered to large audiences, and then printed in pamphlet form and distributed through the mails. He was in touch with the times, and this was one secret of his success as a speaker. He was accorded that respect by the public which a man should always receive whom wide learning and extended observation have specially

---

[16] Minutes of the University of Nashville, 1850.

adapted to form wise judgments. He spoke with great earnestness, was a man of strong convictions, and did not hesitate to express them. His style was clear, forceful, cumulative. He had a copious vocabulary and a discriminating command of synonyms that obviated the harshness of repetition. A dignified bearing lent weight to his words.[17]

His personal appearance was exceedingly fine. It might well be called commanding, though he was slender and not above the medium stature. His form was perfectly erect and symmetrical. His features were chiselled after the finest Grecian mold. He had full-black hair and a spacious forehead of almost marble smoothness. His dark, penetrating eye flashed with indescribable emotion as he spoke; while his whole frame seemed to dilate and rise with majesty. His voice was rich and musical alike in its highest and its lowest notes; and there was a peculiar play of expression about the mouth, indicative of decision and conscious mental power, which no painter's art could ever catch. All these outward attributes, aside from his rare intellectual gifts and attainments, contributed to make him attractive and eloquent as a preacher.[18]

His addresses were almost invariably upon education. Even his sermons bore upon it. He never tired of it. He had given his life to it and it filled his life. But the term as used by him had no narrow signification. The difference between the new-born babe and the full-grown man is merely one of education. Education is almost synonymous with acquisition. It comprises every step, every process in a man's physical, intellectual, and moral development. No kind of knowledge is to be despised. Our minds are to be cultivated to the furthest extent. If it were not so God would not have created in us such vast possibilities. "Educate your son in the best manner possible, because you expect him to be a man and not a horse or an ox." As for himself, he held that "learning was the birthright of man." But he had a whole storehouse of utilitarian arguments to use in converting the multitude to his views. To the demagogic plea of the enemies of the university in Tennessee, that colleges are for the exclusive benefit of the rich, he made the counter assertion: "Colleges are the genuine levelers of all distinctions created by mere wealth." He saw that farmers and mechanics, forming as they do a majority of the electors, would be the governing power in the state if they were only more intelligent. Therefore none should welcome education more heartily than they.[18a]

---

[17] Merriam, *op. cit.*, p. 28.
[18] Halsey, *op. cit.*, II, 11 ff.   [18a] Merriam, *op. cit.*, p. 29.

Philip Lindsley was the father of six children, two daughters and four sons, five of whom survived him. The youngest child, Philip, died in early childhood. Margaret Lawrence married Samuel Crockett, a business man of Nashville, who always manifested an active interest in the university. Adrian Van Sinderen graduated from the university in the class of 1831 and became one of Nashville's foremost lawyers. He served the institution as a member of the Board of Trustees continuously from February 19, 1839, to the time of his death, January 22, 1885. Nathaniel Lawrence, the second son, graduated in the class of 1836 and tutored for two years at the university. John Berrien, the third son, received the B.S. degree from the university in 1839 and the A.M. degree in 1841. In 1850 he organized the medical school which became such a potent factor in the development of organized medicine in the South and Southwest. In 1855 he was elected chancellor of the university, over which he presided until 1870.[19]

With this background we now turn to John Berrien Lindsley and the part he played in the affairs of the University of Nashville.

The medical school was organized in 1850 immediately after suspension of the literary department—thus far the only department of the university. Even the most optimistic could not at this time have visualized the brilliant future that lay ahead. John Berrien Lindsley was the guiding spirit in the founding of this earliest of medical schools in the state of Tennessee, a school which became in its day the most notable in the Mississippi Valley. The organization of a medical school had been a matter of consideration much earlier in the history of the University of Nashville, but not until the organizing genius of John Berrien Lindsley became active did anything take definite shape. As early as 1829 Philip Lindsley had included a medical school in his plans for what he called his "ideal university." In his baccalaureate address of 1829, in discussing this question, he said, "Nash-

[19] *Catalogue of the University of Nashville,* 1870.

ville is the only place where a medical school would even be thought of, and physicians know full well that this is a fact."[20] He argued that a medical school would flourish only in a city, and even at that time Nashville was no mean metropolis. The question came up several times, and on February 17, 1844, Philip Lindsley submitted the following plan to the Board of Trustees:

1. That it is expedient to establish a medical school in connection with the University of Nashville.

2. That no portion of the funds of the University shall be appropriated to the aid or support of the said medical school and that this board will assume no pecuniary responsibilities whatever in its behalf.

3. That qualifications for degrees shall be equal to those required by the most respectable medical schools in the United States.

4. That no student shall be admitted to the degree of doctor of medicine under the age of twenty-one.

5. That no person shall be admitted to the degree of doctor of medicine except bachelors of art or such as shall be found on examination to be adequately acquainted with classical literature and the liberal sciences, and that the said examination shall be conducted in the manner hereafter to be described by this board.

6. That the entire supervision and control of the medical school in all respects and for all purposes, together with the power of administration, shall rest with this board and shall be exercised agreeably to the charter and for the best interests of the University and of the commonwealth.[21]

A few days later Dr. Philip Lindsley suggested a medical faculty, and there the matter rested. The medical school did not develop because Philip Lindsley, although he urged absolute control, did not permit the university to assume any financial obligation.

During the winter of 1849, John Berrien Lindsley visited medical schools in Louisville, Philadelphia, and New York, studying their organization, administration, and equipment. Upon his return to Nashville in the spring, he had many conferences with

---

[20] Bowling, *op. cit.*, p. 17.
[21] Minutes of the University of Nashville, 1844.

GERARD TROOST. THE PORTRAIT FROM WHICH THIS PICTURE WAS MADE, PAINTED BY BAKER, WAS PRESENTED BY SAMUEL D. MORGAN TO THE TENNESSEE HISTORICAL SOCIETY IN 1860 AND IS IN THE HALL OF THE SOCIETY IN NASHVILLE

Dr. Charles K. Winston concerning the plan for a medical school as an integral part of the university. Dr. Winston approved fully of the plans he outlined.[22] From the following lines of Dr. Lindsley's diary, later quoted by Dr. Bowling, we find how the medical school was conceived and developed:

> August 30, 1850. Opened my medical project to R. J. Meigs [one of the trustees of the University of Nashville]. Pretty busy at it after this.
> September 2. Called on Dr. D. W. Yandell.
> September 19. Called on Dr. Bowling and Dr. Winston.
> September 20. Dr. Bowling.
> September 21. Doctors.
> September 23. Dr. Bowling.
> September 24. Dr. Bowling.
> September 25. Drs. Bowling, Porter, and evening three hours with doctors' meeting.
> September 26. Evening, doctors' meeting.
> September 27. Dr. Bowling. Evening, Dr. Bowling and Mr. Meigs.
> September 28. Dr. Bowling.

As a result of these meetings, a club of five physicians was organized which later addressed itself to the trustees of the university.

Dr. W. K. Bowling refers to the establishment of the medical school as follows:

> In September, 1850, the name of J. Berrien Lindsley was left on my office slate. I had never seen him. The next day he called while I was in. We had a long conversation upon medical men and medical schools. He was born and reared at the University with the lofty ideals of his father. We were both full of medical schools and rather anxious that a medical school should become partially full of us. By him I was introduced to kindred spirits. We had frequent meetings in my office, all were enthusiastic. . . . The club consisted of Dr. J. Berrien Lindsley, Dr. A. H. Buchanan, Robert Porter, Charles K. Winston, John Watson, and myself. This group was later joined by Dr. Paul F. Eve, a generous scholar and one of the most effective speakers for the cause.[23]

---

[22] Bowling, *op. cit.*, p. 24.   [23] *Op. cit.*, p. 21.

The following extract from a letter to the members of the Board of Trustees of the University of Nashville, signed by the members of the medical club, will indicate the conditions under which this club became a department of the University of Nashville:

To the Trustees of the University of Nashville:

We have no hesitation in believing that the popular voice here is in favor of a medical school. Any attempt has heretofore been made in vain to meet the expectations of the public upon this subject. The great difficulty in the way of this enterprise as is shown by its history, running through a period of fifteen years, has been means to put it into successful operation. We propose to supply this desideratum from our private resources and to chance the results for reimbursement. We ask of you gentlemen only a recognition and the loan of your college buildings for a period of twenty years. We wish to have the sole management of the department ourselves, first,

For the experience and history of similar institutions show that the powers taken by those most interested are most effective; and secondly,

Because it will be an enterprise in which we will have expended no inconsiderable amount of money and would on that account desire to be untrammeled in the management of it.

We herewith exhibit the constitution which, in event of our recognition, is to regulate the internal affairs of the department and which will most clearly illustrate our plan of a medical college. We ask, if our proposition be favorably received, such agreement on your part as will insure us against molestation by your successors in the possession of the buildings and the professorships which you will confer upon us.

We ask of the University extraordinary powers, the entire control of our department for a term of years. We render to the University in return extraordinary advantages, making ourselves liable to heavy expenses for the sake of starting this department when it is quite uncertain whether the success will pay for our venture. For the time being, we serve as active agents for the University in securing funds to erect additional buildings for the medical department and in getting up a medical library and museum, all of which will be the absolute property of the University.

We respectfully solicit your early action in the matter with the assurance that whatever that action may be, we shall continue to maintain the approval of your wise body.

(Signed) JOHN M. WATSON, M.D.
W. K. BOWLING, M.D.
ROBERT M. PORTER, M.D.
A. H. BUCHANAN, M.D.
CHARLES K. WINSTON, M.D.
J. BERRIEN LINDSLEY, M.D.[24]

NASHVILLE, Sept. 28, 1850

Immediately after this proposal was received from the medical club, a committee was appointed by the Board of Trustees of the University of Nashville to take the question under consideration and make a report. The committee reported, on October 11, 1850, as follows:

RESOLVED, That a medical department be established in connection with the University and that a committee be appointed to draw the articles of agreement between the University and the professors of the medical department as created.[25]

Messrs. Ewing, Bass, and Meigs were members of this committee.

The board then proceeded to elect the following professors to fill the various chairs in the medical department of the university: John M. Watson, M.D., obstetrics and the diseases of women and children; A. H. Buchanan, M.D., surgery; W. K. Bowling, M.D., history and practice of medicine; C. K. Winston, M.D., materia medica and pharmacy; Robert M. Porter, M.D., anatomy and physiology; J. Berrien Lindsley, M.D., chemistry and pharmacy.[26]

Immediately after this contract was entered into, the medical faculty met and elected John Berrien Lindsley dean of the faculty. Thus, at the age of twenty-eight, it was given him to organize and direct the first great medical school of the state. Upon him "devolved the duty of managing the entire machinery at home and of representing the institution abroad." In January, 1851,

---

[24] Minutes of the University of Nashville, 1850.
[25] Ibid.
[26] Nashville Journal of Medicine and Surgery, LXX (1898), 47.

he sent Dr. A. H. Buchanan to Europe to purchase apparatus, books, specimens, and other equipment. It has been mentioned that before the beginning of the first session, in 1851, Dr. Paul Eve had been added to the faculty as professor of surgical anatomy and clinical surgery. A short time later, Dr. William T. Briggs was added as demonstrator of anatomy.[27] The next new chair was created in 1854, when Dr. Thomas R. Jennings was elected professor of history of medicine and clinical medicine.

John Berrien Lindsley lost no time in getting things started after the medical school was organized. Money was badly needed and there were several ways of getting it. One of them was by actual solicitation of the citizens of Nashville. The following extracts from Dr. Lindsley's diary of 1850 indicate the zeal with which he worked and something of the results of his labors:

November 1, 1850. Faculty meeting. The trustees ratified our lease.
November 2. Medical business several hours.
November 3. Worked at the college, moving equipment.
November 7. Commenced begging for the new building of the medical department. Got $750 from four individuals.
November 8. Begging; $500 from three persons. Evening, preached for Dr. Edgar.
November 10. Preached twice for Dr. Lapsley.
November 12. At the college.
November 14. Begging all day; $400 from four persons.
November 15. Three hundred dollars from three persons.
November 16. One hundred dollars from one person.
November 25. Begging one and one-half hours; $100 from one person.
November 26. Begging forenoon; $200 from three persons.
November 27. Begging three hours; heavy rain; $2.50 at night.

The next entry concerning the medical school followed an interval of two weeks:

December 14. Busy all day with medical college business.
December 17. Begged half day; $100 from two persons.

The begging continued into 1851. In the diary we find:

January 13. Faculty meeting.

[27] Minutes of the University of Nashville, 1851.

January 15. Begged two hours; nothing. Begged four hours; nothing. Begged five hours; $150 from two persons.

The next successful begging recorded in his diary is on March 11 and 12, when he received $230 from seven persons. On March 26 he begged half a day and received nothing. On April 11 he collected $210. We find him again begging on April 19, but with no results. Later in the year, in July, we find him receiving $110; and then he was busy all one week begging and collecting $220. On October 15 he was pledged $55 and collected $50. On October 16 he collected $50. This phase of his work continued throughout his administration. He never hesitated to ask for money in the cause of education. He thus set a pattern which was to be followed by many American college presidents, some to succeed gloriously and others to fail miserably.

John Berrien Lindsley's activities in raising money for the institution called forth a letter from Philip, his father, dated March 14, 1855, New Albany, Indiana, stating that this was sorry work in which he was engaged, for which he would receive no credit. An extract from the letter follows:

I am afraid you have undertaken too much in the begging line. It is, at best, a sorry business, and seldom yields any return of profit or thanks to even the most disinterested and successful beggar. As you have, however, engaged in the work, I wish you all the consolation, and all the benefit which can result from a zealous and faithful discharge of your duty.

Ma is hugely pleased with your new title and honours and dignities, etc. Ladies however know little about such sad realities and look chiefly at the outside. Our best love to you all.

Your affectionate Father,
P. Lindsley[28]

On this point John Berrien was wiser than his father. Had Philip Lindsley actually engaged in personal solicitation for funds back in those early days, instead of contenting himself with dignified addresses on the subject, he would no doubt have come nearer to realizing his *ideal university*.

[28] The Lindsley Papers.

There is no record to indicate that other members of the faculty met with any success in soliciting money.

During the earlier years of the medical college, there was never a surplus of funds. It was the duty of the dean to handle all financial matters. When the tuition fees and other resources were not sufficient to meet the operating expenses of the college, the difference was supplied by a pro rata assessment on each professor. During these earlier years, when the museum had to be furnished and equipment bought, the assessments were often very heavy. The money that John Berrien Lindsley was constantly securing from the public was of great help in these troublesome times.

The government of the college provided that a majority of the professors should rule, but that they should have no power to make the fees of the different chairs unequal. A majority of the faculty members could assess the professors any amount. A professor's only recourse, if he did not like the assessment, was resignation. Failure to meet the assessment within three months after it was imposed upon him by the majority of the faculty and recorded by the dean was accepted as resignation without further action of the faculty.[29]

The requirements for graduation from the medical school of the University of Nashville in the early days included the following stipulations: (1) three years of service in the office of a practicing physician; (2) two full years' attendance upon lectures in a medical school, the last year of which must be in that institution; (3) four years' successful experience in the practice of medicine would be accepted in lieu of one course of lectures; (4) the candidate for graduation must write a thesis on some medical topic and must file it with the dean by the middle of the year (many of these theses may be found in the library vault of Peabody College); (5) the candidate must be twenty-one years of age and of good moral character. Because of the pressure exerted by the American Medical Association for a longer course of study,

---

[29] Minutes of the University of Nashville, 1850.

UNIVERSITY OF NASHVILLE 39

a summer school was inaugurated in 1855. This course was advertised as one largely of a practical nature. The students enrolled in the winter term were compelled to pay tuition fees for the course and received no refund if they did not attend the summer quarter.[30] This in a sense made attendance compulsory.

Hospital facilities for the medical school were secured in the beginning through the use of St. John's Hospital. In 1851-52 the Tennessee legislature passed an act which converted the lunatic asylum in Nashville into a state hospital, and this also was used by the medical school. A library, to which all the students had access, was collected within a short time. The faculty in all spent thousands of dollars upon buildings, equipment, and grounds; but it was a good investment, for they made money on the medical school.

The first year opened with 121 students and closed with 33 graduates. The attendance grew steadily until 1859, when 456 students were enrolled in the medical school. As far as numbers were concerned, the medical school of the University of Nashville ranked among the leading medical colleges of America. Every southern state was represented in the enrollment and, in addition, California, Pennsylvania, and the District of Columbia.[31]

Early recognizing the fact that he had a part in directing the destiny of an institution whose possibilities were very great, John Berrien Lindsley spent the winter of 1851 in Louisville and other cities studying medical schools, and the interim between sessions of 1852-53 and 1858-59 in the medical schools of Germany and France seeking the best these schools had to offer for his own institution.

From his diary we have a very good record of his European trips. He left Nashville by stagecoach at 4:00 A.M. on Tuesday morning, February 10, 1852, in a rain which continued all day, and arrived in Louisville the next evening, February 11, at 7:00 P.M. Five days later he was dining in Pittsburgh at the

---

[30] Merriam, *op. cit.*, p. 44. [31] *Ibid.*, p. 45.

Monongahela House, "an excellent hotel," and then on to New York, where he took passage for Liverpool on February 21.

On Saturday, April 3, 1852, we find him in London calling on George Peabody, who gave him tickets to the Royal Botanical Gardens.[32] (This was fifteen years before George Peabody's gift to the South.) Then he went to Bartholomew's Hospital, where he saw a Mr. Lloyd exsect a tumor, using chloroform. "There were fifty or sixty spectators in the Amphitheatre."

On Monday, April 5, a chemistry professor at the University of London, "an exceedingly poor lecturer," discoursed on "specimens and experiments."

On Wednesday, April 8, Dr. Lindsley spent the whole day at the Royal College of Surgeons. "The Hunterian Museum was rich in comparative anatomy and wet preparations." A description of the building and the lecturer followed.

In Paris, a week later, he rambled about for several hours and heard Wurtz on chemistry at L'École de Médecine. "Would find the language a dull business had I not studied it previously. As it is, when spoken slowly, I comprehend it very well, and can make myself understood a little."

On April 16 he heard Nelaton at the *clinique* of the faculty of surgery, after which he witnessed several operations.

On April 22 he again heard Wurtz and understood him better than before.

The next day he spent five hours in the laboratory—the rest of the day "home studying."

On April 27 he spent six hours in the laboratory and one hour at Wurtz's lecture.

Almost every day for several weeks there is an entry in his diary about a lecture attended or laboratory work done.

Dr. Lindsley's diary of 1856 begins in October with an evening at the McGavock's, which was followed by many evenings at the McGavock's until that evening of February 9, 1857, when

---

[32] Dr. Lindsley again visited George Peabody while in London in 1859, and eight years later, in 1867, he called on him, through the Peabody Education Fund, for financial assistance in establishing a normal school.

he was married by the Rev. T. J. Edgar to the beautiful Sarah McGavock, "daughter of Jacob McGavock," with only the family and a few friends present. (Sarah McGavock was a granddaughter of Felix Grundy.) All were very happy. A honeymoon trip to the East included a stopover at Richmond. On February 16, Dr. Lindsley walked the streets of Richmond with Mrs. Lindsley. Not forgetting the medical school even on his honeymoon, he makes the following entry in his diary:

> Went to the Medical College of Virginia. Dr. Gibson had a review quiz—Dr. Scott, professor of chemistry, lectures three times a week. Dr. Gibson lectures six times a week. About 78 students yield the professors about $1,000 each. The State endowed the school, and the current expenses are light. The Dean is paid $500 a year. The building is a handsome Egyptian edifice—lecture rooms small and an infirmary with beds is also in the University.

Any attempt to evaluate the life of John Berrien Lindsley must necessarily involve an appraisal of the medical school of the University of Nashville. It was in a large measure his achievement. He had to be as much concerned with buildings and grounds as with curriculum matters. He brought back with him from Europe the plan for the beautiful gray stone building which was completed in 1853. A joint editorial by Dr. W. K. Bowling and Dr. Paul F. Eve concerning Dr. Lindsley and this building appeared in the *Nashville Journal of Medicine and Surgery* in April, 1855. It read:

> The brilliant success of the medical school here is greatly indebted to his brain. The beautiful building of stone, known here as the new university, was fashioned in his brain before the corner stone was quarried. The magnificent structure known as the medical school is the legitimate offspring of the same fertile source. The activity of the man compared with the leisurely quiet of the student is amazing.

The service rendered by the medical school under the administration of John Berrien Lindsley may be indicated by the fact that there were 3,199 matriculants and 999 graduates during the first ten years of its existence. The succeeding decade increased these numbers to 4,401 and 1,317 respectively. There is ample evidence that the instruction given in this institution was as thorough, practical, and efficient as that given in any other institution of its type in the country.[33]

While the medical school was flourishing on the campus of the University of Nashville, the literary department, which had closed its doors in 1850, was still in a state of suspended activity. The buildings had been destroyed in order to make way for a fast-growing city. On account of considerable agitation for the renewal of the collegiate department, the Board of Trustees, in February, 1853, appointed a committee with power to erect a college building, nominate professors, and plan for the reopening of this department. As a result of this decisive action on the part of the board, a plan of reorganization was submitted by the committee and was approved by the Board of Trustees. Four professorships were created and filled as follows: John Berrien Lindsley was asked to accept the chair of chemistry and natural sciences; Joseph A. Eaton was appointed to the chair of natural philosophy and mathematics; Dr. J. W. McCulloch was appointed professor of ancient languages; and Dr. Edward Wadsworth was appointed professor of ethics and belles-lettres. Professor Eaton resigned the chair of mathematics soon after and A. P. Stewart, of Cumberland University, was appointed to fill his place. The venture did not succeed, for, in February, 1855, every member of the literary faculty resigned. This department was to take on new life under a more carefully laid plan conceived by John Berrien Lindsley.

Upon the resignation of the literary faculty on February 10, 1855, the Board of Trustees realized that careful plans had not been made for the reorganization. On February 19, the board met and it was recommended that John Berrien Lindsley be elected chancellor of the university and be given broad powers. Immediately after the name of Dr. Lindsley was proposed, his medical colleagues made the following recommendation to the board:

[33] *Southern Practitioner*, XIX (1897), 223.

UNIVERSITY OF NASHVILLE—MEDICAL DEPARTMENT.

FROM THE CATALOGUE OF 1855. THE BUILDING WAS PLANNED BY DR. LINDSLEY.

Having been informed that Dr. Lindsley, our colleague, has been mentioned in your honorable body as a suitable person to fill the important and responsible station of Chancellor of the University, we deem it due to him and the Board to say that the appointment to that office would meet with our most cordial approbation. We can assure the Board that if untiring perseverance, consummate prudence and unflinching integrity, combined with finished scholarship and a capacity for business that anticipates and provides for every thing, great or small, are the qualities which they desire in such an officer, Dr. L. possesses them to an eminent degree.

As the working man of our Faculty from the beginning, we have reposed unlimited confidence in him and can therefore speak from experience.

Should he receive the appointment and undertake the duties of the office, it will be no fault of his if the most brilliant success fails to crown his administration.

(Signed) PAUL F. EVE   A. H. BUCHANAN
ROBERT M. PORTER   JOHN M. WATSON
THOS. R. JENNINGS   CHAS. K. WINSTON
W. K. BOWLING[34]

John Berrien Lindsley was thereupon unanimously elected chancellor of the University of Nashville, February 19, 1855.

The board then proceeded to ballot for an executive committee, and the following gentlemen were elected: James Woods, L. D. Morgan, and Russell Houston.

The chancellor was now in full control. He was chairman of the different faculties of the university and represented the academic as well as the medical faculty. It was his duty to work out the plans of reorganization for the university, to select faculty members, to raise funds, advertise the school, and represent the institution in every way before the public. Remembering the causes which led to the closing of the literary department, among which were the competitive institutions springing up all over the country, Dr. Lindsley felt that little opportunity existed for an ordinary literary and scientific college unless it were heavily endowed and magnificently equipped. If the University of

---

[34] This and the following statements are from Minutes of the University of Nashville, 1855.

Nashville was to be successfully reinstated, it must be by meeting some special need. After giving this question serious consideration, Dr. Lindsley conceived the idea of a military college in connection with the university. This plan he confidently expected to succeed.

On March 9, 1855, he submitted to the Board of Trustees a plan for reorganization of the university. This plan recommended the immediate addition of three departments to the institution: an academic department, a law department, and a department of science and philosophy. In submitting these recommendations Dr. Lindsley referred to the fact that the medical department was terminating its fourth session with every evidence of prosperity and success. The law department had closed its doors because of failure to complete its organization the previous year. The academic department was without professors because of the action of the board in accepting the resignations of the faculty, which had been tendered for various reasons.

Dr. Lindsley's first proposal was that the literary department be organized on such a plan as to make it self-sustaining. In other words, he was recommending the same plan for the collegiate department that had been worked out for the medical school. This, he told the board, could be done by simply organizing this department on the military system. He supported the plan before the board with the following arguments:

1. That the Americans most unwisely neglect the cultivation of military science; that, as a matter of national preparedness, the young men should learn military discipline. (This argument was hardly consistent with some of his earlier utterances on peace.)

2. That the military system in the school would help to preserve good discipline, which was well-nigh impossible among immature boys.

3. That if the university was to succeed it must of necessity undertake something more than the twenty-five or thirty so-called colleges clustered around the institution were pretending to do.

4. That the Western Military Institute was seeking a new connection and would accept the invitation to join the University of Nashville without imposing any financial burden upon it.

Dr. Lindsley's second recommendation was that a new department, to be known as the department of science and philosophy, be organized, in which all the branches of knowledge not included in the other three departments would be taught, either with reference to their practical application or to fuller theoretical development. He felt that this department would be of great importance to the institution because of the high standing it would give the university as a scientific center and because of the great favor with which the wealthy landowners and intelligent farmers, manufacturers, and industrial men of the South would regard it. It would be the purpose of this department to furnish such knowledge of any branch of science as might be needed for the successful pursuit of industries calling upon scientific principles. To the civil engineer, for instance, this department would furnish a knowledge of mathematics, mechanics, surveying, and draughting. To the iron manufacturer it would furnish a knowledge of chemistry, geology, metallurgy; to the farmer and planter a knowledge of agriculture, chemistry, botany, zoology; to the teacher a knowledge of languages, philosophy, etc. Dr. Lindsley recommended that this department should ultimately include professorships in civil engineering, mathematics, physics, astronomy (with an observatory), analytical chemistry, agricultural chemistry, geology and mineralogy, botany, zoology, ancient and modern languages, political economy, history, etc.

The third department recommended in his report was the law department. He felt that this department would appeal especially to the wealthy and liberal-minded youth of the South.

Dr. Lindsley believed if the board would approve the completion of his plans it would soon have a university with three professional faculties of high standing whose lecture rooms would be filled with students gathered from all the southern states, together with a collegiate department as flourishing as

Cambridge, New Haven, or Charlottesville. He prophesied that under this plan the University of Nashville would within a few years have the following number of faculty members and students: medical department, 10 instructors, 400 students; law department, 4 instructors, 100 students; scientific department, 7 instructors, 100 students; collegiate department, 15 instructors, 300 students; total, 36 instructors, 900 students. This, he felt, could surely happen if the Board of Trustees and the citizens of Nashville would subscribe $50,000 toward the immediate improvement of buildings and the purchase of equipment for the institution. He said:

> This plan is neither novel nor crude nor hastily conceived on my part. It is the result of several years' constant and interested study of the subject, aided by extended facilities of observation furnished by travel at home and abroad. This long period of attention to the subject in general has been in connection with the peculiar conditions of our own university and also the educational wants of this whole region.

After outlining the financial condition of the institution he concluded his report by saying that if his program were given consideration he would not hold a professorship in the school but would prefer to give up the chair hitherto his own in order to advance the general scheme. He also would subscribe his first year's salary toward a fund to be used in the scientific department. His report closed with this remark:

> I esteem the work in which we are now engaged worthy of enthusiastic devotion through its justly claiming largely of our time and our attention, affecting as it does the highest interest of thousands living and yet unborn, reaching down through remote ages and connecting the present by a crystal stream of knowledge with the far distant future.

The following resolution was passed by the board: "*Resolved*, That the plans proposed by Chancellor J. Berrien Lindsley for reorganizing the University of Nashville be and the same are hereby adopted by the Board of Trustees."

A committee composed of the following gentlemen was then appointed to solicit subscriptions: R. C. Foster III, J. M. Lea, and C. K. Winston.

Dr. Lindsley delivered an address before the alumni society of the University of Nashville on October 3, 1854, in which he outlined his idea of an educational program for the university and made an appeal for its support. This report was later published by the Board of Trustees.[35] In answer to the questions, "What next do we need? what is the work of the future?" he stated that the most imperative need at that time was endowment with which to support students who could devote themselves entirely to the study of special branches of science and letters and thereby gain such proficiency as would enable them to become authorities in their several fields, that they might add to the domain of knowledge by making new discoveries. The number of students eager for and able to pay for such training, he said, "must always be too small to enable men dependent upon student patronage to devote themselves to such studies, and yet this is precisely the type of student that constitutes the crowning glory of a university."

In the department of letters and science he would have at least twenty fellowships to enable worthy students of this type to educate themselves. In letters he would have professorships in Hebrew, Greek, Latin, German, and Anglo-Saxon. In science he recommended the need of professors of astronomy, botany, geology, zoology, and chemistry. He would spend one hundred thousand dollars on a library and develop a plan to insure its permanency by making it productive. As to philosophical, astronomical, and chemical instruments, he believed that the proceeds of an endowment of fifty thousand dollars would be a "rather decent outfit." A university theatre (auditorium) should be provided, he said, which would seat such audiences as assemble on commencement occasions and in which all exercises of the university could be held. He felt that such a building would

---

[35] This and the following statements are from Dr. Lindsley's *Address Before the Alumni Society of the University of Nashville*, 1854.

prove indispensable. He would spend one hundred thousand dollars for an astronomical observatory, a suitable library in connection therewith, and a museum hall. To give the university the endowment needed and such buildings as its friends would wish to see it have, would require not less than a million dollars. "Such an institution there is not in the United States, unless Harvard may claim this right," he said. After outlining the needs of the university, he proceeded to give the sources from which the money must come. Wealthy men, foundations, a plan of leasing the unproductive real estate of the university, aid from the city, the county, and the state are some of the sources mentioned. He said:

Our wealthy planters and merchants and professional men may become imbued with a fondness for science, polite letters and theological lore, as well as those of Massachusetts or New York. . . .

Due patience and proper exertion on our part may show that there are among us men whose names will be as worthily and gratefully held in remembrance and veneration by future generations of professors and students of Nashville as are those of Harvard, Hollis, Boylston, Elliott, Hartman, Royall, Rumford, Dane, Lawrence, and many others at Cambridge. . . .

Why should you not emulate the example of the alumni of other colleges and by general and continual though not burdensome contributions add to its resources? Why grows so slowly the endowment of the Winchester Professorship? And why should not scholarships and prizes keep fresh the memories of our brethren who have devoted, yea sacrificed their lives to the cause of education and religion? Are you willing to forget the Humes, the Allens, and the Ewells, whose names and works and deeds are the richest possessions and brightest ornaments of your society?

The following remarks on the institution of Negro slavery in this appeal for a greater university are not without interest. The same argument was used by many educational institutions of the South.

As a people it is useless to ignore the fact that the inhabitants of the southern part of our Confederacy are distinguished by a social feature without a parallel, as far as history teaches, in any other time and country—the holding in bondage by one race of nearly half their number of a much inferior race—a feature of course intimately connected with the laws, customs, and feelings governing the pursuits and relations of both races. It is equally unwise and vain to conceal the fact that the sympathy of what is called the civilized world is enlisted against the master race because of this relation, and that this sympathy greatly influences the writings and teachings of the said world. [At this time *Uncle Tom's Cabin* had enjoyed a record-breaking sale for three years, and the abolitionist literature was pouring into the South.] We may indeed be said to be an isolated people, whose true situation cannot be rightly appreciated by those at a distance, and who are consequently always liable to be very grossly misrepresented. If, then, we wish our ministers, lawyers, physicians, and others who are to be leading men in all the walks of life, trained up with proper notions of home affairs, it will not answer to educate them abroad, where they can hardly fail to be prejudiced in several ways. Either they will become dissatisfied with the existence of slavery at home, and converts to wild, radical and impracticable schemes of reform; or else from the necessity under which they are placed of defending the custom of their fathers against oft repeated attacks, they will become intolerant bigots the other way, averse even to any Christian schemes of ameliorating the condition of the inferior servile race. By home education both dangers are avoided.

The immediate interest of John Berrien Lindsley when he submitted his plan for reorganization to the Board of Trustees was the merging of the Western Military Institute with the University of Nashville as the literary department of that institution. For the details of this merger, we now return to the diary of Dr. Lindsley.

The Western Military Institute had been incorporated by the state of Kentucky in 1847.

In the fifteen years of its existence the school had five different homes. It began in September, 1847, in Georgetown, Kentucky, under the presidency of its founder, Colonel Thornton F. Johnson, and in 1850 was moved to Blue Lick Springs, and in 1851 to Drennon Springs, Kentucky. In 1854 the school was taken to Tyree Springs, Tennessee, and in 1855 to Nashville, where, in 1861, it ended its career as a part of the University of Nashville.[86]

The proprietors of the Western Military Institute were Colonel Bushrod R. Johnson and Lieutenant Colonel Richard Owen.[87]

Dr. Lindsley had no doubt been watching this institution for some time with keen interest and covetous eyes, and, being ever alert to further the interests of the University of Nashville, he was quick to take advantage of the opportunity when it came. The following extracts are taken from his diary of 1855:

February 23. Colonel Owen spent two hours with me yesterday, and the following night.

February 24. Executive committee met. Explained my plans. Approved them. Board met. Read my plans and received personal explanations. Board surprised; still my plans well received.

February 26. Executive committee met. Captain Foster was sent out after big subscriptions. Obtained $8,000.

March 3. Board met to consider my proposition about the University. Some opposition. Adjourned until Friday. Forenoon with Colonel Bushrod Johnson. All about the College.

March 6. To Tyree—after dinner with Mr. Hoyt. [This is presumably Tyree Springs.]

March 7. Returned home after dinner. Long conference with Colonels Johnson and Owen.

March 8. Very busy writing out my first report to the board fully.

March 9. Forenoon waited with Colonel Owen on many members of the board. Afternoon board met. Read my first formal report. All opposition withdrawn. Unanimously and cordially approved and adopted.

March 10. Forenoon with Colonel Owen at the University. Afternoon executive committee met and approved articles of union between Western Military Institute and the University of Nashville which had been the result of my conferences with Colonels Johnson and Owen. Moved my lodgings to Market Street in a larger residence. Eleven thousand dollars. Captain Foster working like a Turk.

---

[86] Mabel Altstetter and Gladys Watson, "Western Military Institute, 1847-1861," *Filson Club History Quarterly*, X (1936), 100.

[87] *Rules and Regulations of the Western Military Institute*, 1854.

On March 10, 1855, John Berrien Lindsley wrote his father concerning the new enterprise. We quote from Philip Lindsley's reply:

> Yours of the 10th inst. is at hand. The recollection of Prof. Owen is utterly at fault. I never wrote to Col. J. or to any mortal whatever, a syllable about military schools or military discipline—much less about connecting such an institute with the University. I never thought or dreamed of such a thing. Possibly President Linsley, late of Marietta College, may have written, said or done something to occasion Prof. Owen's mistake—though I know nothing of the matter.
>
> I repeat what I said in my last letter that, as I know nothing about military government or modes of action & study in military institutions, so I offer no opinion or advice upon the subject. The Military Academy at Lexington, Virginia, has no official connection, I believe, with Washington College, in the same town.
>
> My motto or rule has been: "I dictate to no man: I allow no man to dictate to me." To learn all we can, from friend or foe, from the dead and the living, from old fogies or young America—is right and wise and very becoming. But then, the responsible head or general in chief must decide for himself. I never decided against my own judgment—or yielded my own deliberate convictions—to please any body, for any consideration, without having cause to regret it afterwards. Whenever you are fully satisfied of the vertitude, expediency or necessity of any course or system or measure—stand by it, through evil and through good report. If others will not sustain you, or choose to overrule or defeat you, let them assume the responsibility and meet the consequences.[88]

Thus on April 4, 1855, Western Military Institute became the literary department of the University of Nashville.

The Articles of Union contained the following provisions:

1. Western Military Institute was to become a part of the University of Nashville.

2. Western Military faculty was to pay no rent for the use of the university buildings or grounds.

3. The faculty of Western Military Institute was to have no set salary, but the fees of the collegiate department were to be divided among them.

---

[88] The Lindsley Papers.

4. Four professors were to be allowed for each hundred students.

5. Fees were to be divided so as to give Colonel Johnson and Major Owen not less than $1,750 a year for each hundred students, not less than $2,000 a year for each hundred and fifty students, and not less than $2,500 a year for each two hundred students. The two proprietors were to live in the old house formerly occupied by the president.

6. The boarding establishment was to meet all expenses for food, servants, lights, and fuel, but was not to be a source of income to the faculty.

7. The Board of Trustees was to designate the fees of the cadets.

8. In store and shop service, 10 per cent of the net profit was to go to Johnson and Owen. The remainder was to help cover any deficit of the institute; otherwise the profit was to buy equipment for Western Military Institute.

9. The University of Nashville was not responsible for any debts incurred by Western Military Institute.

10. The authorities of the University of Nashville were to have supervision over the activities of the institute.[39]

In addition, the military department was to erect suitable buildings for the accommodation of the cadets and to guarantee that the university property would be kept in good order. At this time a building costing $32,000 was constructed. Eighteen thousand dollars of this amount had been subscribed by the citizens of Nashville, leaving an indebtedness of $14,000 to rise up and haunt the proprietors in years to come. Despite many difficulties, this department of the university justified the hopes held for it by John Berrien Lindsley. The student enrollment increased from 154 in 1855 to 648 in 1859-60. These figures included the medical students. Gradually the university was approaching a sound financial condition. Tuition fees were sufficient to pay the professors' salaries and most contingent expenses.

---

[39] Minutes of the University of Nashville, 1855.

When the war began, the military department was paying interest on the building debt at the rate of $1,000 a year, and it was expected that within a short time this indebtedness would be retired. The war brought the literary department again to an untimely end.

Dr. Lindsley delivered an address at the Masonic Hall in Nashville on the occasion of the opening of the sixteenth session of the medical department of the University of Nashville, November 6, 1865. It was a thoughtful address on the history and development of the older universities, and again included an appeal to the citizens for adequate financial support. He discussed at some length the University of Michigan at Ann Arbor, "the admiration of the entire Northwest," whose doors were thrown open to all who would come and partake of the free tuition offered. This great seat of learning was a result of national munificence and wise state legislation. Nashville, he said, could offer far greater advantages than Ann Arbor, if only the legislature would do what it ought to do.

It is significant that in this address, in 1865, he proposed a normal school and a polytechnic school as two departments which would attract many hundreds of students and would add greatly to the usefulness of the university.

On June 21, 1867, at the first meeting of the Board of Trustees of the University of Nashville after the close of the Civil War, Chancellor Lindsley recommended that there be "no further delay in the performance of the obligation imposed by the legacy of Montgomery Bell." In 1855, Montgomery Bell, the iron capitalist of Davidson County, Tennessee, had left in trust to the University of Nashville the sum of twenty thousand dollars to be invested in state bonds. The interest on this sum was to be used in maintaining an academy to be known as "Montgomery Bell Academy." According to the stipulations of the will, this fund was to be used for the purpose of educating male children who were "not able to support and educate themselves and whose parents were not able to do so." The children were to be selected by the trustees.[40] The will further stipulated that preference be given to ten children from Davidson County and five each from Williamson, Dickson, and Montgomery counties. No child below ten or above fourteen years of age was to be considered, and the children were to be permitted to remain in the school until they were eighteen years of age.

The original sum left in trust had been carefully invested by the members of the board and, in 1867, amounted to approximately forty thousand dollars. The board accepted the recommendation of Chancellor Lindsley, and Montgomery Bell Academy was opened in September, 1868. Le Roy Halsey was elected principal and was given three assistant teachers.[41]

There had been some discussion concerning the restoration of the literary department in 1867, but nothing definite had been accomplished. General E. Kirby Smith and Bushrod R. Johnson made a proposition to the Board of Trustees in May, 1870, to reopen the literary department and use Montgomery Bell Academy as a preparatory school to support it. This was the first definite move made to resuscitate this department of the university. The Board of Trustees rejected the offer, and this brought forth a communication from the pen of John Berrien Lindsley to the board, which was published in advance to the citizens of Nashville. In this open letter, entitled "The Present Conditions and Prospects of the University," Chancellor Lindsley urged the acceptance of the proposal made by Messrs. Smith and Johnson to reorganize the collegiate department. He reviewed at length the origin and development of the university, and showed how the original grant of 60,000 acres made by Congress had by legislative manipulation been rendered unavailable to the university for many years. He explained how, after a delay of thirty years, the General Assembly, during the session of 1837-38, had finally agreed to allow the university half of a township, or 11,520 acres of land in the Ocoee District (then recently secured from the Cherokee Nation) in lieu of its claim upon the state for the

---

[40] Merriam, *op. cit.*, p. 50. [41] *Ibid.*

principal (not less than $100,000) and the interest for thirty years. This compromise on the part of the university and the legislature, he said, yielded to the university its college fund, which, in 1870, amounted to some $50,000 invested in Tennessee bonds. This gave an annual income of about $2,220. Dr. Lindsley argued that the property and funds held in trust by the board were intended by their donors to keep in operation a college in the generally accepted sense of the word (a literary department) which would serve all the people of the state. In other words, he urged that when the state of North Carolina and the government yielded this fund through land, they did so in order to perpetuate a standard college for the people of Tennessee. The board, he said, was obligated to keep open the literary department of the university rather than the professional schools.[42] Under the plan submitted by Messrs. Smith and Johnson, the literary department would be reopened and the board would thereby fulfill its obligation and trust without incurring the risk of further debts. Dr. Lindsley said:

> In 1870 the board finds itself very much in the same situation as in 1855, with large and valuable college buildings most beautifully situated within the limits of a wealthy, refined, and growing city, and with an income from its college fund not sufficient to pay one-half the salary of the principal or head of the institution, as such officers are now paid. While to the popular eye the institution is wealthy, its buildings and grounds attracting universal attention, it is in reality poor, very poor. Its endowment is utterly inadequate even to the keeping in repair of its large and costly buildings, and to the proper caring for its libraries, apparatus, et cetera. It has always depended, and must for years continue to depend, upon tuition fees for the payment of its corps of teachers.
>
> And here comes a consideration never to be lost sight of by the board in planning for its college. . . .
>
> By accepting these propositions, the University committed to your charge can in no event be damaged. All the risk is to be borne by the two distinguished gentlemen who propose to conduct

---

[42] This and the following statements are from John Berrien Lindsley, "The Present Conditions and Prospects of the University," *Bulletin of the University of Nashville,* May 21, 1870.

a great school under your charter and with your co-operation, in buildings which are now but partially used, and in the present unsettled financial condition of Tennessee may soon be not used at all. The only guarantee demanded by these gentlemen is that they shall continue in their professorships for the short period of fifteen years, instead of being at the pleasure of the board, and that they shall have the right to nominate their co-adjutors and associate teachers in the school. When it is considered that these gentlemen must at once obtain from the public several thousand dollars to place the buildings in good repair, that by their individual influence and efforts they are to draw students from distant states to fill these buildings, and that the salaries of the teaching corps will depend entirely upon their success in so doing, surely nothing less could be asked. As the board does not guarantee any pay, it is but fair that a reasonable time should be secured to these gentlemen so that after having faithfully and patiently sown the seed through a number of years, they may hope to reap the harvest through a second more remunerative period. As to nominating their associates, this is a courtesy usually conceded to heads of colleges by boards of trustees. . . .

He recalled the consolidation of the Western Military Institute with the university in 1855 upon the basis proposed by Messrs. Smith and Johnson, and reminded the board how successful this arrangement had become by 1860, when the war started. "The records of the department from 1855 to 1860 show conclusively that but for the great political misfortune which engulfed the whole southern country, the entire plan would have been an eminent success. . . ."

He reviewed the history of the medical school and showed how the Smith-Johnson proposal was almost identical with the plan submitted by the group of physicians who had opened and kept the medical school in operation during the twenty years.

By accepting the propositions now before us for the establishment of a collegiate department upon a plan somewhat analogous to that which has proved so brilliant a success in the medical branch of the institution, the board will meet the just expectations of the public, which has the right to demand the reopening of the college, with its commencements, its honors, its exhibitions, its academic life and animation. . . .

He not only recommended the plan, but he praised highly the gentlemen who were making the proposal. With reference to E. Kirby Smith, he said:

The gentlemen who are to head this important undertaking are known, honored, and esteemed throughout the entire land from whence students are expected to come, not merely as famous upon the great theater of public life, but as accomplished and experienced educators. The one, a member of a distinguished Connecticut family, though a native of Florida, was graduated with high honor at the National Academy at the early age of nineteen. After serving with distinction through the Mexican War, he was assigned a position as assistant professor at West Point, where for three years he taught the graduating classes, gaining well-merited eminence in this laborious work. For some eight years subsequently, he was stationed upon the Mexican frontier and in the Indian country, generally with a detached or independent command. Here he made high character for executive ability and for attainments in natural science. From the great civil strife he emerged with the happy and rare reputation, universally conceded, of a brilliant military genius combined with untarnished humanity and unblemished integrity. Among the various pursuits open to his choice, he hesitated for a season between taking orders in the Protestant Episcopal Church, or devoting himself to the work of teaching. He selected the latter as his calling. Having refused the presidency of several well-known institutions, he opened an establishment upon his own premises in Kentucky some year or two since. In consequence of the recent destruction of a large edifice by fire, he has, after visiting Nashville and consulting with friends, determined to unite in the propositions now before the board. . . .

He spoke of Colonel Bushrod R. Johnson's qualifications in the following words:

His associate in this proposition has so long been a resident of Nashville, and is so well known as identified with collegiate education, that it is hardly necessary to detail his antecedents. In early life he earned, by teaching, the means which enabled him to prepare for West Point, where he obtained a thorough scientific training, which characterizes the United States Military Academy. For a period of thirteen years previous to 1861, he was engaged in the work of education. He thus became personally acquainted with large classes of young men from the entire valley of the Mississippi. As a governor of boys and young men, the difficult work in all colleges, he made a high reputation. Retiring, and perhaps diffident when appearing in public, slow and cautious in his utterances, he has doubtless been too lightly appreciated by the careless or prejudiced observer. Amid the excitement of the battlefield, his rare powers of command and discipline have been fully acknowledged. Calm, conscientious, unflinching and firm in the discharge of irksome and onerous duty, he has uniformly won the confidence and respect, no less than the esteem, of many who have been associated with him as colleagues, or have been under his care as pupils. The two gentlemen well combine the qualifications essential to the management of a populous college. . . .

Dr. Lindsley had the feeling that it was entirely utopian to attempt to maintain a school for the humanities without a large and productive endowment, and again he appealed to the generosity of the public to raise such an endowment for the literary department of the institution. He again called attention to four departments which he felt the university could very well support if given encouragement by the public; namely, the literary department, the medical department (which was then going very well), the law department (which he had recommended in his earlier report), and a new department of agriculture and mechanical arts. With proper effort, he said, and with the co-operation of the people, he believed the agricultural and mechanical arts department would thrive.

Common sense, which is profound philosophy, teaches us that all institutions, including those designed to advance letters and science, must be adapted to the wants, desires, and prejudices, if you choose, of the people upon whose good will and fostering care they depend. Tropical plants will not flourish in temperate climates. We are called upon in Tennessee to build up a great seat of learning for Tennesseans, Kentuckians, Mississippians, and the citizens of other kindred and contiguous states. If we prudently, energetically, and without further loss of time address ourselves to this work, we shall undoubtedly succeed. For no city can surpass Nashville in eligibility as the site for such an institution; none has as yet outstripped us in the race. . . .

Having thus outlined to the Board of Trustees the broad field and great work of the University of Nashville, Dr. Lindsley resigned the office of chancellor, saying that imperative calls upon his time and attention from the medical department and private business left him no choice in the matter. He retained his chair in the medical faculty until 1873, when he retired as professor emeritus. He remained to the end a loyal and untiring friend of the university.

Upon his recommendation, the board accepted the proposal of Messrs. Smith and Johnson, but reserved the right to elect the faculty, approve or reject courses of study, and assume jurisdiction over the methods of discipline. The board was to furnish free of rent the use of the grounds and buildings, provide apparatus and all facilities for collegiate instruction, and make appropriations for twenty-five students for Montgomery Bell Academy. On the other hand, Messrs. Smith and Johnson agreed to make the undergraduate department, which included the college and academy, self-sustaining, the university assuming no liabilities beyond that of guaranteeing the salaries of the professors. For the first year or two under this management, the literary department met with some degree of success, but the need for a larger endowment and the financial crisis of 1873, which exhausted the South, compelled the institution to close its doors at the end of the fourth year, June 11, 1874. Thus the literary department of the University of Nashville came to another untimely end. It was to be reopened a year later, in 1875, through the co-operation of the trustees of the University of Nashville and the trustees of the Peabody Education Fund. The part played by John Berrien Lindsley in bringing these two boards together for the purpose of establishing Peabody College is told in a subsequent chapter.

CHAPTER III

DURING THE CIVIL WAR

IT WILL BE RECALLED that Dr. John Berrien Lindsley, as chancellor of the University of Nashville from 1855 to 1870, presided also over Western Military Institute, the literary department of the university, which was under the immediate direction of Colonel Bushrod Johnson and Lieutenant Colonel Richard Owen.

The winter of 1861 found the university with an enrollment of approximately six hundred students.[1] When the war clouds gathered and the call to arms came in the spring of that year, many of these students enrolled for military service. Young men with military training were sought for responsible assignments.[2] Under the command of their old instructors, Colonel Johnson and Lieutenant Colonel Owen, they answered the call, going as drill masters, commissioned officers, and on other assignments of importance. The military records of the South reveal many names found on the rolls of this student body, among them the name of Sam Davis, boy hero of the Confederacy.

The work of the literary department of the University of Nashville ceased in the spring of 1862. The medical school remained open throughout the Civil War.

We now return to Dr. Lindsley's diary, in which he wrote regularly for a period of more than thirteen years. Because of an avid interest in public affairs, he included in this diary many facts and references of social and political significance. His mature scholarship, intellectual honesty, and ability to present clearly the salient facts of a given situation ensure the integrity of this record.

Dr. Lindsley did not believe in secession. His position was that of many other distinguished Southerners. During the winter of 1861, Robert E. Lee wrote to his son Custis:

[1] *Catalogue of the University of Nashville*, 1861.
[2] Minutes of the University of Nashville and Western Military Institute, 1861.

LITERARY AND MILITARY DEPARTMENT OF THE UNIVERSITY OF NASHVILLE, 1858. TAKEN FROM THE CATALOGUE OF THAT YEAR

But I can anticipate no greater calamity for the country than a dissolution of the Union. . . .

Still, a Union that can only be maintained by swords and bayonets, and in which strife and civil war are to take the place of brotherly love and kindness, has no charm for me. . . . If the Union is dissolved, and the Government disrupted, I shall return to my native State and share the miseries of my people, and save in defence will draw my sword on none.[3]

In January, 1860, Dr. Lindsley accompanied members of the Tennessee and Kentucky legislatures on an excursion of good will into Ohio.[4] He gives in his diary a detailed account of this trip, and concludes with the statement: "The whole affair was undoubtedly the greatest Union demonstration of the season."[5] Although he believed in the preservation of the Union, and had little patience with the extreme state sovereign philosophy represented by the "South Carolina group," his sympathies and interests were with the South from the beginning to the end of the war. In an editorial written on November 9, 1860, and found in his unpublished work, "Thoughts and Hints," he condemns the separate secession of South Carolina as treason to the South as well as to the Federal Union:

South Carolina is now making preparations for separate secession. Admitting as we must that taking possession of the Federal power by a sectional party, omnipotent throughout nearly the entire North, and proclaiming loudly that free labor and slave labor—that is, white

---

[3] Douglas Southall Freeman, *R. E. Lee*, I, 420-421.

[4] *Nashville Gazette*, January 26, 1860: "The Tennessee legislature has gone abroad—gone to Louisville, Cincinnati, and perhaps to Columbus. They have ceased for a time to legislate for the good of the state, and have gone off on the state's time to eat sumptuous dinners at the expense of sister states."

[5] *Ibid.*, January 28, 1860: "Louisville, Ky., Jan. 25.—The banquet given at the Masonic Temple last night to the delegates from the various states was one of the grandest affairs that ever came off in the United States. Four states were largely represented—Ohio, Indiana, Kentucky, and Tennessee, with many others in various parts of the country. It was a genuine Union festival."

"Dayton, Ohio, Jan. 26.—The citizens of Dayton had made partial arrangements for the giving of a dinner tomorrow to the distinguished guests from Kentucky and Tennessee. . . ."

"Cincinnati, Ohio, Jan. 26.—The Kentucky and Tennessee legislatures reached Columbus at three o'clock this afternoon. They were conducted to the Hall of the House of Representatives and were received by the General Assembly in joint convention."

labor and African labor—are in irresistible and everlasting conflict, is cause for serious alarm and watchfulness in the slaveholding portion of the Union, yet it by no means follows that this alone creates a necessity for a revolution. There is every reason to be assured that the united action of the Southern states authoritatively announced would secure from the Free states the faithful execution of the fugitive slave law, and the acknowledgment of the right to create new slave states.

A special or particular league to demand and obtain and protect our rights in the Union would now be perfectly justifiable; inasmuch as a party professing hostility to our views and wishes has either obtained or is in the way of obtaining control of the entire machinery of government federal.

This species of league requires concert of action between all the states interested—and this course is alone just and proper now. All the slaveholding states are alike interested, all are alike threatened, all should have the opportunity of meeting together in council, of expressing their views, and finally agreeing to the course of action seeming best to the majority.

Separate state action, or even that of two or three or four states, is justifiable under no pretext whatever. It is in fact both discourteous and disloyal to the sister slaveholding states—and indicates plainly an overweening self conceit in judgment and an intention to compel the other slave states to follow whether willing or not.

It is an attempt to overbear, browbeat and dragoon Tennessee, Virginia, and other states into a separate confederacy with them, even when it is evident that the vast majority of the people of these states are opposed bitterly to secession, and wish to maintain the present grand and splendid imperial Confederation.

Separate secession by South Carolina is treason to the slaveholding sister states as well as to the Federal Union, which as yet has not given cause for revolution, whatever party leaders have threatened.

If South Carolina now goes out alone, it will be clear that she merely makes Mr. Lincoln's election a pretext for breaking up a government which she has long detested, notwithstanding her close affiliation with the party administering that government for years past, and in which she has had a controlling voice. It will prove that all her declaration of loyalty to the Constitution, and of a desire to secure only constitutional rights, have been false and hollow-hearted; and that she is really controlled by men who from selfish or theoretical views believe a slaveholding confederacy would best promote their welfare.[6]

The University of Nashville, to which John Berrien Lindsley and his father before him had dedicated their lives, was located in the very center of the war zone. As chancellor of the institution, Dr. Lindsley determined, and wisely, that it was his duty to remain and protect the buildings, grounds, equipment, and very life of the institution during the fratricidal conflict. This decision was not made, however, until after his return from Richmond, where he went to see if volunteer surgeons were needed.

The medical school of the university, therefore, kept its doors open during the five years of hostilities. And because of Dr. Lindsley's vigilance its buildings, grounds, library, and equipment were in a fair state when the war closed. His position as a noncombatant rebel no doubt saved the university from total destruction. Had he assumed the position taken by Dr. C. D. Elliott, president of the Nashville Female Academy, the University of Nashville would in all probability have gone the way of that institution and its notable history would have terminated in 1861.

Dr. Lindsley's faithfulness in recording the events of these stirring times enables us to follow him through the dark days of the war. On April 20, 1861, he makes this entry in his diary: "All of this week the city intensely excited." On July 8 of that year, he again expressed his thoughts on secession in an editorial, in which he placed the responsibility directly on the South Carolina ordinance:

The enormous war preparations are now coming to a head, and rumors of great battles are afloat. Whatever may be the remote causes of this (Slavery, Tariff, State-rights, etc.), is not the Secession ordinance of S. C. the direct cause of it all? Would not years of patient & united effort on the part of the slaveholding states to secure their rights in the Union have been infinitely better than the present fearful war?

[6] I, 1-2.

Many think such an effort would have been successful. It ought at all events to have been tried, before this awful appeal to arms was made; for that secession meant war our Northern States uniformly declared, and we should have taken them at their word. The S. C. Ordinance in Dec. 1860 was de facto a declaration of war against the U. S. A.; even regarding the Constitution merely as a treaty—the Union as a league—such an ordinance for such causes was a declaration of war.[7]

Then follows an account of the trip to Richmond, Virginia, to find out if volunteer surgeons would be needed. He left Nashville on July 29, at 3:15 P.M., eight days after Bull Run. After an interview with Surgeon General Moore in Richmond and much observation, he became convinced that volunteer surgeons were not welcome. He returned to Nashville on the morning of September 5, and recommended to the ladies of Nashville that the best agent for managing their contributions was the army committee of the Young Men's Christian Association.

The entries in his diary during the summer and fall of 1861 deal for the most part with interests not related to war. Politics, gardening, faculty meetings, field trips, lectures, funerals, finance, education, the weather, and domestic affairs are some of the topics recorded.

On December 2 he refers to the excitement caused by militia drafting, which disturbed both departments of the university; and then, on December 28, he tells us that the gun factory on College Street is near completion.[8] The last entry in 1861 reads: "A year of confusion and trouble."

If the year 1861 had been one of confusion and trouble, the following year was to prove more trying. On January 23, 1862, "there is great excitement about Zollicoffer's disaster"; and on February 1, "General Zollicoffer's remains arrived in Nashville." A few days before, Henry Fogg's body had arrived and there

---

[7] *Ibid.*, p. 14.
[8] There were three gun factories of importance in the South during the Civil War. One was located in Nashville; one in Selma, Alabama; and one in Augusta, Georgia.

had been a large delegation at the depot to receive it.[9] February 7, "gave the fifty-seventh and last lecture of my course. Great apprehension for the safety of Nashville."[10]

On February 12, 1862, Dr. Lindsley was notified that the university buildings were needed for hospitals. By working a large force all day he succeeded in clearing the buildings and moving the library. At four o'clock in the afternoon he was visited by Dr. Pim, who requested him to act as surgeon. Two days later he notified Dr. Pim that the hospitals would be ready by the sixteenth. He was then ordered to be ready for convalescents immediately, as the Bowling Green troops were arriving in large numbers. Upon further conversation with Dr. Pim, he discovered that an encampment was also being established on the university grounds. Dr. Lindsley took the position that the hospitals and the encampment would greatly interfere with each other, so he hastened to Captain A. J. Lindsay, commander of the post, and after much persistent argument got an order to remove the encampment. He hurried back to the university with the order and presented it to Captain Cattles, who received him "civilly" and agreed to carry out the order if Dr. Lindsley would provide shelter for his men that night. Snow was on the ground and it was bitterly cold. All day crowds of forty, fifty, or a hundred had been pouring in from the Bowling Green army. These men were tired and hungry. Dr. Lindsley and his hospital staff fed seven hundred who were quartered in barracks in the stone college that night, and gave to each man a gill of brandy from the hospital stores.

On Saturday, February 15, when all were worn out with the task of feeding some six hundred convalescents, rumor came of the battle of Fort Donelson. A great mass meeting was held at the Capitol that evening to celebrate the repulse of the gunboats, but the joy was short-lived. News came the next day of the fall of Fort Donelson. "During all Sunday from 10:00 A.M.,

[9] Will T. Hale and Dixon L. Merritt, *A History of Tennessee and Tennesseans*, III, 108.

[10] This and the following statements are from Dr. Lindsley's diary.

when the news of the fall of Fort Donelson reached here, the wildest excitement prevailed in the city. There were many persons fled the city in vehicles—many on the cars. The Governor and legislature decamped. Nashville was a panic-stricken city. The Union men alone seemed to have their heads about them." "Johnston's army passing by the university from 10:00 A.M. until dark; camped out near Mill Creek. Light of campfires very bright that night." The army was in rapid retreat. The Southern army regretted bitterly the necessity of abandoning the city without a struggle, but it was too small to make a stand against the overwhelmingly superior numbers of the Union troops.

During the confusion and panic in Nashville, Dr. Lindsley assumed a position of heavy responsibility.[11] Early on that Sabbath morning he was ordered to assemble all the men in the hospital who were able to walk and to place them under a sergeant, with orders to report at once to the camp on the Murfreesboro Pike. This order was executed, and by two o'clock he had scarcely more than a hundred men left. Immediately all hands were set to work cleaning the buildings for the reception of the wounded from Fort Donelson, who were expected to arrive at any time. At daybreak on February 17, Dr. Lindsley issued a requisition for food sufficient to feed 750 men for 90 days. This requisition was issued on the assumption that many wounded would arrive from Fort Donelson and that when the Federal army occupied the city the hospital would have some 400 or 500 patients. In case these men were not recognized as prisoners of war, the provisions would supply the hospital for six or seven weeks, until they were well; or, in case the rules of war were observed, the hospitals would be turned over to the Federals well supplied. The requisition was approved, and when

[11] When news of the surrender of Fort Donelson on February 16, 1862, reached Nashville, Dr. C. D. Elliott, president of the Nashville Female Academy, was attending services at McKendree Methodist Church. He went immediately to the academy and gave orders that all trunks be packed for the exodus. With the effective cooperation of the railroads, by midnight more than four hundred girls, representing the South's proudest families, were speeding homeward.—J. E. Windrow, "Collins D. Elliott and the Nashville Female Academy," *Tennessee Historical Magazine*, Vol. III (1935), No. 2, p. 74.

Dr. Lindsley arrived at the commissary department he found a great crowd there, "carrying off bacon." There was a mad scramble for supplies. Vehicles of all kinds were used for transporting them. Stout men were walking off with sides of bacon and hams. Some persons secured large amounts. This promiscuous and irregular scramble was stopped by General Floyd at noon.[12]

At noon on February 17, Dr. Lindsley was summoned to a conference with Dr. Yandell, who appointed him post surgeon of all the hospitals in Nashville, stating that Dr. Pim was obliged to accompany General Albert Sidney Johnston. This work was taken over with the understanding that Dr. Pim would attend to the duties of the office for two days in order to give Dr. Lindsley time to get his hospital in readiness. It was also understood that Dr. Lindsley was to retain his post as acting surgeon at the university. Later that same afternoon, Dr. Lindsley talked with Dr. Pim, who told him that the hospitals were in great confusion as several of the surgeons and assistants had left suddenly and it would be necessary to send someone to each hospital to ascertain the true condition:

> As a day of panic and terrified confusion, this was equal to the preceding. Large bodies of the retreating army were hastening through and getting their supplies as they passed. Many citizens and their families left on the cars and in vehicles. So absorbed was I with my special work as to be but little conscious of all this. . . .
>
> What I saw of Johnston's army today and yesterday fully equaled any description I have ever read of an army in hurried retreat before a superior force whose fangs they must avoid. There was hurry, confusion, alarm, and on the part of many a sullen dissatisfaction at not being able to fight.

On Tuesday, February 18, there was "a great deal of pressing of all kinds of vehicles." A carriage, a wagon, or a vehicle of any description was retained with great difficulty, even when carefully guarded. Dr. Lindsley made up a guard of ten or fifteen of his convalescents and armed them, in order that they

---

[12] This and the following statements are from Dr. Lindsley's diary.

might protect his vehicles and help to secure supplies from the public stores. He issued a handbill of appeal in behalf of the sick and wounded, then at the close of the evening went to headquarters to ascertain the number of men for whom his hospitals were responsible. He found that there were perhaps one thousand sick and wounded in the several hospitals.

On Thursday, February 20, at 2:00 A.M., Nelson, Dr. Lindsley's colored servant, gave him a nice breakfast, which was shared by Dr. Bowlecock and Mr. Colvin, both from Memphis. He had met these gentlemen at the corner of Cherry and Deaderick streets inquiring for a coffeehouse. He enjoyed his chat with them because "the Doctor was with Walker in Nicaragua." It will be remembered that Dr. Lindsley and William Walker, "the Gray-eyed Man of Destiny," were boyhood friends and classmates in college.

At 4:00 A.M. the suspension and railroad bridges across the Cumberland were in flames.

I have never witnessed a more strikingly beautiful scene than that which met my eyes while standing on the platform of the door of the college mess hall about 4:00 A.M. The wire bridge was a line of flooring on fire, the railroad bridge a perfect framework of flame. The whole lit up brilliantly the scarred fringe of the city.

At this moment the ordnance works just west of the State Prison burst into flames and added to the brightness of the illumination. The day was spent in transferring supplies and food from the downtown storehouses to the hospital and university.

Passing A. V. S. Lindsley's office, saw a group of men coming out of the cellar. One of them proved to be Bradley, Van's waiter. Told him if he would open the office for us and attend on us all day he could have $100. He went along at once.

Since the exodus which followed the fall of Fort Donelson, when most of the vehicles were taken from the city, there were few left to be used for transporting supplies and the wounded soldiers to the hospitals.

As I was driving down Market Street below the medical college, Captain Hawkins' company of Home Guards was marching up the hill on their way to the army. The company was quite full, and I recognized many familiar faces. They gave in response to my bows a hearty farewell cheer. It was very sad indeed to see these poor fellows, in obedience to stern military rule, leaving their homes and families just on the eve of the enemy's advance.

The scenes of confusion and pilfering witnessed in the government storehouses on this day baffled description. At the commissary warehouses, as on Monday, bacon and other stores were freely given away. This occasioned a rush after provisions which interfered seriously with the soldiers who were getting supplies for the Confederate troops leaving for the south. An officer with whom Dr. Lindsley talked told him that he had thirty-six starving men near the Chattanooga depot to feed and that he could get neither food nor conveyance. "I told him to press a small contraption which was hauling bacon for a citizen, and went with him to Broad Street, where we got supplies. He then went on his way happy enough."

On February 22, Dr. Lindsley wrote the following letter to Dr. Yandell, expressing concern over the existing conditions and asking for an authenticated document from Albert Sidney Johnston that would make his actions legal:

MEDICAL HEAD QUARTERS
NASHVILLE, Feb. 22, 1862

Your despatch of the 21, duly received. It is utterly impossible to get any servants to follow the army.

Your second despatch same date received to day. There is some mistake; *I sent no men* by Dr. Childers. In all cases I impress upon them the necessity of taking every thing possible with them. But what can the poor fellows do! all the government offices are in the greatest confusion—a perfect *panic and stampede:* most valuable stores of every description scattered to the winds, pillaged by drunken soldiers . . . & stolen by shop lifters. By great labor and several fortuitous combinations I have secured a large amount of provisions, and some valuable quartermaster's stores. These if not taken away by Confederate or Federal authority will be enough prudently administered to save us from becoming beggars whether to the people, or the Federals. Send me instructions by Dr. Thomas as to how I shall manage to support the hospitals, and meet all the engagements & expenses necessarily made and incurred.

The authority of Post Surgeon is just now quite extensive—heavy, very heavy responsibilities, & I am no military man and could easily involve myself in difficulties with the Richmond or Washington Governments. Therefore as I am redeeming my pledge to aid you, do you get a document properly authenticated, from Gen. A. S. Johnston, which will make my actions legal.

My Apothecary, Dr. Thomas, can note full the events of the past week. I also refer you to Col. Morehead, 2nd Reg. for particulars.

Today I despatched the Steamer Hillman to Clarksville for our wounded. Cave Johnson and others have written very pressingly to this effect.

Very respectfully
Your friend in haste
J. BERRIEN LINDSLEY

To Dr. D. W. Yandell, M.D.

P.S. Dr. Thomas goes on business for my father-in-law, Jacob McGavock, Clerk of the Confederate Court—any aid you can give him will be a personal favour.[13]

This letter was returned to Dr. Lindsley two days later bearing on the reverse side the following notations:

Dr. Lindsley will take all necessary steps for the comfort of the sick now, or that may hereafter come under his charge. Of course Dr. L. will exercise all proper economy, but will obtain such supplies as may be required for the welfare of Confederate sick in hospitals at Nashville.

D. W. YANDELL
HEAD QUARTERS W. DEPT.
M'BORO, Feb. 24, 1862

Dr. D. W. Yandell
  Med. Division
What authority he thinks proper in the premises
            by command [ALBERT SIDNEY] JOHNSTON

Friday, Saturday, Sunday, and Monday were spent preparing for the wounded expected from Clarksville. It was thought there

---

[13] The Lindsley Papers. Italics mine.

would be about three hundred. Letters from Cave Johnson and others represented the condition there as most deplorable.[14] Doubtless the condition was as described during the panic and campaign just previous to Federal occupation, but when the steamer "Hillman," which had been dispatched to Clarksville, returned there were only four wounded on it, and it was reported that the people of Clarksville were taking good care of their sick and wounded. Late in the afternoon of February 24, it was reported that the Federal fleet was near at hand and that the Federal cavalry pickets had come to Edgefield. The next morning Dr. Lindsley "witnessed from University Hill the arrival of a Federal fleet, a noble but distressing sight. Nelson's brigade of five thousand passed by the university about 4:00 P.M. Quite a number of Federal surgeons came to the university during the day, Dr. Gay, of Columbus, Ohio, among them. They asked leave to send some sick men the next day between 9:00 and 11:00 A.M. The university now presented a fine hospital garb, clean-swept, four hundred nicely arranged cots, and neat grounds. Being directly in the way of the army, it was not surprising that the surgeons so quickly took it."

Wednesday, February 26, "troops passing all day. All the air and assumption of a conquering host. The surgeon with whom I had to do not a little truculent—Taylor and Johnson perfect brutes."

On Friday, February 28, Dr. Lindsley surrendered the university hospital and stores to Surgeon Johnson. A few days later, on Tuesday, March 4, he accompanied Dr. Murray, who was the senior medical officer and director of Buell's staff, to the hospital buildings and later to Van Lindsley's office, where he instructed him concerning the quartermaster's stores. "This wound up my business as acting surgeon of the Confederate army."

His official duties as post surgeon having come to an end, we find Dr. Lindsley's interest turning again to the university

---

[14] This and the following statements are from Dr. Lindsley's diary.

and the grounds. On March 17, he wrote, "Saw Horn about fixing my two rooms in the Faculty House. Set workmen to repairing the fence around university grounds." Later a new hydrant was put in the grounds, and the fencing continued until it was completed.

On April 2 Dr. Lindsley wrote in his journal the following editorial, which succinctly explains the European dilemma with reference to our war between the states:

Both Northern and Southern partisans are disappointed at the unsympathising attitude of European writers in periodicals. This should not excite surprise. The South is fighting for the right of governing themselves: while at the same time they deny to four millions of Africans the right of owning themselves. Now to European thinkers, the latter is a much more indefeasible right than the former.

On the other hand the North is fighting to force upon the South a supreme or federal government which with great unanimity they desire to throw off. Yet Northern statesmen and people all contend for the principle announced and demonstrated in and by the American Revolution—the right of the people to govern themselves—that government was made for the people, and not the people for the government—the great American political maxim. They are thus fighting right in the face of the very principle upon which the union which they are defending is avowedly based.

Need we wonder that the rather biased lookers-on beyond the Atlantic should be tempted to exclaim, O ye wicked hypocrites, who so coolly deny to others rights and privileges ye so loudly claim and fiercely fight about. God hath in just judgment given you up to blind rage that thus you may work out for each other a mutual and deserved destruction.[15]

Shortly after this time Dr. Lindsley left with Jacob McGavock for Washington, where he secured a pass from the War Department to see his brother-in-law, Randall McGavock, who had been captured at Fort Donelson and was imprisoned at Fort Warren. He returned to Nashville several weeks later, in time to hear the report of the Confederate capture of Murfreesboro on July 13, and to witness the preparations made in Nashville

[15] "Thoughts and Hints," I, 22-23.

to receive an attack from the Confederate army on July 14. Cannon were planted around the university, the Capitol, Hume School, and on the principal streets. Companies were stationed to support the artillery. Federal officials announced that the city would be destroyed if it were attacked.[16]

A few days later, July 21, there was another scare about a battle in the direction of Murfreesboro, and Dr. Lindsley tells of the artillery that was planted all around his house—"not very comfortable." And then, on July 22, he made this entry: "General Forrest with his cavalry drew up opposite the Insane Asylum about 5:00 P.M. and sent detachments to destroy railroad bridges. Here streets are barricaded with wagons. Every effort made to resist General Forrest. Twelve-pounder rifles command the principal streets."[17]

There had been much skirmishing throughout the week in and around Nashville, particularly along Mill Creek. The weather was unusually hot and heavy rains fell. The city was in a state of real alarm until reinforcements began to arrive on July 23.

Again there was excitement in Nashville on December 6, occasioned by the news from Washington and by the passing of Buell's army through the city. Twelve regiments camped on the university and Lindsley grounds. On September 13, Dr. Lindsley secured an interview with General Thomas and was assured by him that the Lindsley house would not be demolished without an official order, and only in case of an impending battle. General Thomas also assured him that he would place a soldier at the door of every room of the university that contained books.

[16] John Berrien Lindsley, MS Diary.
[17] *Nashville Dispatch*, July 23, 1862: "In the past day or two, we have had a repetition of the late Murfreesboro alarm. Gen. Forrest, with a large force of cavalry, has turned up at Lebanon, Wilson County. On Monday evening, six of the Federal pickets were attacked by a body of twenty of Forrest's men in an orchard on the Lebanon Pike, a short distance from the city. Five of the pickets were captured, the other escaping. Later in the evening, three bridges on the Chattanooga Railroad, within eight miles of the city, were burned down. Forrest is said to have a force of from 1200 to 2000, and on yesterday he was reported only five or six miles distant. The Union troops here are under arms and preparations are making to resist any attack that may be made. Unusual vigilance is displayed by the Provost Guard, and they have already arrested many rashly jubilant citizens, among whom are some who claim to have had interviews with Gen. Forrest."

Later in the day after he had consulted with Mr. Wood, Dr. Lindsley gave orders that the books and apparatus should be boxed, and the next day his orders were carried out. At two o'clock on the morning of September 15, General Thomas' division began to move, and by daylight the university grounds were completely deserted. "University property much damaged by the move yesterday. Faculty furniture and fixtures badly abused, although myself and assistants did all we could to protect it." On September 18, we find this entry:

> Rifle pits dug all across my garden. Noticed that Dr. McMasters, chaplain, had no chairs or table in his room while the niggers had—the latter are quartered in the barracks and recitation buildings—negro men, women, and children occupying the handsomest college building in the State. What vandalism! How little in accordance with Northern devotion to education.

On September 19, he estimated the damage done to the university by the encampment thus far to be as follows: "To fencing, over 6,000 feet, $1,500; to furniture carried off, $1,000; heating and washing apparatus, $500; boxing up books and apparatus, approximately $200."[18]

On Thursday, October 2, Dr. William James Bass was killed in a most brutal manner at his home on the outskirts of the city. Dr. Lindsley sat up with the remains that night and attended the funeral the following day. A few days later he wrote in his diary under the name of William James Bass two lines from Swift:

> The soldier smiling hears the widow's cries,
> And stabs the son before the mother's eyes.

A large Federal force left Nashville at midnight on October 7, and evidently won a victory over the Confederates quartered about thirteen miles out on the Murfreesboro Pike. They returned about 2:00 P.M. with prisoners and plunder and "big tales of the fight."[19]

---

[18] John Berrien Lindsley, MS Diary.
[19] *Nashville Dispatch*, October 8, 1862: "The city was thrown into an unusual state of excitement yesterday morning, by the current rumor that a number of Confederate

Phil Sheridan's entire baggage train camped on the university grounds on December 26, and shortly thereafter a great forward movement was launched. Half of the wagon train, Dr. Lindsley said, went with the army, and the other half remained in the city. All day the long trains were going out and coming in on all the streets in view of his house.

Ministering to the sick, filling the pulpit each Sunday, laboring day and night to protect the buildings of the university, and using his influence and energy to care for his people, Dr. Lindsley closes his diary for 1862 with this entry: "So ends this year of the horrors of war, forever memorable in the annals of the world as stamping indelibly upon the Northern faction the mark of Cain. Unable to conquer, they endeavor to exterminate a people."

New Year's Day, 1863, brought no relief from the "horrors of war." Dr. Lindsley wrote: "Federal soldiers are reporting a great battle near Murfreesboro in which they have driven all before them. . . . Federal wounded are continually being brought in. Intense anxiety among our own people about their relations and friends in the battle. Mrs. Josiah Nichol has thirteen grandsons there."

In the midst of tragedy and confusion, Dr. Lindsley wrote in his journal on March 13, 1863, the following editorial, in which he turns to history and the Supreme Ruler for a renewal of hope for the future:

Looking at what is now, and has for more than two years been passing before our eyes, we are apt to be overwhelmed with deep melancholy, sadness of soul, and utter despair for the future of our country.

In a fit of sudden madness under the guidance of corrupt, of selfish, or ambitious leaders, we have seen the splendid fabric of American

---

prisoners had been brought into town. It was generally known that a large force had left about midnight on Monday, taking the Murfreesboro Pike, and as it was known that the Confederates were in force at Lavergne, a fight was of course expected. Forty or 50 Confederates were killed and 240 taken prisoners. Federals captured all the camp equipage. All the prisoners are located in Nashville at penitentiary and workhouse."

nationality and constitutional freedom suddenly level with the ground. We have seen peculation and corruption in their most abominable forms prevailing among government officials, even those occupying the highest stations, as seats in the senate or the cabinet. We have seen mob violence widely diffused and devoted to the most devilish ends, as in the persecution of the poor helpless negro race, or to the suppression of freedom of speech and thought in the destruction of printing offices. We have seen all the guarantees for personal liberty, freedom of conscience and freedom of speech, so carefully and solemnly provided by the American Constitution swept away, and absolute, irresponsible power given to a party and a dictator. We have seen vast and beautiful regions, lately blooming in all the pride of agricultural wealth, given over to desolation and pillage and visited with all the horrors of war in its most savage, pitiless and unrelentive forms. We have seen all the sacredness of private life contemned and a system of examining letters, spying, deleting, entrapping, practised quite equalling any Russian or Austrian practices in this line, which in times past have excited our warmest indignation and surprise at the baseness of government and its minions. We have seen the whole available strength of the nation called to the battle field, miserably to perish there in fratricidal strife.

Such is a faint picture of the condition to which their violent political passions and their wicked unprincipled leaders have reduced the thirty or forty millions of American citizens lately the most prosperous and the happiest people on the globe. Truly we have fallen on evil days.

But is there no hope for the future? Have not other nations had their days of tribulation and fearful trial, and yet emerged therefrom and resumed their pristine glory with even greater brilliance than before, purified and exalted by the fiery trials through which they had passed? The horrors of the Thirty Years' War are a familiar tale, yet Germany owed her liberty, and her subsequent intellectual pre-eminence, influence, and glory to that fearful contest. Where were English freedom and institutions during the calamitous period of civil war, 1640-1660, with its exiles, confiscations, executions, and military despotism. What over-turning and chaotic changes in church and state and social life! Yet how gradually and surely did English constitutional liberty work its way back! And how wonderfully did those times of woe and trouble and fearful dissension lay a broad and deep and solid foundation for British freedom and empire, so that this very period is the starting point from whence we date her steady and rapid growth in empire and renown abroad and her settlement in greater internal peace and happiness than has ever blessed any nation with whose history we are acquainted. The struggles, woes, calamities and horrors, internal and external, through which Revolutionary France passed during a period of twenty-five years are as familiar to all as a twice told tale. Their end is not yet. But one thing is certain, it was the period of her greatest influence upon the affairs of the world, and has left her a renown and intellectual might which still place her second to no other nation in the world.

Germany, England, France, the three great centers of modern power and civilization, have thus in turn passed through the fiery furnace of evil days as exhibited in the worst form of revolutionary civil wars with all their concomitant horrors. Why should America be exempt from a similar lot? Of a certainty our present calamitous condition is not singular and unprecedented. And thus looking at other nations and other countries in other times we may have hope for our own beloved land in this its day of tribulation.

Wonderful is the Providence of the Supreme Ruler, still from evil educing good, still restraining the wrath of man and causing the remainder thereof to praise him.

The Lord reigneth, let the earth rejoice, let the multitude of isles be glad thereof![20]

Nashville was in a state of trouble and alarm in April, many citizens having been arrested for engaging in politics. Many others were required at this time to take the oath of allegiance. In addition, a bond had to be posted. The Lindsleys and McGavocks were required to give a five-thousand-dollar bond for each member of the family, including Dr. Lindsley. Many who could not execute a bond were thrown into prison.

Dr. Lindsley sent in a claim for the university before the United States commissioner on March 25, and on April 16 he was requested to hand to Captain Driver his declaration of citizenship to accompany the claim. He spoke also at this time in behalf of the claim of Moses B. Stevens and his estate. Captain Driver appeared "interested and agreeable."[21]

May 16, 1863, was a sad day in the Lindsley and McGavock

---

[20] The Lindsley Papers.
[21] This and the following statements are from Dr. Lindsley's diary.

families. While out walking with Dr. Hoyt, Dr. Lindsley bought a copy of the *Louisville Democrat* from a newsboy. In looking over the telegraphic column, he saw that Colonel McGavock of the Tenth Tennessee had been killed. He hurried home and was met at the door by Fanny, the servant, who told him that "Marse Randall" had been killed.

Randall McGavock, Dr. Lindsley's brother-in-law, was the eldest son and the pride of the McGavock family. It was he who organized the Robertson Association, the purpose of which was to alleviate suffering in times of epidemics and financial stress in the city and county. The work of this association locally was very much the same as that of the American Red Cross today. It was later reorganized and kept alive by Dr. Lindsley. Randall McGavock was one of the most popular young men of his day in Nashville and served at one time as mayor of the city. He was killed in the battle of Raymond, Mississippi.

On June 8, 1863, Dr. Lindsley spent three hours, from nine until twelve in the morning, before the commission on claims, chiefly in behalf of the university. He found the men "business-like and civil." He was again called before this commission on June 11, this time in behalf of the medical college. A few days later he received a letter from Grundy McGavock, of Memphis, confirming the report of Randall McGavock's death and stating that he had his seal ring and knew where he was buried. On July 30, Dr. Lindsley received from Russell Houston, chairman of the Federal Commission, the promise of a proper certificate respecting the claim of the university.

On September 20, 1863, the diary reads: "It is a custom of the military authorities to go to the colored people's churches on Sunday when they wish to make a big haul of pressed men." A few days later Dr. Lindsley refers to a "horrible catastrophe" at the Maxwell House, where the stairs gave way and precipitated two hundred Confederate prisoners from the fifth to the second floor.[22]

[22] *Nashville Dispatch*, September 20, 1863: "A dreadful accident occurred yesterday morning about eight o'clock at the Maxwell House, called Barracks No. 1." Con-

On October 22, a medical faculty meeting was held, at which time Drs. Bowling, Winston, Briggs, and Lindsley were present.[28]

Dr. Lindsley's diary of 1864 is a recital of long hours of watchfulness and labor in protecting the campus of the university. But his optimism is still assertive. "Dr. Bowling and myself are both settled in the conviction that when peace comes we should put the medical department on the same basis as that of the University of Michigan, and thus render it, as formerly, a great school."

He had to be ever alert to retain possession of the grounds. During the latter part of 1864, it was necessary to arrange the center buildings of the medical college for tenants in order to exclude squatters and keep control of the campus for the faculty. Many families were therefore permitted to use the buildings and Dr. Lindsley's problem was so to place them that they would not interfere with the medical and collegiate schools. On April 10 of that year, he had succeeded in getting the university buildings on the government roll at a monthly rental of three hundred and fifty dollars.

Reference is made, on September 1, to great excitement which prevailed because the city was threatened by the Confederates, and, on September 2, the occupation of Atlanta by Sherman is recorded.

On December 2 there was a great army movement in and around Nashville. A large force of government employees was at work on entrenchments from the reservoir through the university grounds. The trenches were staked off directly through Dr. Lindsley's yard. Captains Barlow and Wilcox, of the Missouri Engineers, who were in charge, were very kind and considerate. "They took pains to make the trenches run so as to destroy as few homes as possible." The homes of Dr. Lindsley

---

federate soldiers were housed in the building. When going down to breakfast, too many crowded on the stairway and the steps collapsed.

[28] This and the following statements are from Dr. Lindsley's diary.

and Dr. Hoyt were directly in line, but the trenches were diverted to run immediately behind these houses.[24]

On December 3 Dr. Lindsley states: "Citizens expect General Hood to attack the place; breastworks through our place; considerable cannonading." Then, on December 4, he refers to skirmishing and cannonading, and tells us that about seventy-five hundred men are working on the fortifications through his garden and the university grounds.

On December 6 Captain Barlow told him that orders had been issued to make the fortifications permanent, and recommended the removal of the servants' house and shed. Skirmishing was going on in and around the edge of town.

On Wednesday, December 7, there was heavy skirmishing at 10:00 A.M. between the Murfreesboro and Nolensville turnpikes. Smoke from the musketry of both lines was plainly visible from the Lindsley home. The weather was turning cold. Work on the fortifications continued through Thursday, December 8. Dr. Lindsley refers to Captain J. W. Root, who was in charge of the hands walling up the new work. Then, on Friday, a very cold day with sleet on the ground, the servants' house, which was being moved and pushed through a ditch by a large number of men, was stopped halfway because of the cold. On Saturday, December 10, work was resumed and the house reached its final resting place. The cold was still bitter—"ice everywhere." Sunday, December 11, continued cold. On Monday, at 7:00 A.M., the weather was moderating, and Tuesday the skirmishing in and around the city continued. The trenches were now in readiness but were not yet occupied.

On Thursday morning, December 15, Dr. Lindsley was awakened about two o'clock in the morning by brisk musketry and artillery firing, and by daylight the Union soldiers could be seen filing into position behind the breastworks.[25] A brigade of five

---

[24] Dr. Lindsley's home at this time was located in the block which he owned, bordered on the north by Lindsley Avenue, on the south by Carroll Street, on the east by Maple Street, and on the west by Market Street (now Second Avenue).

[25] *Daily Union* (Nashville), December 16, 1864: "At early dawn yesterday, our troops were all in line of battle, and an advance commenced soon after daylight. Little

regiments occupied the grounds in and around Dr. Lindsley's home. The One Hundred and Forty-second Indiana was stationed immediately in front of the house. Mrs. Lindsley and the two children were hurriedly sent to the home of Jacob McGavock, Dr. Lindsley's father-in-law, who lived on what is now Fourth Avenue between Union and Church streets.

Thus began the first day of the battle of Nashville. There was a heavy roar of artillery on the center all day, with intermittent skirmishing on the left. Federal batteries occupied Love and Foster's hills. By night all was quiet and the soldiers slept in the muddy trenches.

During the forenoon of Friday, December 16, cannon could be heard constantly. In the afternoon the battle was fierce, "one continuous roar of artillery." The mercury registered sixty-five degrees. There was a shower of rain in the evening.

The next day, December 17, there was heavy rain and mud, the weather was warmer, the battle was over, and Hood was gone.

Immediately after the battle of Nashville, Dr. Lindsley obtained permission from Captain J. W. Barlow to rebuild the fences around the university and repair the damage done to the campus and buildings.

On April 3, 1865, we are told that there was great rejoicing among the Union people in Nashville over the capture of Richmond and Petersburg, and the surrender of General Lee. The rejoicing came to an abrupt end when news of the assassination of President Lincoln reached Nashville at 10:00 A.M. on Saturday, April 15. "A day of festival turned into one of mourning." Four days later there was a memorial procession in Nashville for the President. The line was formed for the most part of soldiers and government employees.

---

was done except reconnoitering till after noon; but at twenty minutes till one, the order to advance was given and the whole column moved forward. The Fifteenth Ohio, of Col. Straight's brigade, commanded by Col. Frank Askew, captured five guns on the extreme left, near McCeedy's house, on the Granny White Pike. The Confederates were driven back. Eighteen guns were captured and twelve hundred prisoners. . . ." (This paper was in sympathy with the Union; "our" means "Union.")

On June 2 Dr. Lindsley makes this interesting observation: "A notable feature in the history of Nashville during the past two weeks is the return of large numbers of former citizens who have cast their fortunes with the Confederate cause."

After the war Dr. Lindsley edited the *Confederate Military Annals of Tennessee,* a splendid volume of about nine hundred pages, in which was given a review of military operations in Tennessee with regimental histories and a memorial roll call. This book, published in 1886, was the first volume of an encyclopedia of Tennessee history which he planned to publish and upon which he no doubt did a vast amount of research work. The second volume, which was scheduled for publication a year later, in 1887, was to be an index of the officers and men who served in the Confederate army of Tennessee. This, he said, would include an alphabetical list of about eight thousand officers and approximately sixty thousand soldiers. The third volume of the series was to complete the regimental histories and memorial rolls begun in the first and carry biographical data on the more prominent Confederate officers and soldiers. The three volumes were to constitute an exhaustive record of Confederate Tennessee.

Unfortunately, the first volume was the only one ever published—for perhaps two reasons. First, the Tennessee public did not respond in a financial way with sufficient generosity to encourage the author to do the vast amount of work and assume the heavy responsibility necessary to continue the series. And second, Dr. Lindsley was at this time engaged in promoting a health program for the state of Tennessee, the possibilities of which were so challenging that he devoted the greater portion of his time thereafter to its development. Nor did he ever find the time to write a volume of the encyclopedia dealing with the civil and political phases of Tennessee history, although there is evidence that he had collected and arranged much of the material.

In protecting the buildings, equipment, and grounds of the

University of Nashville during the years of the Civil War, Dr. Lindsley rendered a significant service to the cause of public education in the South. One of the determining factors in the establishment of Peabody College in Nashville in 1875 was the offer of this plant to the trustees of the Peabody Education Fund. The offer was made in lieu of a state appropriation, which the Tennessee legislature had consistently refused to make. Had the plant not been available in 1875, the founding of Peabody College, as far as Nashville was concerned, might have been delayed for a decade—perhaps forever. Many private and public buildings in Nashville were completely destroyed during the years of the war, and the plant of the University of Nashville could easily have been among them but for the vigilance of John Berrien Lindsley. In an article on "Prison Discipline and Penal Legislation," which appeared in the *Theological Medium,* the Cumberland Presbyterian quarterly, in July, 1874, he says:

> In February, 1862, at the instance of Dr. David W. Yandell, then on Gen. A. S. Johnston's staff, the writer took charge of the sick and wounded Confederate soldiers and Federal prisoners just after the fall of Fort Donelson. It was the first great disaster on the one side, and triumph on the other—a time of panic and confusion. Two weeks afterward, he received the Federal medical director's certificate that these sick and wounded were all well cared for. During the whole war period it was his duty to watch the University of Nashville—all the large buildings most of the time being used as hospitals or for camps. At the battle of Nashville, rifle pits ran through its campus; yet it lost not a specimen, a book, nor a dollar. Buildings and grounds were injured by use, not by abuse.

CHAPTER IV

PIONEER IN PUBLIC EDUCATION

DR. LINDSLEY devoted much of his time and effort to the cause of public education in Tennessee. As early as 1851 he was working in behalf of the public schools of Nashville.[1] In 1856 he became a member of the City Board of Education and for many years served as one of its most active workers.[2] In 1865 he was elected superintendent of the Nashville city schools.[3] His election took place at a crucial period in the history of the schools when his services were needed to reorganize the system, which had disintegrated as a result of the war.[4] In 1875 he prepared the bill which created Tennessee's first State Board of Education and served this board as secretary from 1875 to 1887.[5] He was one of the leaders in the organization of the Tennessee State Teachers' Association in Knoxville on July 21, 1865, and was a charter member of the organization.[6] He presided at the first meeting, which was held in Nashville the following October.[7] He later served the association as president and delivered many addresses before its sessions.[8] He was early an advocate of nor-

---

[1] The Lindsley Papers.

[2] W. W. Clayton, *History of Davidson County, Tennessee*, p. 253.

[3] Minutes of the Nashville City Board of Education, July 6, 1866. Dr. Lindsley was elected superintendent of the Nashville city schools on December 13, 1865, at a salary of $250 per month. He assumed the duties of this office on January 2, 1866, and resigned on July 6 of that year. Upon his resignation, the city board passed the following resolution: "*Resolved*, That the thanks of the board of education and the gratitude of the people of Nashville are due to Dr. J. B. Lindsley for the zeal and ability with which he undertook and discharged the duties of superintendent of public schools, though called unexpectedly to the office, for the past six months."

[4] Deering J. Roberts, editorial, *Southern Practitioner*, XX (1898), 35: "In 1866, a most critical period in the history of our public schools, Dr. Lindsley was the superintendent and so boldly faced opposition in the city government as to effectually warn ward politicians that the schools of the city were above and beyond political manipulation."

[5] W. R. Garrett, "The Genesis of Peabody College for Teachers," *American Historical Magazine*, VIII (1903), 18.   [6] The Lindsley Papers.

[7] *Nashville Daily Press and Times*, October 13, 1865.

[8] John Eaton, Jr., *First Report of the Superintendent of Public Instruction of the State of Tennessee*, 1869, Appendix, p. CVI.

WILLIAM WALKER. PAINTED BY WASHINGTON COOPER, AND PRESENTED BY WALKER TO HIS FRIEND, JOHN BERRIEN LINDSLEY. NOW IN THE POSSESSION OF LOUISE G. LINDSLEY, OF NASHVILLE, TENNESSEE

PIONEER IN PUBLIC EDUCATION   85

mal schools, at a time when the concept of professional education for teachers was not familiar to the Southern mind.[9] As chancellor of the University of Nashville, he frequently delivered addresses and worked in behalf of the public schools. He accepted the training of leaders for public education as one of the important services of the university. In 1867 he made the first contact with the Peabody Education Fund with reference to a plan for the establishment of a normal school in connection with the University of Nashville.[10] He worked with Barnas Sears, W. P. Jones, and others in presenting the plan that was finally accepted by the trustees of the Peabody Education Fund, the trustees of the University of Nashville, and the State Board of Education, and that resulted in the establishment of Peabody Normal College in 1875.[11] Dr. Lindsley inherited the educational philosophy of his father, which had been expressed as early as 1825 to the effect that "education is the rightful inheritance of every human being." He believed, however, that there could be no public school system without the stimulation of an institution of higher learning. "The stream cannot rise higher than the fountain nor the day be brighter than the sun." In an address delivered before the State Teachers' Association and the Tennessee State Grange in 1875, he attempted to show the scope and function of normal schools in the scheme of public education.[12] The purpose of this address was to create sentiment for a normal school in Tennessee.[13]

Dr. Lindsley was largely instrumental in founding and organizing five educational institutions, two of them active today. In 1850 he organized the medical school of the University of Nashville.[14] In 1855, he was responsible for the plan which merged the Western Military Institute with the University of

---

[9] The Lindsley Papers.
[10] Minutes of the University of Nashville, 1867.
[11] Garrett, *op. cit.*, pp. 16-19.
[12] *Nashville Union and American*, May 26, 1875.
[13] *Address on Popular Education Before the Tennessee State Teachers' Association, May 25, 1875*; reprints among The Lindsley Papers.
[14] Minutes of the University of Nashville, 1850.

Nashville and thus created a new literary department which operated successfully until 1860.[15] In 1867 he set up the plan for the organization of Montgomery Bell Academy, which became the preparatory department of the University of Nashville and which still operates under the charter of the university.[16] In 1870 he helped to organize the Tennessee College of Pharmacy and served for several years on the faculty as professor of materia medica.[17]

Dr. Lindsley's greatest achievement, however, in behalf of the public schools, and the one which no doubt gave him the most lasting satisfaction, was the part he played in connection with the founding of Peabody College in 1875.

The cause of public education in Tennessee was indeed at a low ebb in the early fifties when John Berrien Lindsley and his colleagues began their efforts in its behalf. The office of state superintendent of public instruction had been abolished in 1844,[18] and for more than two decades thereafter there was no unifying head to stimulate interest and manage satisfactorily the affairs of public education in Tennessee. The state treasurer allocated the limited funds for public school purposes.

A memorial to the legislature by the common school convention held in Knoxville in 1847 suggests the dismal conditions of the time.[19] This memorial states that in 1840 the white population of Tennessee was 640,797, of whom 240,008 were over twenty years of age. Of those over twenty years of age, 58,531 could neither read nor write. This constituted one in every eleven of the total white population of the state, and one in every four and one fourth of those above twenty years of age. In 1849 there were 278,049 children over six and under twenty-one years of age. The school fund was $113,431, making a per capita distribution of 40¾ cents per child.[20] Ten years later the per capita

[15] *Ibid.*, 1855.
[16] *Ibid.* Also Merriam, *op. cit.*, p. 50.   [17] Little, *op. cit.*, pp. 38-39.
[18] Robert H. White, *Development of the Tennessee Educational Organization*, p. 77.
[19] *Tennessee Senate Journal*, 1847-48, Appendix, pp. 388-99.
[20] *Tennessee House Journal*, 1849-50, Appendix, pp. 78-82.

distribution for public education was increased to 70 cents per student.[21]

On October 12, 1869, John Berrien Lindsley, speaking before the State Teachers' Association in Nashville, discussed the weaknesses of the public school system and suggested the causes for its deplorable condition. He placed the responsibility directly on the state legislature when he said:

> It has so happened, that while prudence and liberality have characterized the past legislation of Tennessee on several points of public moment, her record in this respect is one of reproach and regret from the beginning to the ending. Going back to the early acts of her General Assembly, we find that higher or university education was deprived by repeated legislation—all the while protested against—of the just and handsome provision made for it by the parent State—North Carolina—and by the National Congress. And as popular education has ever been an outgrowth from the university, and never flourished without the university, it need not excite surprise that ever from that day to this, the hopes of the masses have been deceived by futile and nugatory legislation—that ambitious and selfish political leaders have ever promised the people a good system of public schools and have ever falsified these promises, until at length Tennessee has fastened upon her magnificent and heaven-blessed domain the *meanest, poorest, most fruitless school system in America, ranking her among the very foremost States in the Union for deficiency in the elemental arts of reading and writing.*[22]

Dr. Lindsley was one of a small pioneer group which furnished the leadership in organizing the Tennessee State Teachers' Association, which in turn created the sentiment for Tennessee's public school system.

On July 21, 1865, a "few friends of a liberal and systematic education met in Knoxville, Tennessee, at the old Female Institute and organized the Tennessee State Teachers' Association." John Berrien Lindsley was among them. In fact, Dr. Lindsley "warmly seconded Governor W. G. Brownlow's motion to organize this association."[23] We quote from his diary of that year:

---

[21] *Tennessee Senate Journal*, 1857-58, Appendix, pp. 233-35.
[22] Eaton, *op. cit.*, Appendix, p. CVII. Italics mine.
[23] Clayton, *op. cit.*, p. 405.

July 19. Left for teachers' convention. . . . Free passage.

July 20. 7:00 A.M. at Knoxville. . . . Evening at speaking. Villainous politics.

July 21. All day meeting. See proceedings.

July 22. 7:30 A.M., left Knoxville in box cars; 8:48 P.M., at Nashville.

After establishing objectives and discussing plans, this little group of pioneers adjourned, to meet three months later in Nashville.

On October 12, 1865, at nine o'clock in the morning, the Tennessee State Teachers' Association convened in the hall of the House of Representatives at the Capitol in Nashville. The executive committee met in the committee room with Dr. Lindsley presiding as chairman. On motion, Nashville was recommended as the place for the second annual meeting of the association. It was then proposed that the following topic be discussed at the Friday afternoon session: "What Form of Organization for a Bureau of Public Instruction for the State Is Best?" At this meeting Dr. Lindsley announced that any teacher or active friend of education could become a member of the association by signing the constitution and contributing one dollar. "This is an adjournment [from the Knoxville meeting] and is hence but a continuation of the first meeting of the association. All persons joining now will be considered original members and founders of the first body of the kind ever formed in Tennessee." During the program an interval of fifteen minutes was announced to permit the reception of the public school children of Nashville. In the auditorium and halls were 2,000 children and approximately fifty city teachers. Dr. Lindsley said: "It gives me much pleasure to receive this visit from the children of the schools. I welcome you in the name of the Association."[24] It will be recalled that Dr. Lindsley had been a member of the City Board of Education for a number of years and was vitally interested in the progress being made in the public schools.

At this first meeting the delegates went on record as (1) favoring free schools; (2) honoring the profession of teaching;

[24] *Nashville Daily Press and Times*, October 13, 1865.

and (3) endorsing the need for normal schools. "They urged the Legislature to a liberal provision for education and pressed the doctrine that *the property of the State should educate the children of the State*."²⁵ When we observe that this organization meeting of the Tennessee State Teachers' Association went on record as *favoring free public schools,* we get a significant glimpse of the educational system of Tennessee prior to 1865. The concept of free public schools for all the children had made little progress in the Southern states prior to the Civil War, and Tennessee was no exception.

After the convention adjourned, the plans which had been made were set in motion. For eight years following this first meeting, the members of the association worked toward the realization of their program. The general school law of 1873, which provided the foundation of the state's present school system, resulted from the efforts of the little group which organized the State Teachers' Association in 1865. In 1875 Dr. Lindsley summarized the progress made in public education in the decade 1865-1875 in the following paragraph:

Nearly ten years ago, Gov. Brownlow called a convention, which became the State Teachers' Association. Gov. Brownlow's object was so to organize the advocates of popular education as to keep prominently before the voting masses a fundamental topic of legislation, which had hitherto been slurred over, by being freely endorsed in word and ignored in action. So far the idea has accomplished all, if not more, than he could have hoped. Look at the century's history of this goodly State, and tell me in what other ten years has the subject of education for the toiling masses been so fully discussed in the newspapers, so much referred to upon the stump, so much acted upon in the State House? As a fact, during all this eventful and exciting ten years it has been second to no other topic whatever. This of itself indicates progress, wonderful progress.[26]

Dr. Lindsley's philosophy of educational administration was that of his father Philip, who had stated as early as 1825 that "a

---

[25] Eaton, *op. cit.,* p. 85.
[26] *Address on Popular Education Before the Tennessee State Teachers' Association,* May 25, 1875.

free, republican, representative government can be permanently sustained only by an enlightened and virtuous people."[27]

Both Philip and John Berrien Lindsley had read widely and critically upon educational problems. In one of his famous lectures, which appeared in the *Nashville Republican* of 1831, Philip Lindsley said:

> The intelligent public are aware that much has been done also towards improving the methods of instruction, in all its stages, and in every department of every species of school or college. Education itself has become a science; and it deserves the most profound study of all who wish to be esteemed skilful and thorough educators. It is well known that Edgeworth, Bell, Lancaster, Pestalozzi, Fellenberg, Jardine, Pillans, Dufief, Lasteyrie, Degerando, Wilderspin, Hamilton, Harnisch, Jacotot, Brougham, and others, have, in our times, been zealously labouring to benefit the world by their experiments and publications on this subject. . . .
>
> I have not been able, however, to discover in any of the authors already named much that is really useful which had not been previously and forcibly exhibited in the pages of Montaigne, Comenius, Cowley, Carew, Ascham, Bacon, Locke, Milton, Fenelon, Dumarsais, Tanaquil, Faber, Bossuet, Lowe, Clarke, J. T. Philipps, D'Alembert, Condillac, and others of a preceding generation. And whether these have added much to the science or art of education, as unfolded by a still more ancient school—by the Quinctilians and Ciceros and Xenophons and Aristotles and Solomons of Rome and Greece and Judea—may also admit of question. I am not sure that even our modern Bacons and Lockes and Miltons are entitled to higher praise than that of modestly following in the orbit of the great luminaries just cited. . . .
>
> But however wise men may speculate about systems or modes of education or about modern improvements in the art, in one most essential point they all agree. And this one point involves the whole mystery or philosophy of education under every rational system. *No man can teach what he does not himself understand.* Every man can teach, *if he will,* what he does perfectly understand. The teacher then must be able and willing, or apt, to teach. He must possess the requisite intellectual furniture, and also moral principle—or he cannot be trustworthy. He must be able to do the work, and he must also love the work.

[27] Philip Lindsley, *Lecture on Popular Education,* 1837.

Socrates, Plato, Aristotle, were the master spirits and the master pedagogues of Greece—and their illustrious disciples did honor to their schooling. Give us such a constellation of glorious intellect—refined and purified by Christian ethics—elevated and expanded by Christian hope and Christian charity—and the republic will live forever.[28]

The following quotation is taken from the private journal of John Berrien Lindsley:

In order to insure to the people the greatest possible amount of rational well-being, Fichte taught that the introduction of the most universal popular education was one of the principal duties of the State. In regard to this subject his urgent appeals to the German government have been highly successful. Kant, Fichte, Schelling, and Hegel were the quarto of immortal German philosophers whose gigantic intellects and profound thought have made an indelible impress on their country. Popular education in Germany descended from the university to the multitudes.

Both John Berrien Lindsley and his father had an exalted conception of what the teaching profession should be and deplored its lack of standards and the conditions which attracted to its ranks only the inadequate and unqualified. In one of his addresses Philip Lindsley referred to the teaching personnel of the state as follows:

At present the great mass of our teachers are mere adventurers—either young men who are looking forward to some less laborious and more respectable vocation and who, of course, have no ambition to excel in the business of teaching and no motive for exertion but a brief and temporary pecuniary embarrassment, or men who despair of doing better or who have failed in other pursuits or who are wandering from place to place, teaching a year here and a year there, and gathering up what they can from the ignorance and credulity of their employers. . . .

Give us men competent to teach, and desirous to teach for a living; and they will work their way to public favour and patronage. The universal complaint, even in the older States, is, that the teachers of common schools are, in nine cases out of ten, utterly unfit for their vocation; and bad teachers are worse than none. To commit children to bungling, lazy, intemperate, swaggering, vagabonds, knaves, and

---
[28] *Ibid.* Italics mine.

smatterers, is very like perpetrating intellectual and moral treason or assassination with malice prepense. If there be one object under the whole heaven which parents should be eager to purchase at any price or sacrifice—which is indeed above all price—it is the proper education of their children. If there be one good object, which preeminently demands the profoundest attention of the legislature—it is this.[29]

In this same address, which was delivered in 1835, four years before the opening of the first state normal school in America, Philip Lindsley recognized the need for professional schools for the education of teachers.

Our country needs teaching seminaries, purposely to train and qualify young men for the profession of teaching. We have our theological seminaries, our medical and law schools, which receive the graduates of our colleges and fit them for their respective professions; and whenever the profession of teaching shall be duly honored and appreciated, it is not doubted that it will receive similar attention and be favored with equal advantages.

In 1875, forty years later, John Berrien Lindsley was much more specific with reference to the needs of Tennessee for professional education for teachers.

We can now see the position of the normal college in the Tennessee system of education . . . an efficient system of district schools being in operation throughout the State, institutions will be needed to train teachers for these schools. These are an essential part of the district school system, and hence with that should be provided for by the State. . . . These are the only institutions above the district schools which our State need assist, and as through the district schools these come in contact with all the citizens of the State, is it asking too much that they should be projected upon a scale commensurate with their object? The public school system of Tennessee being well established, the present population of one million and a quarter would require four normal colleges, each at an annual cost at least equal to those of New York. As in many States, these may be placed where the best offers of lots and buildings are made to the State, thus making the outfit to fall upon the localities desiring the normal college. One of these four should be for American citizens of African descent, who constitute

[29] *Address on Public Schools.*

PIONEER IN PUBLIC EDUCATION 93

about one-fourth of the population of the State, and whose labors fully produce one-fourth of the annual wealth of the State.[30]

As indicated, John Berrien Lindsley believed, as did his father, that the college or university was essential to the existence of "a system of primary or common school education." He believed that it was impossible to create a general demand for education among the people or to supply the teachers needed for the public schools without the stimulus afforded by higher learning to the common school system. "One brilliant, blazing sun in the firmament will shed around and beneath infinitely more light than a thousand twinkling stars. Plant a noble university in our midst, and from its portals will issue streams of cheering light upon every dark corner of the land."[31]

On October 28, 1871, Dr. Lindsley, in his *Report to the Nashville Board of Trade,* discussed at length the possibilities of Nashville as an educational center. He emphasized, as one of the greatest contributing factors to the educational wealth of Nashville, the system of public schools, which he said was "mainly founded by the beloved and venerated Alfred Hume, and was the direct outgrowth of the University." Following his graduation from the University of Nashville in 1835, Dr. Hume opened a school for boys in Nashville.

He [Dr. Hume] was a member of the city's first board of education and, as its representative in 1852, visited many of the famous public school systems of the country. His study of these formed the basis of the report whose recommendations were consolidated in Nashville's initial attempt at public education. This report remains as one of the most important of the city's contributions to educational literature.[32]

In 1851 Nashville could hardly be said to have a public school system. In 1871, however, the citizens were contributing over $50,000 in tax money and were employing fifty-nine teachers, who were occupying six large buildings and giving instruction to 3,561

---
[30] *Nashville Union and American,* May 26, 1875.
[31] Halsey, *op. cit.*, I, 452.
[32] A. L. Crabb, "Lines to a Teacher," *Peabody Reflector and Alumni News,* VI (1933), 115.

children between the ages of seven and eighteen years. Judging by what was taking place in other American cities, Dr. Lindsley predicted that by 1891 the city school system would be the most popular and useful department of the whole city government.

He recommended, in October, 1871, that the citizens and Board of Trade of Nashville build a municipal university. When we consider what American cities have done in the past few years in building municipal colleges and universities, we must give Dr. Lindsley credit for seeing far in advance of his time. His plan for a municipal university included the University of Nashville, from which he had resigned as chancellor. His arguments for such an institution follow.

He believed that boys and girls were carried through the primary and grammar grades of the elementary schools in a satisfactory manner. The high schools for both the boys and girls, however, were sadly neglected because of the small number of students and the expense of financing them. He recommended, therefore, that the preparatory instruction given in the public schools be considered the foundation for the great municipal university.

This University of Nashville would embrace within its curriculum the entire range of human experience and knowledge, with emphasis upon the application to man's daily needs. It would be the function of the university to affiliate more or less with all the special and higher schools then in operation in the city, whether under public charter or as individual property, and with all others that might thereafter be established. The subdivisions of this municipal university were to be free of charge to every pupil resident within the city limits, the higher and special schools to non-residents upon payment of the required fees. If such an institution should be established, he said, Nashville would at once take high rank among other cities and in a few years would without doubt become a city of colleges and professional schools. Under his plan the city government would finance an undergraduate department of the university and would pay each year the tuition of a limited number of students from the grammar schools. In this way the institution would become a part of the public school system and the advantages of higher education would be accessible to even the poorest children. The only requirement would be that they present the proper scholastic records from the grammar grades.

He proposed, in addition, to establish, in connection with the university, a girls' high school and a normal school department. The normal school department would find support not only from the citizens of Nashville but also from the Peabody trustees and the state. It would be open not only to the girls and boys of the local community, but to students from over the entire South. In this municipal university venture, Dr. Lindsley wished to provide free public education from the grades through the university.

In the fall of 1871, when Dr. Lindsley made this report to the Nashville Board of Trade, the University of Nashville was under the direction of General E. Kirby Smith and Bushrod R. Johnson, who were assisted by a corps of instructors. The first year under the new administration had just closed. The outlook appeared hopeful, in spite of the poverty-stricken condition of the country from which patronage was drawn. Dr. Lindsley's report was widely disseminated but its recommendations were never incorporated into the university and public school system.

When the Peabody Education Fund was announced, it was Dr. Lindsley who made the first contact with the trustees of this fund with reference to the establishment of a normal school in connection with the University of Nashville. This movement led to the founding of Peabody College. As early as June, 1867, Dr. Lindsley advised the Board of Trustees of the University of Nashville "to correspond with the trustees of the Peabody Fund in reference to co-operating with them in this field."[33] He was

---

[33] Merriam, *op. cit.*, p. 53; also Minutes of the University of Nashville, 1869.

appointed by the board as the one best fitted to present the matter, and immediately opened correspondence with Barnas Sears, agent for the Peabody Fund.

There was, perhaps, no man in the state of Tennessee during this period better qualified to assume the leadership in public education than John Berrien Lindsley. As a student of education, he was conversant with the facts concerning school systems of other states and countries, and was aware of the need for raising the level of intelligence of the common people. He contrasted the better school systems of other countries and states, notably that of Massachusetts, with the school system of Tennessee, in order to show the inadequacy of the public schools of the state and to challenge the people to further effort. The following quotation from one of his addresses on public education will serve to illustrate this point:

> ... Tennessee can just as readily provide a thorough and efficient system of public instruction for all her inhabitants as can her sister States of Massachusetts and Michigan; or the European kingdoms of Saxony and Prussia; or the mountain-bound republic of Switzerland. In the latter, a State system of instruction went into operation so recently as 1833, the result of which is, that in a population of over two million, hardly a boy or girl can be found who cannot read and write. The same statement is made of Prussia, with its population of more than sixteen million. Indeed, Northern and Western Germany, the land of great Universities and deep learning, is also, by all odds, the land of common schools and universal intelligence. What a wonderful contrast to our own lovely State, where, in a population of rather more than eight hundred thousand white people, there are, at this day, more than eighty thousand adults who can neither read nor write.[34]

At a meeting of the State Teachers' Association held on Lookout Mountain at Chattanooga in 1869, Dr. Lindsley was appointed chairman of a committee to memorialize the state legislature, the Governor, and the people of Tennessee in behalf of

---

[34] "Address to the People of Tennessee on Popular Education," in Eaton, *First Report of the Superintendent of Public Instruction of the State of Tennessee*, 1869, Appendix, p. CVIII.

public education.³⁵ His arguments were predicated upon the assumption that *education for the masses was bound up in all the highest and best interests of the state.* He said, "A calm and comprehensive view of this matter will invariably lead to this conclusion." A summary of the arguments presented in this memorial follows:

1. Education is the cheapest defense of nations. No police expenditures are so effective as those of an educational nature.

2. In order to eliminate crime and poverty and the attendant burden of taxation, we must educate the masses. He argued that school houses were much less expensive in the long run than pauper houses and "school teachers and school books cost much less than jails and penitentiaries and criminal courts."

3. Education is one of the most prolific sources of wealth among people. "That power created by education and made available in all the forms of labor and in all processes of art and science is worth many times its cost."

4. A good system of public education would favorably affect immigration. Regardless of how poor and humble the immigrant may be, he is always mindful of the educational opportunities offered by a new region; "and generally," Dr. Lindsley said, "the immigrant goes where the State is not backward in educational matters."³⁶

---

[35] "Address of the State Teachers' Association to the Governor, Legislature and People of Tennessee," in Eaton, *op. cit.,* Appendix, p. XLV.

[36] In a brochure *On Prison Discipline and Penal Legislation,* pp. 3-4, Dr. Lindsley says: "In 1852 it was my good fortune so to time my movements as to be in Manchester, England, on September 2nd, the day appointed for the opening of a great free library for the working-classes. The morning assembly was for those who had made large donations to the cause. Upon stating to the door-keeper that I was from an interior State of the Great Republic, and much interested in education, he at once sent in my card. Word was immediately returned to assign me an excellent seat. To an utter stranger this was a pleasant recognition. Among the speakers were the noted philanthropist and statesman, the Earl of Shaftesbury; the great novelists, Bulwer-Lytton, Dickens, and Thackeray; Sir James Stevens, the historian; Monckton Milnes and John Bright of Parliamentary fame; Knight, the great publisher; and others of similar prominence. Time and again, by bishop, by lord, and by commoner, was America commended and cited as an example worthy of emulation for good works connected with the elevation of the masses. To an American this, also, was gratifying and none the less so, though in each particular case it was some great achievement of Massachusetts which elicited applause. For years, as a member of the Nashville Board of Education, and hence as a student of public school systems,

5. The educational character of the state has much to do with the good name and credit of the state, and capitalists seeking an opportunity to invest in industry and commerce would be influenced largely by the state's educational reputation.

An intelligent people are a thrifty people. It is this which sets all the wheels of ingenuity and enterprise in motion, which stirs the mind with new activities and inventions and enables it to unfold new projects and lay a firm grasp upon all the resources of nature and art.

The memorial closed with the assurance that, although the Tennessee State Teachers' Association represented almost every shade of political sentiment, it sought no partizan gains but was interested only in the highest welfare of the people.

We greatly desire that our honored and beloved commonwealth may move steadily forward in the pathway of peace, prosperity, and true greatness, and it is our profound conviction that this can only be attained by fostering with a kindly care the public school system.

In his presidential address before the State Teachers' Association and the Tennessee State Grange in 1875, Dr. Lindsley attempted to describe the scope and function of normal schools in the scheme of public education.[37] His address was a plea not only for normal schools, but for the whole system of public education. Immediately after it was delivered, Mr. J. O. Griffith, chairman of the publications committee of the Tennessee State Teachers' Association, received the following letter from Leon Trousdale, state superintendent of public instruction, R. W. Winston, superintendent of Davidson County schools, and S. Y. Caldwell, superintendent of the Nashville city schools:

I found the Massachusetts State Reports recognized authorities and Horace Mann the acknowledged master of the subject. . . . What has not the church, the university and the common school done for Massachusetts?

"Tennessee has the church, and, through the remarkable combination of churches, north and south, is destined soon to have the university, complete and full-appointed. *Let the common school be added, and then may our children see this splendid State what it ought to be—in education and manufactures, the Massachusetts, in agriculture and mines, the Pennsylvania of the South!"*

[37] *Address on Popular Education Before the Tennessee State Teachers' Association,* May 25, 1875.

NASHVILLE, TENNESSEE
May 23, 1875

DEAR MR. GRIFFITH:

Having recently examined the admirably lucid address of Dr. J. Berrien Lindsley, before the Tennessee Grange on the subject of State normal colleges, we deem it important that it should be published in our city and State journals at the present time when the great movement to establish a central normal college at Nashville through the enlightened co-operation of the Trustees of the University of Nashville and the Trustees of the Peabody Education Fund, has, at length, culminated. . . . The public is now naturally seeking for more light on a subject so fruitful of promise and success to our common school system. Dr. Lindsley's address furnished that light, and we respectfully ask that you will, therefore, at this most appropriate and opportune moment, as chairman of the Committee on Publications of the State Teachers' Association of Tennessee, immediately secure its publication for popular reading and information.[38]

On May 25, 1875, Mr. Griffith wrote to these gentlemen, stating that the address would be given widespread distribution over the state and calling attention to the fact that the editor of the *Union and American,* Nashville daily, had tendered the columns of that paper for its immediate publication.

In this address Dr. Lindsley reviewed the development of the normal school movement in Massachusetts, New York, Illinois, and Wisconsin, having purposely selected two of the eastern states, where commerce and manufacturing predominated, and two of the western, which were mostly agricultural. He quoted freely from the 1873 report of the United States Commissioner of Education. At that time, there were 119 normal schools in operation. Fifty-five of these normal schools were supported in whole or in part by state aid, six by city aid, and four by county aid. The others were private institutions attached to colleges or universities. Dr. Lindsley called attention to the fact that Massachusetts had for many years maintained four normal schools and that a new one was being established that year (1875) at Worces-

---

[38] This and the following statements are from the *Nashville Union and American,* May 26, 1875.

ter. He stated that the city of Boston, which had long conducted a normal school in connection with its girls' high school, had just finished a large building for the separate use of the normal school, at a cost of $300,000.

The state of New York in 1873 had eight normal schools. The average annual cost of each was $18,000. Dr. Lindsley referred to the one in Albany, established in 1844, as an institution which ranked high throughout the entire educational world. Its staff of sixteen included a president, a superintendent of the model school, a principal of the primary school, a professor of mental and moral philosophy, a professor of natural science, a professor of mathematics, teachers of mathematics, vocal music, geography, hand-drawing and penmanship, ethics and elocution, rhetoric and English literature, English grammar and history, arithmetic and geometry, an associate teacher of rhetoric and English grammar, and an associate teacher of algebra. These instructors taught 524 pupils in the normal school, 102 in the model school, and 46 in the primary school. In the seven other state normal schools in New York, "the corps of teachers ranged from fourteen to eighteen, with annual salaries varying from $600 to $2,500, and with large academic, intermediate, and primary departments attached for practice training." These normal schools were opened between 1867 and 1871.

In Illinois, which was chiefly an agricultural and rural commonwealth, Dr. Lindsley referred to the State Normal University which had been established in 1857. Bloomington and McLean counties had secured the university by offering $140,000 in a rather spirited contest with the cities. Dr. Lindsley discussed the annual appropriation of this institution, which amounted to $29,000, its faculty of 13 members, its student body in the normal department of 450, its model school with an enrollment of 316, subdivided into 112 in the high school, 147 in the grammar school, and 57 in the intermediate and primary school. Reference was made to the fact that the normal school at Carbondale was being organized at that time with an extensive program.

Wisconsin's four normal schools were discussed, with particular emphasis on the one at Oshkosh, which had that year 10 teachers and 527 students, 268 of whom were in the normal department and the remainder in the grammar and lower departments.

Having dealt with the curriculum and administration of these schools, Dr. Lindsley interpreted their scope and function under four important heads: (1) academic character; (2) training character; (3) collegiate character; and (4) their far-reaching influence.

1. *The academic character of these schools.*—They are not merely intended to teach how to use knowledge, art, or practice. A leading part of their work is to impart knowledge, science, or theory. They are then, as all professional schools should be, scientific and practical. Their true function is analogous to that of our medical colleges, in their fullest development, in which the student is taught the elementary principles of science only indirectly, yet essentially, connected with his profession; and then the phenomena, causes and treatment of the various maladies to which flesh is heir; and as a crowning initiation is called upon to apply this knowledge to the living patient; so in the ordinary two years' course at the normal school the pupil must not be content with such knowledge of the elementary branches as was acquired when a child, and as may be sufficient for the entering examination. These studies must again be gone over with mature minds and with a special view.

2. *The training character of these schools.*—To the medical college, hospitals are indispensable as schools of practice; so must the normal college have its model schools, in which are practically exhibited the best methods of teaching, and in which the pupils have due opportunity of exercising these methods. As an instance of how this is done, a passage from the Fifth Annual Report of the Fredonia, New York, State Normal School, 1874, may be cited: "To furnish the requisite practice for the training classes, it is necessary to have on the premises a series of schools, representing every grade of our public schools, and each grade should be sufficiently large to furnish appropriate exercise for the practicing teachers, in both instructing and governing. These schools for practice should be organized on the best plan known, and be under the most able, industrious and faithful teachers that can be procured. When properly organized and operated, they will make, with the normal department, one consistent sympathetic organism,

where every member will feel the joy or the sorrow of the other. Such an organism will go far to exalt and expand the thoughts of every practicing teacher, and to fit him to become the animating soul of whatever school he manages. To carry out this idea we have a primary department of about 120 children; a junior department of about 120, a senior department of about 140 students. The principals and assistants of these departments are also the critics over the practicing portion of the training classes."

3. *The collegiate character of these schools.*—Intended to train for the most niggardly compensated of all professions, they are attended by pupils of very limited means. Hence arises the necessity for that mode of living, which, as experience everywhere has shown, gives more comfort for less money than any other, and which is known as collegiate. Another powerful reason why normal schools have ordinarily created great colleges as part of their organism, even though often commencing without them, is the fact that a large majority of their pupils are young ladies, who of course, much prefer residing with their teachers and aloof from the world. Thus it happens that even when situated in villages, these schools become collegiate establishments.

4. *The wide-reaching influence of these schools growing out of comparatively a small work accomplished.*—Take the states in which the oldest and most liberal provision has been made, and yet very few of the teachers employed have been in the normal school. Indeed, in all such states, a pressing question, very eagerly discussed, is how to supplement this deficiency. In Massachusetts and New York various modes of training teachers are called into requisition, such as teachers' institutes, which may be styled short term, migratory normal schools; and the introduction of normal training into high schools and academies. Yet all the while the normal school proper in these very states is being pushed to greater and still greater development. For it is found that as a little leaven leaveneth the whole lump, so do the relatively few, though intrinsically numerous, graduates of these institutions infuse a new life and spirit into the entire educational corps of a state. Each one becomes a model teacher. Each one establishes a model school. Thus an influence of good goes out which literally is never ending. We can hence understand why it is that these seminaries have so rapidly increased in number, magnitude and public appreciation during the last thirty years.

Having reviewed the favorable progress of these four states in establishing and fostering normal schools, Dr. Lindsley turned to Tennessee and contrasted the state's utter lack of facilities for the education of teachers. "In our State of Tennessee," he lamented, "our legislators and even our laws have always promised more than the people have enjoyed." He told of the efforts that had been made in the interest of the common schools. He praised Robert Hatton, who had almost succeeded in getting a bill passed in 1855-56 for the establishment of a normal school, and Dr. William P. Jones, senator from Davidson County, who had introduced a bill in 1873 for a normal school in each division of the state.

The bill of 1873 had passed the Senate, but too late in the session to be considered by the House. While Dr. Lindsley lamented the indifference which had defeated the cause of the public schools, and particularly of the normal schools, in Tennessee, he saw definite signs of encouragement. "Look at the history of this state and tell me in what other ten years has the subject of education for the toiling masses been so fully discussed in the newspapers, so much referred to upon the stump, so much acted upon in the State House." Progress was being made. He paid a tribute to the liberal contribution of George Peabody, who perhaps "next to George Washington will be the best known and most loved by future generations of Americans." More than one hundred thousand dollars of the Peabody Education Fund had been distributed for educational purposes in Tennessee in 1875. But for the aid held out by the Peabody trustees, the efforts to strengthen the public school system of Tennessee at that time would perhaps have been abandoned. "Certainly," Dr. Lindsley said, "the present attempt to create a system of normal colleges whose beneficent influence shall reach without a doubt every household in the State results from their liberal action."

He recommended in 1875 that higher education in Tennessee be left to the churches and private institutions, and that public effort be concentrated upon the development of a primary and elementary school system. This, of course, included the normal school, which he considered essential to the development of the public schools. He believed that after the public school system of the state was well established, with the population of 1,250,000, four normal colleges would be required to meet the needs, the annual cost of each to be at least equal to those of New York ($18,000 per year). "One of these four," he said, "should be for American citizens of African descent, who constitute about one-fourth of the population of the State and whose labors fully produce one-fourth of the annual wealth of the State." He recommended that a normal school be established in East Tennessee, one in West Tennessee, and two at Nashville in Middle Tennessee. In referring to the Negro institution, he said, "Fisk University can accommodate a first-class normal school and not miss the room." Thirty-four years later, in 1909, his recommendations became reality when the Tennessee legislature passed an act establishing the normal schools at Johnson City, Murfreesboro, and Memphis, and the A. & I. Normal School for Negroes at Nashville. Dr. Lindsley predicted that at the end of thirty years the normal colleges would be second to no other educational institutions in America.

John Berrien Lindsley made a vital contribution to the founding of Peabody College. We know that as early as 1852 Dr. Lindsley, while in London, had called on George Peabody and had received from him complimentary tickets to the Royal Botanical Gardens.[39] In 1859, after he became chancellor of the University of Nashville, he was again in London and again visited Mr. Peabody.[40]

Dr. Lindsley's visits with Mr. Peabody perhaps in no way led to his later contacts with the Peabody Education Board. But

[39] *Proceedings of the Peabody Education Fund*, 1888, III, 422-423. "Dr. Lindsley knew George Peabody in 1852. Upon one occasion he was going to London, and was asked by a Southwestern physician to carry the philanthropist $250 that he had loaned the physician to come home on. He had exacted no note or security, but when he saw a man needing his aid he had extended it without question; and perhaps this man was only one of many whom he had helped in his way."

[40] John Berrien Lindsley, MS Diary.

we do know that when the Peabody Education Fund was announced in 1867 Dr. Lindsley, as chancellor of the University of Nashville, immediately opened correspondence with the trustees of this fund concerning the establishment of a normal school in connection with the university.[41]

L. S. Merriam said: "The eyes of the trustees of the Peabody Education Fund were first turned toward Tennessee by the representation of John Berrien Lindsley and the trustees of the University of Nashville."[42]

W. R. Garrett stated:

The first conception of converting the old University of Nashville into an institution for the training of teachers originated in the mind of Dr. J. Berrien Lindsley, chancellor of the University of Nashville, as early as 1867. The year in which the gift of Mr. Peabody was made, he suggested to the board of trustees that correspondence should be opened with the Peabody Education Board and was appointed to correspond with Barnas Sears, the general agent.[43]

In 1884 Dr. Lindsley wrote to Robert C. Winthrop the following letter, which was later published in connection with the *Proceedings of the Peabody Education Fund*:

HONORED SIR;—With high respect I transmit the enclosed. The State Normal College of Tennessee is peculiarly the offspring of the Peabody Education Fund. So soon as this fund was established, the idea of the present scheme was outlined in a *Report made by myself to the Board of Trustees of the University of Nashville, which Board I had then the honor of serving as Chancellor of the University*. Your agent, the illustrious Sears, *with his usual solid prudence and far-sighted wisdom, at once grasped both the brilliancy and the weaknesses of the scheme. Under his guidance your Board made it a reality*. . . .[44]

We find, therefore, that as early as June, 1867, Dr. Lindsley had written to Barnas Sears and had received from him encouragement for his plan of establishing a normal school in connection with the University of Nashville. Barnas Sears believed,

---

[41] Minutes of the University of Nashville, 1867.
[42] *Op. cit.*, p. 53.
[43] *Op. cit.*, p. 14.
[44] III, 256. Italics mine.

however, that such a school, in order to participate in the Peabody Education Fund, should be a part of the public school system, under the administration of the state, from which it would also receive financial aid. In taking this position Mr. Sears placed the responsibility directly upon the state, and the long fight for a normal school was begun.[45]

A bill to found a normal school had been introduced in the legislative session of Tennessee in 1855-56 by the brilliant young legislator, Robert Hatton. It passed the House, but failed in the Senate by one vote.[46] Robert Hatton had been a student of Nathaniel Lawrence Lindsley, brother of John Berrien, at Cumberland University, and had received from him much inspiration and assistance in this first legislative effort to establish a normal school in Tennessee. After the defeat of his bill in 1855, he wrote the following letter to Dr. Lindsley:

Your book on Normal Schools came to me in good time. I regret, however, that all my efforts with your book to aid me failed in the accomplishment of an object which I had much at heart. As you saw by the papers, my bill was defeated in the Senate by one vote. . . . Degenerate times these.

Truly your friend
ROBERT HATTON[47]

Dr. Lindsley, in his address before the State Teachers' Association in 1875, paid a tribute to Robert Hatton's efforts in the following words:

Among the statesmen of Tennessee, one is found in whose brief but brilliant career a whole-souled effort to promote popular education constitutes a prominent episode. Robert Hatton, gifted, eloquent, brave . . . was a true Democrat. He knew full well that it was education which transferred "the plow boy of Long Hollow" into the halls of legislation and enabled him to appear cool and self-reliant, the peer of any in the crowd. He wished all to have the equal opportunity at least with himself. Therefore, in his first and only term in the General

---

[45] Garrett, *op. cit.*, pp. 14-25.
[46] John Berrien Lindsley, *Address on Popular Education Before the Tennessee State Teachers' Association*.
[47] Samuel Francis Drake, *The Life of General Robert Hatton*, p. 87.

Assembly, session 1855-56, we find him bending all his energies toward the establishment of a State normal school so successfully that it passed his own body, the Lower House, and failed of becoming a law for want of only one vote in the Senate. It was a sore disappointment to the generous Hatton.

Eight years had now passed since Dr. Lindsley's first proposal to the Peabody Board in 1867, years in which the educational forces of the state had been most vigorous. Sentiment in favor of the normal school had become too strong to be ignored. In the spring of 1875, Dr. W. P. Jones, a former member of the legislature and a friend of the public school movement, wrote to Dr. Lindsley, then president of the State Teachers' Association, suggesting the possibility of passing a bill through the legislature "creating the normal school" without an appropriation. This was a clue. Aided by Barnas Sears and others, Dr. Lindsley prepared the bill "creating Tennessee's first State Board of Education," and thereby made possible the organization of Peabody Normal College.

It happened in this way. The newly elected legislature met and James D. Porter was inaugurated governor. Dr. Lindsley, accompanied by Barnas Sears, called at the executive office. "Governor Porter received us cordially." At this conference the plans assumed final shape. Governor Porter refused to recommend a state appropriation, and gave his reasons for so doing, but he assured them, as a member of the Board of Trustees of the University of Nashville, that the university, through its income and the use of its valuable grounds and buildings, would give more than was asked of the state. This proposition was satisfactory to Dr. Sears and a bill was prepared by Dr. Lindsley in accordance with their agreement. This bill passed the legislature on March 23, 1875. There now remained many details but no legal barrier to delay the plans for the normal school.

The State Board of Education held its first meeting in the Governor's office at Nashville at eleven o'clock on the morning of April 8, 1875. Those present at this meeting were: J. B. Lindsley, S. Watson, E. H. Ewing, L. G. Tarbox, and Governor Porter. On a motion made by Mr. Tarbox, J. B. Lindsley was unanimously elected secretary. Mr. Watson made a motion that Dr. Lindsley announce that the board was ready to receive propositions offering the funds, buildings, and grounds for the normal school project. Dr. Lindsley, Mr. Tarbox, and Mr. Watson were appointed a committee to draw up a plan of organization for the normal school.[48]

Following Mr. Watson's resolution, Dr. Lindsley prepared the announcement, which was the next day approved by the president of the board. It appeared in the Nashville dailies on April 10, and was copied by the press throughout the state of Tennessee. It read:

Address to the Public

At the recent session of the General Assembly an act was passed to provide for the establishment and to prescribe rules for the government of a normal school, or schools, in the State of Tennessee, in connection with the public school system thereof.

The law contains the following provisions, among others:

That in the location of said normal school, or schools, the State Board of Education shall give preference to such locality, accessible to all parts of the State, as shall offer gratuitously the most suitable ground and buildings for the establishment of the same, provided that nothing in this act shall be so construed as to authorize the expenditure of money from the State Treasury or school fund of the State.

That said State Board of Education may receive contributions of money from the trustees of the Peabody Education Fund, or donation of property or funds from any sources for the benefit of the enterprise, which they shall in good faith dispose of and disburse, in accordance with the conditions of the donation.

That the trustees of colleges and universities, or other educational institutions, shall have power to give the use of their property to the State Board of Education for the benefit of the normal schools.

In pursuance with the above provisions, the State Board of Education will receive propositions until May 11, 1875, offering buildings and sites for the school or schools. Other donations will be received at any time. In these normal schools accommodations must be provided for

---

[48] Minutes of the Tennessee State Board of Education, 1875.

young ladies, as the ranks of teachers in the primary schools are mainly filled by these.

Propositions will be received for normal schools for white and colored pupils, entirely distinct and separate, in accordance with the provision of the school law of Tennessee.

Communications may be addressed to his Excellency, James D. Porter, ex-officio president of the State Board of Education or to

J. B. LINDSLEY, *Secretary*

In 1875 the University of Nashville owned, in South Nashville, beautiful grounds and substantial buildings, suitable for educational purposes, but had no endowment with which to carry on the work. The preparatory school for boys was the only department in operation, and this was made possible only by the will of Montgomery Bell. The trustees of the Peabody Education Fund possessed money for endowment and operation, but had no funds for extensive buildings and grounds. It was, therefore, logical for these two boards to enter into a co-operative educational program. A proposal to this effect was made by Dr. Lindsley in 1867, but because of the insistence of Dr. Sears upon state aid and supervision it was not until after the creation of the Tennessee State Board of Education in 1875 that a plan acceptable to both sides was submitted. The general program of cooperation had been agreed upon in advance by Barnas Sears, James D. Porter, and Dr. Lindsley. When, therefore, Dr. Lindsley's proposal reached the Board of Trustees of the University of Nashville, it remained only for them to meet and formally accept the proposition, which they did on May 26, 1875. George Peabody College for Teachers was now in the process of evolution.

During the early days of this institution, when it was struggling for a place in the sun, Dr. Lindsley was ever thoughtful of its welfare. As executive officer of the State Board of Education, he watched over it with a personal and professional interest that no doubt saved it from much embarrassment. It required nothing short of a personal devotion to develop an institution under the auspices of three separate boards. Dr. Lindsley acted as liaison officer among the three agencies responsible for the institution. The following paragraphs from the Minutes of the Tennessee State Board of Education, September 27, 1884, suggest with what care he endeavored to maintain a happy relationship among the contracting parties:

WHEREAS, It is provided by Chapter CCLV, Acts of 1883, Section 3, "that the State Board of Education shall, at proper times, inspect the management of the State Normal College, and audit the accounts for the disbursement of the funds and make a bi-ennial statement through the Governor to the Legislature showing its condition, and otherwise guard the State's interest in the same;

Therefore Resolved, That this Board appoint a Commission to make the inspection required by the fore-going section, at the present meeting, and that in order to produce harmony and co-operation between the several Boards, having a common interest in and guardianship over the Normal College, the Trustees of the Peabody Education Fund, and the Trustees of the University of Nashville, be respectfully and earnestly invited to appoint a similar Commission, each to unite with that appointed by this Board, to make a joint inspection and report as thus provided, and said inspection and report shall be made before the meeting of the Tennessee Legislature in January next.

Resolved, That the above preamble and resolution be transmitted by the Secretary to the Presidents of the respective Boards before mentioned.

J. BERRIEN LINDSLEY,
Secretary[49]

In his correspondence with the executive officers of the various boards, and in the resolutions which he presented from time to time, we discover a skill and diplomacy which no doubt created and held for the institution many friends at a time when they were sorely needed. When it became necessary to have assistance from any one of the three boards, Dr. Lindsley did not hesitate to present the needs of the institution in a direct and vigorous manner. On August 20, 1789, he presented to the Tennessee State Board of Education the following resolutions, which were unanimously adopted:

WHEREAS, The Tennessee State Normal College has now completed four years under great difficulties as a pioneer institution in a wide

[49] *Proceedings of the Peabody Education Fund,* 1888, III, 257.

PIONEER IN PUBLIC EDUCATION

extended field and with work first-class in its character and fruits, therefore

Resolved, That in the opinion of the Board, Dr. B. Sears, Agent, has exhibited great patience, prudence, and wisdom in the general oversight of this institution.

Resolved, That Chancellor Stearns has been all that could be desired as President of the school. His oversight has been vigilant and paternal. He has the confidence of the community as head and guide.

Resolved, That the Trustees of the University of Nashville have shown uniformly a cordial desire to co-operate with the agent of the Peabody Fund, with the President of the College, and with the Board in all measures for the advancement of the college.

Resolved, That the most pressing want now is more extended facilities in the way of class rooms; and that we may reasonably hope that this deficiency may be remedied by the University Board at an early day, as that Board has uniformly granted every request made by the Board within their power.

Resolved, That in view of the growing interest manifested in the welfare of the college by our people, and the fair prospects of co-operation hereafter from the State, it would in every point of view be disastrous now to move the college to a new and experimental field.

Resolved, That copies of the above resolutions be sent to the Agent of the Peabody Education Fund, to the President of the Normal College, to the President of the University Board of Trustees, and to the President of the Board of Trustees of the Peabody Education Fund.[49a]

There were moments, no doubt, when those entrusted with the administration of the Peabody Education Fund became discouraged because of the many annoying problems which grew out of local prejudices. At such moments Dr. Lindsley filled a strategic position in co-ordinating the efforts of the various groups. The following letter to Robert C. Winthrop, president of the Board of Trustees of the Peabody Education Fund, was written at a crucial moment in the history of the institution:

HONORED SIR,—With high respect I transmit the enclosed. I beg your Board to bear in mind that the Public School idea as well as system has yet to take hold of the Southern mind. Without just such a lever as the immortal *Peabody* has placed in your hands, generations would be required to permeate the vast area embraced by the revolutionary

---
[49a] Minutes of the Tennessee State Board of Education, 1879.

Confederate States with this idea. You are doing a grand work. You are making great progress. Be patient and persevering. In twenty more years your efforts will have redeemed this land.

Most respectfully yours,
J. BERRIEN LINDSLEY
Sec'y S. B. of Ed.[50]

Appreciation of Dr. Lindsley's contribution to Peabody Normal College and to public education was expressed by the first two presidents of the college, Dr. Ebens S. Stearns and Dr. W. H. Payne.

In an address on the ninth anniversary of the founding of the college, December 1, 1884, President Stearns said: "The whole South is greatly indebted to Dr. Lindsley's early and persistent efforts in behalf of popular education."[51]

President William H. Payne, in his report to the Peabody Education Fund on September 1, 1898, said:

Since the writing of my last report, the College has suffered the loss of two of its best friends, Dr. William P. Jones and Dr. J. Berrien Lindsley. Dr. Lindsley inherited from his illustrious father the most enlightened views concerning the higher professional education of teachers, and by his wise and enthusiastic co-operation with Dr. Sears he was largely instrumental in perfecting the establishment of a college within the old university organization. At that early date he foresaw, as but very few did, the possibilities of a school supported by the Peabody Board of Trustees, the State of Tennessee, and the Trustees of the University of Nashville.[52]

---

[50] *Proceedings of the Peabody Education Fund*, 1881, II, 246. Italics mine.
[51] *Ibid.*, 1888, III, 300. [52] *Ibid.*, 1900, V, 351.

CHAPTER V

CHAMPION FOR PUBLIC HEALTH

The American Democracy will, beyond a doubt, long before the next century becomes old, vote that each man, woman, and child of its many millions everywhere upon its imperial domain shall breathe the pure air of heaven and enjoy that bright sunshine which is the truest emblem of the divine giver of all life.
—JOHN BERRIEN LINDSLEY, 1889

DR. LINDSLEY devoted the last twenty years of his life to the cause of public health education.[1] His training, experience, and temperament combined to equip him for service in this field.[2] By nature he was a philanthropist and humanitarian, ever seeking the emancipation of the masses. He had seen his fellow-citizens die by the score as a result of frequent epidemics of Asiatic cholera, yellow fever, and other diseases. He served as a physician in Nashville during the cholera epidemics of 1849,[3] 1854, and 1866[4] and was in charge of the yellow-fever refugees received in the city in 1878.[5] His scientific mind and broad training enabled him to see more clearly than others that a modicum of common

---

[1] Minutes of the Tennessee State Board of Health, 1897, pp. 253-259.

[2] *Southern Practitioner*, XX (1898), 40.

[3] *Nashville True Whig*, June 14, 1849: "The cholera is in a more malignant form in our city at this time than on any former occasion. On Tuesday there were 12 deaths; on Wednesday, 7."

[4] *Nashville Dispatch*, September 18, 1866: "Health Report, Sept. 16, 7:00 P.M. During the twenty-four hours ending this 7:00 P.M., there have been officially reported 12 new cases of cholera occurring among the whites, and 5 cases among the colored, making a total of 17 new cases, with 2 deaths, both of which were white. Of the cases heretofore reported, there were 6 deaths, all colored. By order of the Board of Health, F. D. Plunkett, Sec'y." The *Nashville Dispatch* of September 23, 1866, states that on September 22 the number of deaths per day had reached 67. The same paper on October 13, 1866, gives the following figures: "Cholera in Nashville, 1835, 66 victims; 1849, 311; 1850, 316; 1854, about 150." The epidemic of 1866 broke out on August 31 and lasted until October 9, the total number of deaths being "753 plus 57 burials in the Catholic Cemetery." "With the single exception of Memphis, the mortality has been greater in Nashville, according to population, than in any city yet visited in this country."

[5] DeWitt, *op. cit.*

sense on the part of the people would in a large measure prevent the ravages of these visitations.[6] His thoughts on a program of public health education had matured long before the opportunity came to translate them into action. In an address delivered before the forty-third annual meeting of the American Medical Association in Detroit, Michigan, on June 7, 1892, Dr. Lindsley told of an incident which early increased his interest in sanitary science. While a student in the medical school of the University of Pennsylvania in 1842-43, he found himself one day examining the literature displayed at a second-hand bookstore. A little volume entitled *An Inquiry into the Sanitary Condition of the Laboring Population of Great Britain* arrested his attention. He purchased the book, went home, and read it with avid interest. He stated that no other book had so influenced the thoughts, studies, and actions of his life as had that government document. The report was written by Edwin Chadwick and was dated London, May, 1842. In it the author set forth the extent and operation of the evils facing the common people of London and discussed means by which the sanitary condition of the laboring classes could be improved. At that time, the number of deaths caused by Asiatic cholera among the poorer and laboring classes of the British Isles was still a matter of grave concern, and public health measures were commonly discussed and advocated by the leading statesmen of the day.

On June 5, 1866, the first Board of Health in the state of Tennessee was organized in Nashville.[7] Organization of the board took place at this time because a note of warning had been sounded that Asiatic cholera was in the United States and would probably reach Nashville.[8] Dr. C. K. Winston, president of the

[6] With reference to the cholera epidemic in Nashville in 1866, we find on page 12 of the *Second Report of the Nashville Board of Health* (1877) the following: "By October 13, the epidemic was a thing of the past. The *Dispatch* of that date estimates at over 800 deaths the harvest which the pestilence gathered while it held high carnival in the city, and states that 'the pestilence raged with greater force than during the former visitations'."

[7] *First Report of the Tennessee State Board of Health*, 1880.

[8] *Second Report of the Nashville Board of Health*, 1877. J. C. Newman was elected president, T. L. Madden vice-president, and J. D. Plunkett secretary of this board.

Nashville Medical Society and a former professor in the University of Nashville Medical School, was one of the moving spirits in this organization. On April 11, 1867, the ordinance passed the previous year organizing a Board of Health was amended to provide for a health officer with a salary of $1,800 per annum.[9] This officer was to give his entire time to the cause of public health, with the exception of a few months during the winter when he would be permitted to engage in private practice. He was to be nominated by the Board of Health and elected by a joint vote of the board and the City Council.[10] On April 15, 1867, Dr. Joseph Jones, professor of physiology in the medical school of the University of Nashville, was named the first health officer.[11] He was a scientist and a physician and had served for four years in the Confederate army, where he learned the value of sanitary science. It seemed now that Nashville had entered earnestly into the business of arranging for an effective health unit. And then things went awry.

John Berrien Lindsley, in his first report to the City Board of Health, wrote: "All this was frustrated by the strange political anomaly which disfranchised the wealth, intellect, and virtue, while it enfranchised the vice, ignorance, and misery of the city of Nashville." It appears that Dr. Jones was unanimously reelected health officer in 1868 by the City Board of Health, but the city government deferred his nomination and elected a man of their own choice. The board did not contest the election, and thereby virtually came to an end.

An attempt was made to revive the board in 1869, when John M. Bass secured control of the city government, but it was unsuccessful. Dr. Lindsley said that Mr. Bass made the fatal mis-

---

A number of meetings were held in June, and regular conferences with the city government took place during that month. The expected cholera epidemic came in July and by the end of October nearly eight hundred had died in the city. Under this severe punishment, the municipal authorities of Nashville took the matter up seriously and the Board of Health became a reality.

[9] *Nashville Union and American*, April 12, 1867.
[10] Clayton, *op. cit.*, p. 295.
[11] *Second Report of the Nashville Board of Health*, 1877.

JOHN BERRIEN LINDSLEY

take of economizing while in power at the expense of the public health. With the machinery thus disrupted, interest in the city health program waned until 1873, when Asiatic cholera again made its appearance and taught the people another lesson on the importance of sanitary common sense.[12] On May 27, 1874, a new ordinance creating a City Board of Health became law.[13] Dr. J. D. Plunkett was elected president of the board. Dr. John Watson Morton was chosen health officer, on June 3, 1874,[14] and served until June 10, 1876, when Dr. Lindsley was asked to succeed him. The opportunity had come, and we find Dr. Lindsley accepting the appointment as city health officer for Nashville on June 7, 1876.[15] He was later to serve the state in a broader capacity as president of the State Board of Health and as executive secretary of this board.

When Dr. Lindsley became active in promoting a city health program for Nashville, he and his colleagues encountered many deep-seated prejudices on the part of the people. The cost of such a program, of course, was stressed as a major objection by those who opposed it.[16] Some argued that Nashville was too small a city to need sanitary reform, and others could not see why doctors should have any interest in eliminating sickness in a community. The question of public health itself was at that time in an experimental stage. Massachusetts, the pioneer in public health measures, had issued only her seventh annual report, and other states were just beginning to concern themselves with such a program; withal, there was little literature available and small precedent to follow. Dr. Lindsley and the members

---

[12] *Ibid.*
[13] *Nashville Union and American*, May 27, 1874.
[14] *Ibid.*, June 4, 1874.
[15] *Daily American* (Nashville), June 8, 1876: "The board of health met at five o'clock yesterday [June 7] afternoon and elected Dr. John Berrien Lindsley health officer.... We commend the action of the board of health in its selection of a health officer and congratulate the city upon its acquisition of an officer possessed of such rare qualifications for the proper discharge of the arduous duties devolving upon him. Dr. Lindsley is a man of large medical experience, and of extensive research in those departments of medical science appertaining especially to sanitary medicine."
[16] This and the following statements are from the *Third Report of the Nashville Board of Health*, 1879.

CHAMPION FOR PUBLIC HEALTH 117

of his board realized that one of the first essentials was education of the public mind in the matters of sanitary science. They therefore inaugurated a program of public enlightenment on matters pertaining to disease and its causes, and thus attempted to secure the co-operation of the people rather than impose upon them legislation which might be resented.

One of the first acts of the board was to require the systematic registration of deaths in the city, together with the causes that produced them. This was done through the funeral directors, who were required to produce a certificate, signed by a physician, setting forth the age, name, and cause of death of the deceased person before a burial permit could be obtained from the health officer. Dr. Buist, who was president of the Nashville City Board of Health in 1877, stated that the funeral directors opposed this action vigorously, and even the medical profession jeered at the efforts of the health board. This report was the beginning of the vital statistics of the city of Nashville. When the first vital statistics tables were published by the City Board of Health, many persons took the position that such information should not be made known to the public; that it would be injurious to the city's general welfare and should, therefore, be suppressed.

Dr. Lindsley's first annual report, which was the second report of the Nashville Board of Health, was presented on August 7, 1877. This report, a volume of 230 pages, summarizes the activities of the City Board of Health during the year ending July 4, 1877. It includes a vast amount of scientific data on public health problems. The first 133 pages, which present a summary of the sanitary reforms in Nashville with mortuary statistics for the years 1875 and 1876, were written by Dr. Lindsley. In transmitting the report to the Board of Health, he expressed his appreciation to those colleagues who had contributed papers to be included in the publication. Among them were Wilbur S. Foster, city engineer, who wrote a chapter on the topography of Nashville; Dr. James M. Safford, geologist of Tennessee and professor of chemistry at the time in the medical departments of the University of Nashville and Vanderbilt University, who contributed a paper on the geology of Nashville; Nathaniel Lupton, who submitted a paper on the water supply of the city; and Albert C. Ford, United States Signal Service observer, who wrote a chapter on the climate of Nashville. Finally, Anson Nelson, secretary of the Tennessee Historical Society, prepared a rather extensive chapter on the annals of Nashville, and Dr. George F. Blackie tabulated the analytical index for the report.

During his first year as health officer of Nashville, Dr. Lindsley studied with considerable care the reports of fifty or sixty bulletins of other city and state boards of health; this material he used rather extensively in his first annual report. Excerpts from this report will indicate some of the problems which faced the Board of Health and the progress made in their solution.

> The great object of the board has been to lay a permanent foundation for durable future work. It has endeavored to carry the people with it, commending its labors in the full task of the greatest commercial revulsion America has ever known. It has been exceedingly cautious in urging expensive sanitary measures and has contented itself with keeping before the citizens and the municipal authority the unspeakable importance of cleanliness of all premises, private and public. It has also, in addition to reliable and important mortality statistics, collected a large amount of most important data which will always be of use in the future.[17]

The questions of water supply, drainage, sewerage, and of night and day scavengering were given thoughtful attention and in some cases very satisfactory progress was made.

Dr. Lindsley and the members of the board recognized the importance of mortuary statistics. "The great practical value of mortality registration is demonstrated by the Morton Report of 1876, page 24."[18] (The Commonwealth of Massachusetts issued its first registration report as early as 1841.) Referring to the Nashville mortuary register, Dr. Lindsley said:

[17] *Second Report of the Nashville Board of Health*, 1877.
[18] Clayton, *op. cit.*, p. 299.

CHAMPION FOR PUBLIC HEALTH

Beyond question its mortuary register is honestly kept. The law is stringent and of such a character as to be readily enforced. No one can die within the city limits and be buried without due regard. At the same time great care is taken to separate from the list bodies interred in the City Cemetery from without the limits. As the lessons derived from such statistics are increasingly valuable with the space of time over which they spread, an analysis of the register for 1875 as well as that of 1876 is given in this report.[19]

This was the first mortuary statistical report made by the city of Nashville. The registration of marriages and births, although readily recognized as important by the Board of Health, was not enforced at this time because Dr. Lindsley felt that it would be useless to undertake to do so under the existing laws of the state. He recommended that the medical profession and others who were interested should make a combined effort to secure from the General Assembly in 1879 a law which would make it possible to have marriages and births registered. The death rate in Nashville in 1876 was 33.48 to 1,000 inhabitants. The normal or lowest death rate, as estimated by statisticians at the time, was 11 to 1,000 in rural districts, and 17 to 1,000 in the cities. Dr. Lindsley urged that the death rate in Nashville should not exceed that of Cleveland, St. Louis, or Louisville, which would mean an annual saving of at least 15 lives out of each 1,000 in the city of Nashville.[20] "In other words, 405 lives a year could be saved if sanitary conditions were vastly improved."[21] He called attention to the distress that was placed upon the increasing population by annual immigration and showed how ridiculous it was to allow so many people to die because of insanitary conditions: "For these avoidable 405 deaths annually, for these preventable 11,340 cases of sickness, for these unnecessary 295,650 days of illness, for this enormous useless waste of needed labor, the public authorities of Nashville are to blame."[22]

[19] *Second Report of the Nashville Board of Health*, 1877.
[20] *Daily American* (Nashville), April 11, 1879: "The mortality rate for the month of March, 1879, was 28.34 to 1,000 inhabitants."
[21] *Second Report of the Nashville Board of Health*, 1877.
[22] *Ibid.*

He explained that there were two definite causes for the high death rate in Nashville. First, he said, was the fact that Nashville had grown from a village to a town and from a town to a city without changing her habits.[23] This had caused her to fall into a condition "grossly at variance with the first principle of medical science and common sense." The second cause was the Civil War and its consequent social revolution.

Ten of his important recommendations to the board were:

1. That there be an impartial and rigid enforcement of the ordinance which prohibited the use of a drain for the purpose of getting rid of garbage and kitchen refuse. The subject of the disposal of kitchen garbage received careful study by the Board of Health during its early years. Dr. Lindsley recommended an ordinance which "would prohibit all surface privies and boxes, and allow only water closets, earth closets, and pits, all to be constructed, cleansed, and disinfected as required by the Board of Health."[24]

[23] *Daily American* (Nashville), March 12, 1879: "Health Officer Lindsley submitted his report at a regular meeting of the City Board of Health. He announced that the Third Report of the Nashville Board of Health was ready for the printer.

" 'By direction of the Board I have consulted City Attorney McAllister. He is emphatic that under such clause the Board has the power to declare all the hog-pens within the city nuisances. Hence the suggestion for my report is renewed, to-wit: That the Board do at once declare all hog-pens within the city limits nuisances so that they may be abated before the hot weather comes on.

" 'A radical defect in the present arrangement for scavenger work is the unsatisfactory and perplexing method in which it is divided. In Richmond and other cities the street and alley cleaning is under the Health Department. Here the street scavenger work is done by the Department which makes and repairs streets. This is its proper and main work. The cleaning is done only by spurts. The Board has had much experience in this matter and needs no argument upon it. I would suggest that the City Council be requested to add four carts with attendants to the scavenger force; and that all the cleaning of the public highways be done under the direction of the Board of Health.

" 'The very unhealthy, unsightly, and uncomfortable custom of allaying dust by sprinkling which causes the roadways to wear out rapidly, has given rise to much complaint among our people. I am now prepared to urge that within the crowded business portions of the city this be prohibited, and that, instead, the streets in the said districts be cleaned by sweeping. This should be done every night, either by hand or by machine'."

[24] *Ibid.*, October 15, 1879: "Meeting of City Board of Health in which Lindsley Complains of Old Shanties and Privies.

" 'Many complaints have been made because of the foul odors from stinking surface privies. These are by far the main source of impure air in Nashville. Considering their abounding number and intolerable stench, it is surprising that we are not

CHAMPION FOR PUBLIC HEALTH

2. That the fills of the city be carefully protected against the practice which had prevailed of using them as a means of getting rid of ashes, garbage, household filth, and the scourings of the streets and cellars. He said that this practice constituted one of the serious problems of the city.

These fills also are in the lowest and most ineligible portions of the city, being subject to prevalent overflows from headwaters and backwaters. Besides, these are the portions of Nashville which ought to be most carefully reclaimed and protected from defilement. There is no excuse whatever for this gross violation of common decency. This is utterly laying the foundation for the whole tribe of filth diseases in a region already thickly peopled and claimed to be the heart of a large city.

He further recommended that the best of materials, such as good stone and clay, be used to fill in these low places instead of making them a dump.[25]

3. He called attention to the fact that the machinery of the waterworks had become impaired by age, and referred to the southward growth of the city, which caused a well-founded theory that the river was becoming polluted above the pumphouse. For this reason he recommended that measures be perfected for procuring water from a point above all possibility of foulness. In other words, he recommended that the pumping station be moved up the river above the sources of possible pollution.

4. He pointed to the fact that during the cholera epidemic the portion of the city which suffered most was that which used well and spring water, and he recommended the discontinuance of the use of this water where there was a possiblity of insanitary conditions.[26]

---

visited by epidemic typhoid fever. Our people are stupidly asleep on this vital point. No healthy city without pure air—no pure air with 2,124 boxes of human excreta, all the while exhaling noxious gases'."

[25] *Second Report of the Nashville Board of Health*, 1877.

[26] *Daily American* (Nashville), January 19, 1877: "A plan was submitted for the improvement of Nashville's water supply which is in a large measure responsible for such a high mortality rate."

5. He said that dampness was one of the most universal causes of sickness and death and that it was almost always overlooked as a source of trouble. He recommended a study of the conditions which caused the city to be damp and suggested that these conditions be eliminated. A number of small pools of stagnant water on the outskirts of the city and the condition of the gutters and alleys were listed among the reasons for the dampness of the city of Nashville. "The diseases which are notably favored by undue moisture in soil and air," he said, "are malarial fever, consumption, pneumonia, typhoid fever, rheumatism, neuralgia, scrofula, cerebrospinal meningitis. . . . A glance at this list is enough to show the superlative importance of diminished dampness."[27]

6. He recommended a systematic *check-up and inspection* of the city. "Until the people are better educated on the topic," he said, "it is indispensable that thorough and regular inspection from house to house be enforced." "Keep the city clean. Keep the city dry. Let the people have plenty of pure water to drink. Forbid the use of polluted water. Forbid the overcrowding of people and thus diminished air. These are the four great principles of public hygiene."

7. He recommended a more careful public health program for the city schools of Nashville. "Nashville, which before and since the Civil War has been distinguished as a focal point for public schools, should not be content to follow other cities, but should take the lead in putting health into the schoolroom," he urged. "Above our corps of teachers, the school inspector and lecturer on hygiene should rank second only to the superintendent."

8. He called attention to the necessity for vaccination of the indigent, both white and colored, in and around the city, and recommended diligence in dealing with this problem. He said that during the winter of 1875-76 total vaccinations in the city of Nashville amounted to 10,760, and of this number probably 9,000

[27] This and the following statements are from the *Second Report of the Nashville Board of Health*, 1877.

were gratuitous, a contribution on the part of local physicians. To this group of public servants, he expressed his sincere appreciation.

9. He recommended a hospital for the destitute of the city where medical attention and food and shelter should be given.

Nashville is perhaps the only city of its size in Christendom without a public charity of this kind. All other cities, especially those which are centers of medical education, have great establishments belonging to the public, endowed either by municipal or private generosity, or by both. . . . Would it not be well for the whole community to unite and through one organization provide such an institution for the citizens of Nashville?

In addition to a hospital and dispensary service to relieve human suffering and misery among the poor and destitute, he suggested that the city employ at least two district physicians whose duty it should be to acquaint themselves with the very poor people of the city and to give them medical aid in time to save them from future trouble. These physicians, he was quite sure, would more than save the expense incurred in their salaries by the diminished charges in hospital and dispensary departments. He indicated that they would not necessarily be restricted to this work alone; therefore, their salaries would not of necessity be high. Other cities had employed this type of service and found it a valuable auxiliary to the Board of Health. He referred to Cincinnati, where twenty-five such district physicians were employed, one for each ward in the city.

10. He recommended improvement of the conditions which existed in the jails and workhouses of the city. Dr. Lindsley had published in 1874 a bulletin entitled *On Prison Discipline and Penal Legislation,* and had perhaps made the most exhaustive study of this problem of any of his contemporaries. This study appeared in the July number of the *Theological Medium* in 1874, and was later reprinted and distributed over the State.

Dr. Lindsley's recommendations were favorably received by the citizens of Nashville. In his report, he expressed his appreciation to the two great professions which had sustained him and his colleagues in their efforts; namely, the medical profession and the clergy.

Two great professions, taking the lead and firmly sustained by the intelligent, moral, and industrious of all classes, have in every case carried the day against the stolidity, selfishness, and rascality of the "political bummers" who are the chronic curse of our American cities, and have no issue in seeking office other than to make a dishonest, lazy living at the expense of the honest industry of the community.

He closed his report with a suggestion that indicated his impatience with existing conditions and his faith in the people's desire to have an efficient and effective health program.

After much careful thought and after conferring with the men of prudence and experience, representing all classes and interests, the suggestion is now deliberately made and strongly urged upon the board that a direct appeal be made to the people of Nashville so as to accomplish in a few months and once for all what otherwise would require years of halting and unsatisfactory effort.

Let the board carefully prepare a sanitary code, complete in all respects and carefully adapted to the peculiar conditions of Nashville. Let the city council appoint a date, giving ample time for discussion, for an election by which this code as a whole or in part shall be adopted or rejected. . . . From much talk in the alleys, street corners, and elsewhere, I know that the people, rich and poor, are vastly in advance of the City Hall and am perfectly confident that the vote on this question will do the community as much credit as the decision of the hog question September 27, 1873, or the waterworks extension September 30, 1876. . . . The entire subject will thus be taken away from all complications and from local politics. The people will be fully educated upon the issues and no fears need be entertained for the results.

The *Third Report of the Nashville Board of Health,* compiled and edited by Dr. Lindsley, was published in April, 1879.[28] The greater portion of the material in this volume, he said, was ready for publication in August, 1878, but the sudden epidemic of yel-

---

[28] *Daily American* (Nashville), April 11, 1879: "Subscriptions are taken to the *Third Report of the Nashville Board of Health."*

CHAMPION FOR PUBLIC HEALTH 125

low fever in Memphis made it necessary for him to spend much of his time there and his absence from Nashville delayed the publication for three months. Publication was then further delayed three months in order to incorporate the mortuary statistics of 1878, as well as those of 1879. It thus became a biennial report.

In this volume of 384 pages, Dr. Lindsley endeavored to give the citizens of Nashville an idea of the nature and scope of the work performed by the board and health officials. One hundred and eighty-four pages of the volume were written by Dr. Lindsley himself. He reported (1) on the sanitary progress made in Nashville, giving mortuary statistics for 1877-78; (2) on the mental and physical hygiene of the schools of Nashville; and (3) on the prevention of yellow fever in Nashville during the epidemic of 1878. The remaining chapters, contributed at his solicitation by other authorities, were as follows: "A Plea for Sanitary Reform," by Thomas L. Madden, professor of theory and practice of medicine in the University of Nashville and Vanderbilt University; "The Progress of the Waterworks," by W. F. Foster, city engineer; "The Sanitary Geology of Nashville," by Alexander Winchell, professor of historical geology and zoology in Vanderbilt University; "On Trees and Shrubbery," by August Gattinger, an eminent scientist; and "On Heating and Ventilation of Public Schools," by N. T. Lupton, professor of chemistry in Vanderbilt. The analytical index for this volume was prepared by George F. Blackie, president and professor of chemistry in the University of Nashville Medical College.

In his first report to the Board of Health, it will be recalled that Dr. Lindsley dealt for the most part with the necessities for sanitary reform. In this second report, he gives a summary of the accomplishments of the board in the way of sanitary reforms during the two-year period and continues his discussion of Nashville's sanitary needs.

Dr. Lindsley reviewed briefly the history of the board's efforts to secure a more adequate supply of pure water for the city. When he became health officer, Nashville was using water supplied from springs and the river, there being in addition a few public wells. The investigation of the water conditions by Dr. Lindsley and his board revealed facts which caused the people to revolt and demand pure water. Among other things, it was discovered that Brown's Creek emptied into the river about three-fourths of a mile above and on the same side of the river with the pumping engines which supplied the reservoir. The creek had become the natural drain of all the southern portion of the city. A citizens' committee, appointed by the Nashville Board of Health, reported that the plains above the pumping station for a distance of about a mile and a half were strewn with the carcasses of hundreds of animals of every description. Here, it seemed, were dumped the rubbish and garbage of the southern end of the city, and this area was drained by the creek. The committee discovered that the creek was the natural drain for four cemeteries—the City Cemetery, the Catholic Cemetery, the Federal burying ground, and Mt. Olivet. It was inevitable, therefore, that the water which drained from these resting places of the dead found its way into the creek, into the river, and then into the city reservoir. It also appeared that the cleanings from the privy vaults of the city were deposited not only upon the banks of the creek but actually in the channel of the stream.

Upon further examination it was found that Lick Branch, which ran through North Nashville, was the natural drain for the Tennessee State Penitentiary and for its cesspools, kitchens, and warehouses. Beyond the penitentiary were located several slaughter-houses, the offal from which was discharged into the stream. Wilson Spring Branch, which emptied into the Cumberland south of Broad Street, was also a drain for the refuse of the city.

Besides these menaces, there was in 1878 no guarantee that the city of Nashville would have an adequate supply of water, even of impure water. The pumping station was located at a point on the Cumberland River a short distance above the central part of the city. The water was taken in through suction

CHAMPION FOR PUBLIC HEALTH 127

pipes directly from the river and was pumped into the reservoir, which had a capacity of approximately twenty-two hundred thousand gallons. The reservoir was situated on top of a bluff near the pumping station. From it the water was carried to consumers through street mains, entirely without filtration or any attempt at purification. The daily consumption of water in Nashville was estimated to be about two million gallons a day, or almost the full capacity of the reservoir. This did not permit the water to settle in the reservoir before it was carried on to the consumer. It was also necessary for the engine to work every day, and any accident serious enough to have stopped the machinery for twenty-four hours would have caused the supply in the reservoir to become exhausted and Nashville would have been without water. This was a condition that had to be faced by Dr. Lindsley and his board.[29]

The citizens' committee and the Board of Health, on January 19, 1877, made the following recommendations:

1. That a new filtering plant be constructed up the river above the sources of pollution. The location was to be determined after scientific tests by competent authorities had been made.

2. That the course of Brown's Creek be changed so that it would empty into the river below the island.

3. That a new reservoir with ample dimensions and sufficient elevation be built after a suitable location should be selected.

4. That a more adequate system of sewerage be built.

5. That the legislature be memorialized to construct a proper sewer from the prison to the river in the bed of Lick Branch.

When Dr. Lindsley's report was published, in 1879, he had the satisfaction of knowing that the major portion of these recommendations had been carried out. The city engineer reported that the new pumping machinery had been installed at an approximate cost of one hundred thousand dollars, and an arrangement for filtering the water had been completed.[30] The en-

---
[29] *Second Report of the Nashville Board of Health*, 1877.
[30] Clayton, *op. cit.*, p. 297.

larged reservoir had not been built, but the plan was receiving consideration. With reference to the water supply, Dr. Lindsley says in this third report:

> If during the past few years the board of health had accomplished nothing more than this awakening of public and official sentiment to one of the most vital points connected with the healthy existence of the city, it would have fully justified its claim upon the confidence of the people.[81]

With the completion of the waterworks in view, Dr. Lindsley recommended that every well or spring liable to contamination should be closed by law. This, he said, would make it necessary for many people in limited circumstances who had heretofore gotten their water free of charge to provide hydrants and pay water taxes. If there were families unable to meet this expense, he said, then the city should furnish them water free upon the same principle that it furnished free medicine and hospital service. Each family in Nashville using hydrant water was charged eight dollars a year, regardless of the amount of water used or of the consumer's ability to pay. Dr. Lindsley objected to this method of assessment upon the ground that it was arbitrary and unequal, and recommended that a meter system be installed so that each family would pay for the amount actually used.[82]

Once the improvement of the water system was achieved, Dr. Lindsley took the position that "no municipality should introduce a water system without at the same time providing a correspondingly improved sewer system." An improved drainage system was imperative, or the vast amount of water brought daily into the city would remain stagnant in the gutters and alleys, producing soil moisture and thereby generating the evils of filth and adding greatly to disease and death. The task of getting pure water into the city was accomplished; the problem

---
[81] *Third Report of the Nashville Board of Health*, 1879.
[82] *Ibid.*

CHAMPION FOR PUBLIC HEALTH

of getting it out after it had served its purpose was yet before them.

Dr. Lindsley then lost no time in starting his campaign for a sanitary drainage system for the city. He condemned the downspouts which were so prevalent at the time; that is, the pipes which conveyed rain water from the roofs and terminated a few feet or a few inches above the sidewalks. He recommended that an ordinance be passed by the city government to eliminate this evil, which he considered one of the greatest obstacles to the improvement of public health.

He applauded the decision of the Supreme Court on the "Sidewalk Issue," March 13, 1878, which "upheld laws which had a beneficial effect upon the looks, comfort, and health of Nashville." Immediately after this decision was rendered, a contract was let for several miles of new sidewalks in Nashville. The construction of sidewalks, he said, would be very beneficial to the city in solving its problem of surface drainage.[38]

Dr. Lindsley condemned the use of inferior material for building and repairing the streets of the city; namely, the disintegrated blue limestone which was so plentiful around Nashville. This stone was not cheap, he said, in the long run. It was rapidly ground into dust and was very bright and injurious to the eyes. "When the wind blows," he said, "the atmosphere is usually filled with a powder which irritates the lungs." Then, after sprinkling the streets, which was customary in Nashville, matters were not mended at all. The streets were left rather foul and muddy, and from them "arose usually a disagreeable and malarial effluvia"; then, the streets not being cleared up often, this mud accumulated and choked up the gutters. He recommended for the city streets the excellent gravel found in large quantities up the river. With this material the city could have good macadam streets.

[38] *Daily American* (Nashville), March 14, 1878: "On Wednesday, March 13, the Supreme Court settled the Sidewalk Ordinance in favor of the city and declared that the city had a lien upon the lot upon which they ordered the sidewalks constructed until the owner of the property had paid for the work."

Of all the problems, that of filth riddance and scavenger work was found to be the most annoying. Ignorance, prejudice, and perversity were encountered and had to be overcome. It is not difficult to picture the uncleanliness of 1878 when we consider that Nashville had no systematic way of disposing of kitchen garbage. To clean the city and keep it clean would be, Dr. Lindsley considered, the greatest contribution the health department could make.

In 1878 Nashville was a compact little city with a population of approximately thirty thousand. The force employed at that time to clean the alleys and gutters consisted of five carts, each with a driver and one attendant, who worked under the "scavenger boss." The "boss" was elected by the street committee, not by the Board of Health. In order to strengthen this department, Dr. Lindsley urged that his earlier recommendations be carried out, namely: That a system of careful inspection be established, and the city policemen (at that time there were twelve) be commissioned to observe all infractions of sanitary ordinances within their beats, and to warn or arrest offenders as occasion might develop. "If a policeman is not qualified for sanitary duty," he urged, "he ought to be disqualified for any kind of police duty." Dr. Lindsley felt that the enforcement of sanitary ordinances was, after all, about the greatest service a policeman could render the city.

A three-point program was followed by the board with reference to filth riddance: (1) the improvement of the sewerage system; (2) the visiting of every house by the garbage scavenger; and (3) the organization of a night soil scavenger force. In attempting to develop sentiment in favor of rigid sanitary laws in Nashville, Dr. Lindsley appealed to the poor people by stating that those in moderate circumstances should be more interested in a healthful city than the rich. "When the occasional pestilence or the annual heat of summer comes," he said, "the rich speedily and readily get away to the cool mountains or the seashore resorts, and thus they escape the inconveniences of the epidemic, whereas the working man must remain to face the gloomy days of grimness and dread, and struggle through the summer heat."[34]

Previous to July 1, 1876, according to Dr. Lindsley, a general inspection and cleaning of the city took place only in consequence of epidemics. After that date, however, the Board of Health was more systematic in its inspections. As a result, valuable statistical data had been accumulated, many nuisances of the kind just referred to had been disposed of, and much improvement had been made in eliminating the causes of epidemics. Dr. Lindsley regretted, however, that "cattle still live in town as they did when Nashville was in North Carolina." Then, too, hog pens were still allowed within the city limits.

Another source of regret to him was the fact that the street cleaning committee would sometimes go two or three months before cleaning such thoroughfares as Church Street. In recommending frequent cleaning of the sidewalks, he made the observation that "a reliable citizen who has been a resident of Nashville for three years reports that a pavement on Church Street, daily traversed by hundreds of people, has not been cleaned during that period." Many backyards in the city were evidently in great need of improvement at the time this report was made. Dr. Lindsley said: "For one, two, or three generations these have become receptacles of ashes, garbage, and so on, until they are now nothing but dump heaps." He suggested that these backyards could be turned into beautiful plots of grass, flowers, and shrubs. The ventilation of private grounds was a source of earnest solicitation on his part. He felt that this was of great importance to the health, not only of the occupants, but of all the citizens. The close fences, he said, kept out the sunlight and served to conceal the deposit of insanitary matter which negligent servants and careless housekeepers allowed to remain until it was in a state of decomposition. The widening of the alleys, he contended, would supply the people of Nashville with fresh air and do away with many of the worst nuisances in the city.

[34] This and the following statements are from the *Third Report of the Nashville Board of Health*, 1879.

This was one of the important problems to be considered in view of the city's need for pure air.

Along with the sanitary program, Dr. Lindsley advocated the planting of trees throughout the city. He felt that the comfort and beauty of the city would be very much enhanced by the citizens' efforts in this direction. He called attention to Broad Street, which was so bare of shade and was such a "hot furnace on long summer days," and pictured it with a fine row of forest trees on each side, which would enhance the value of the property tenfold the cost of the trees.

The ordinance to condemn mantraps in the business houses of Nashville was only one of many such measures suggested by him to protect the lives of Nashville citizens. All public buildings were examined with reference to their facilities for ready exit in case of fire. Dr. Lindsley insisted that public buildings of every description should have ample space for exits. His inspection revealed the grossest defects. He discovered that many of the buildings were at variance with the most common-sense laws of sanitation and that even the cardinal principle that doors should open outward and not inward was generally found to be violated. A list of these buildings included nearly all of the churches in town and many of the school buildings. In fact, he said, the only institutions in the city having doors which opened outward as they should were the Grand Opera House, the Masonic Theatre, and the Olympic Theatre.

A systematic examination and vaccination for smallpox of the entire population of the city took place in 1875-76, following the smallpox scare of the previous year. Since that time, Dr. Lindsley said, a large population had moved into Edgefield in the immediate neighborhood of the city and these people had not been vaccinated. This condition was alarming. He felt at the time this second report was issued that there was ample opportunity for smallpox in Nashville, and gave the following warning:

CHAMPION FOR PUBLIC HEALTH 133

Let the city council not remain asleep. Among the several hundred people living contiguous to the city on the northwest, there is abundant material for a plague which would cost us thousands upon thousands. Let the Honorable County Court of Davidson County look at a danger which is most imminent and face a duty which it cannot shirk.

Dr. Lindsley recognized that a registration of vital statistics was the basis and foundation of the future health program of Nashville. Beginning on July 4, 1874, an accurate system of recording deaths in the city was established. In this third report he urges the necessity of adding to this system the registration of marriages and births. He also wanted to add the registration of prevalent diseases. Such a registry of disease, he felt, would bring to light many cases which up to that time had been unrecognized, and would thus give data which would lead to improvement of the public health. An effort was made in January, February, and March, 1877, to get reliable information as to prevalent diseases in Nashville, but it failed. The principal reason for failure, Dr. Lindsley said, was that the health officer did not have sufficient time to devote to this important work, and the attempt was not supported by a city ordinance requiring the medical practitioner to report every case of so-called contagious or infectious disease to the health department. He recommended that proper blanks be furnished to all physicians on which to return full information to the health office after each examination, and that additional clerical help be furnished the office in order to take care of this system of records.

Among his recommendations, Dr. Lindsley also urged that the old City Cemetery, around which lived one sixth of the population of Nashville, be closed and made into a memorial park. He then gave an explanation of his reasons for making this recommendation. A record of burials in the cemetery since its beginning in 1822 totaled 21,421 in 1879. Accompanying his report, he quoted from the reports of other cities, indicating their solution of the same problem, and he strongly recommended that this cemetery be discontinued as a burial place.

Dr. Lindsley was interested in state preventive medicine, and was at this time thinking of the great opportunity which the state of Tennessee would have in beginning such a program. He referred to the efforts of the State Medical Society in developing sentiment for the creation of the State Board of Health. Nashville could not be a healthy city unless her neighbor cities were healthy; hence the necessity for a state-wide program. He recommended, therefore, the support of such a program of preventive medicine.[35]

The four years of civil war he considered a great school for sanitary science. The progress made in public hygiene during the war was due to the fact that the people outside the military lines, as well as those inside, learned by tragic experience the need for sanitary methods. "The important rules of cleanliness and disciplined opposition to filth and intemperance soon prevailed." He felt that all of the surgeons who served in the war on either side became more practically versed in the prevention of disease. Military camps had often to be moved during the war because of epidemics and the diseased condition of the ground on which they were located. This lesson later proved valuable in civil life in the South.

Dr. Lindsley's table of mortuary statistics showed that the death rate among the whites in Nashville was reduced from 25.78 per thousand in 1875 to 17.43 in 1878, and that the colored death rate was reduced from 49.69 to 33.50.[36]

On December 18, 1877, the Nashville Board of Health passed the following resolution:

Resolved, That the health officer be directed to prepare an exhaustive report upon the mental and physical hygiene to which the pupils in the public schools of our city are at present subjected, together with such suggestions as to him may seem proper, looking to the improvement of the same.[37]

[35] *Centennial History of the Tennessee Medical Association,* p. 414.
[36] *Third Report of the Nashville Board of Health,* 1879.
[37] *Daily American* (Nashville), December 19, 1877: "The Nashville Board of Health met yesterday and passed the following resolution: '*Resolved,* That the Health Officer be directed to prepare an exhaustive report. . . .'"

It was further indicated that this report would be included in the third annual report of the City Board of Health. Dr. Lindsley admits that it was with no little trepidation that he undertook the preparation of it. In his characteristic way, he first secured and read carefully the best literature available on the subject. In his preliminary remarks, he quotes from many authorities who had been concerned with the same problem in other cities. Having thus informed himself, he inspected and surveyed the Nashville city schools, with which he was already familiar, and evaluated their condition in terms of the best standard practice elsewhere. His findings and recommendations are given in part.

With respect to the grounds and site of the buildings, he said:

> Two fundamental principles should be followed: (1) the location should be as central as possible for the district to be accommodated; and (2) ample space should be secured for playgrounds and with a view to hygienic and aesthetic points of highest importance.[38]

The Howard, Hume, Hinds, and Trimble were the principal school buildings in the city at the time this report was made. Of the Howard School he said that, under the best management, it was adapted only for a splendid show. Many times he had taken strangers to visit it, and they were always delighted with what they saw and heard. Nevertheless, he thought its style of architecture should in the future be wholly discarded. The Hume School was to be preferred to any of the others. It had four rooms on the first floor and four on the second, which he recommended, but neither did this building meet with his entire approval. The other buildings, he said, were more or less modifications of the Howard plan, and were seriously defective. Lofty school buildings, he urged, should be universally condemned, and instead one-story buildings should be recommended.

In the selection of materials for construction, he recommended that frame houses be used instead of brick. "In this climate, par-

---

[38] This and the following statements are from the *Third Report of the Nashville Board of Health*, 1879.

ticularly," he said, "the best would be frame houses with a layer of brick worked in, thus giving a wall of five layers—plank, air, brick, air, lath and plaster." As to dryness and comfort, he said, there was no comparison between the frame house and the brick.

At Dr. Lindsley's request, Dr. N. T. Lupton, of Vanderbilt University, made a careful survey of the heating and ventilation of the schoolhouses, and the results of this survey were included in Dr. Lindsley's annual report to the board. The report shows that the buildings, grounds, and equipment of the Nashville city schools met with his emphatic disapproval.

With regard to the lighting of the schoolhouses, he found that all the laws of sanitation had been violated. He urged that this problem needed a patient and prolonged investigation, and called attention to the probabilities of injury to the children as a result of insufficient light. He listed as the three most pernicious effects of ineffective lighting: (1) decrease of the range of vision—myopia, or shortsightedness; (2) decrease of the acuteness of vision—amblyopia; (3) decrease of the endurance of vision—asthenopia. These three conditions, he said, came from the same circumstances; that is, from insufficient or poorly arranged lights, or from the child's posture while studying. He felt, however, that great improvement could be made by changing the position and arrangement of the desks in the various schools.

Dr. Lindsley emphasized the injury that could be done to the child by the use of unsuitable furniture and recommended that the furniture in Hinds School be changed. With few exceptions, he found double desks being used in the schools instead of single desks, which he considered preferable. In almost all of the rooms, pupils were found uncomfortably seated. The more common faults of the furniture used he listed as follows: (1) unsuitable backs; (2) too great a distance between the seats and the desks; (3) disproportions generally—too great a difference between the height of the seats and that of the desks; (4) wrong form and slope of the desks.

The outhouses, length of terms, daily sessions, age of admission to school, motives for study, including terror, corporal punishment, pride, emulation, and prizes were discussed at length by Dr. Lindsley in this report. He recommended a term of nine months instead of ten, with two vacations instead of one.

Dr. Lindsley felt that the most important period in the child's life began with the early grades, and he found that in Nashville the most inexperienced teachers, the lowest salaries, and the largest classes were found in the early grades. He recommended that the order be reversed and that, if poor teachers must be used and small salaries paid, this condition should prevail in the upper grades rather than in the lower grades where the work was so important.

In the discussion of motives for study, which included terror and corporal punishment, he said that every happy school child was "a living witness to the imperishable glory and influence of Pestalozzi, who freed the children from that barbaric and cruel system of school discipline which prevailed before his time." It was not, he thought, the introduction of new methods of teaching that would make Pestalozzi live, because he thought it very doubtful whether "the acute and learned Hindoos and their successors in intellectual supremacy, our own immediate predecessors and masters, the Greeks, did not anticipate all possible mere technical modes of communicating thought." "But," he said, "when Pestalozzi observed how Gertrude taught her children he made a moral discovery, not an intellectual one; a child was by his very nature possessed of the same rights as those of a grown-up person. . . . Pestalozzi," he said, "thought very definitely that the chiefest right of the child was to have the door to knowledge opened by the 'gentle, loving hands of a mother and not by those of a merciless, cruel jailor.' Penetrating to the very soul of these new ideas, he touched the heart of all civilized nations. Thus schools ceased to be prisons, and thus Pestalozzi's silent worth has constantly with each successive year become more sharply defined and more gigantic in its proportions."

The use of terror and fear of punishment as a motive for acquiring knowledge should have no place in the public school supervised by Dr. Lindsley. Only a small and constantly diminishing group advocated its retention, he said. He called attention to the fact that in Nashville during the year ending June, 1878, there was only one pupil whipped out of each three hundred in attendance. He felt that this was a highly honorable record and reflected credit upon the administration. Even this blemish, however, he felt should be removed. "It is not right to keep scores, it may be hundreds, of children in fear and trembling lest they should fall short of duty and be punished by the teacher. They still invest the teacher with the ancient odium which made teacher and tyrant synonymous in the youthful vocabulary."

Dr. Lindsley felt that unruly students should be kept at home and not allowed to attend school and that there should be no law which would require teachers to supplement the "laziness or ineptness of parents." While he did not approve of the use of terror and punishment to discipline children, yet he felt that it was equally damaging to use the motives of pride, emulation, and prizes to stimulate study on the part of the children. He felt that this excessive stimulus resulted in rather startling evils and was highly prejudicial to health. The most normal life which could be led by the child while in school was for the best interest of the individual and society. He would substitute for the motives of terror, punishment, emulation, and prizes, the motive of the love of knowledge and duty.

These motives, a sense of duty, and a keen, deep, lofty appreciation of the unspeakably glorious privilege of learning what is in the universe and in one's self, are happy, healthy motives. By them will be produced steady, eager, pleasant, forward steps as each pupil is vouchsafed health and opportunities for learning. It is no disgrace for the feeble to go slowly. It is no cause of pride that the healthy go fast. There is no occasion to despise the former nor to envy the latter. With these few sentences this great theme must be dismissed.

CHAMPION FOR PUBLIC HEALTH 139

Dr. Lindsley believed in physical and health education in the public schools within certain limits. He emphasized his viewpoint by quoting the superintendent of schools of Boston: "The want of proper attention to the health and physical development of our children is the great defect of our system of schools." "At the same time," he said, "we cannot expect our public schools to carry the whole burden of developing the child mentally, physically, morally, and in every other way." To require the already overburdened teachers to be responsible for the health and physical development of the children, he said, was perhaps placing upon them a burden which should be borne by the medical profession.

He also was not sure whether the public school doors should be open to very young children, thus placing upon the teachers the maternal care of the children. He questioned the wisdom of the parents who looked to the teachers for the moral care of their children. "After all, teachers in public schools are teachers simply and have a right to demand that the parents, physicians, and clergy furnish them good, healthy children to educate."

Dr. Lindsley thought that the health of the children could be greatly improved if the Board of Education would come to the rescue and insist that the municipal government make the needed improvements in buildings, grounds, and school equipment.

He believed in co-education and quoted Superintendent W. T. Harris, of St. Louis, to support his views on this subject. It was his opinion that the western states had made a distinct contribution to American education by throwing open the doors of their universities to young women. He also commended the western states for being the first to extend to all the people collegiate and university privileges as an integral part of their public school systems. The report on this question made by Superintendent Harris, he said, indicated clearly that co-education in St. Louis had proved itself to be of value in economy, discipline, instruction, and the individual development of the students.

A serious defect in the school system, he thought, was the fact that it failed to recognize individual differences in children.

> Individuality is the clue which must guide us out of this labyrinth of educational difficulties. Identity of instruction may not be good for groups of boys and girls together. Neither is it good for groups of these separately, thrown together by the haphazard of residence. No two girls and no two boys of the same age are just alike physically or mentally, and in any given pair identical education may produce the worst results.

He would, therefore, relieve the ironbound rigidity of the public schools, which sought at that time to conduct whole classes of children through the mysteries of learning as if there were no more difference in the individuals composing the classes than in so many "peas in a skillet."

In concluding his chapter on the physical and mental hygiene of the public schools, Dr. Lindsley said that the great nations of other days had seen fit to expend the public funds in the support of worship and of standing armies. America was spending hers on a system of public schools, thereby replacing the established church and the armies. This was the only safeguard for a democracy. The public schools, however, were in an experimental stage. It would require several generations to show up the serious mistakes. He warned against one, however, which at this time was obvious even to the layman. He said that the public school system was undertaking too much; that it was spreading out too widely, and was grasping at the work of the family, the church, and the university. "Let the parent, pastor, and physician be held responsible for physical and moral training. Let the public school, and that only for a limited period and curriculum, look to the intellectual."

Dr. Lindsley has been given credit by many for preventing widespread desolation during the yellow fever epidemic of 1878 in Nashville.[39] A rather complete history of the efforts of the

---

[39] *Nashville American*, December 8, 1897: "In 1876, he was elected city health officer and served as such for four years. During his term of office the great yellow fever plague swept over the South, and that it did not reach Nashville was due to

CHAMPION FOR PUBLIC HEALTH 141

health officers in Nashville prior to and during this epidemic is included in the *Third Annual Report of the Nashville Board of Health*. There has not been written a more interesting chapter on the history of Nashville than this one. There is no exaggeration on the part of Dr. Lindsley as to his own contribution in combatting the ravages of this epidemic. The entire citizenship of Nashville was enlisted in a great campaign to prevent the spread of the disease to this city, and to control it once it had arrived. Because of this organization for control of the epidemic, Nashville was able to render valuable assistance to her sister cities in the South and Southwest who were not so fortunate in their efforts to avoid disaster.[40] Twenty thousand dollars contributed by the people of Davidson County was distributed among towns in the South during this plague.

Dr. Lindsley from the beginning followed one great principle from which he never deviated; namely, that the Board of Health should tell the people of the city "the truth, the whole truth, and in timely season." In the beginning, the truth was very unpopular and was resented by some civic-minded persons, but these, too, finally understood that it was to their interest that pitiless publicity be used in dealing with health conditions. The history of the Nashville epidemic and the part Dr. Lindsley played during this memorable year in Nashville will not be further discussed, but it should prove interesting reading to the laymen of Nashville as well as to students of sanitary science.

In April, 1874, the Tennessee State Medical Society appointed a committee to prepare and present to the following session of the legislature a bill which would provide for the establishment of a state board of health. In due time the bill was submitted and passed the lower house, but was defeated in the Senate. In

---

the heroic efforts of Dr. Lindsley as city health officer. The city was made as clean as a swept floor, and all sources of malaria were filled up. By his careful management the death rate of the city was materially reduced and plans of sanitation introduced which have been of incalculable benefit to the city since."

[40] *Daily American* (Nashville), August 30, 1878: "During August the yellow fever epidemic was at its height. Memphis and other Tennessee towns were stricken, but Nashville was left unharmed."

1877, a second bill was introduced, which finally passed with the section providing for an appropriation of funds stricken out. The board was established, but had no executive power and was compelled to act only as an advisory body.[41]

The first meeting of the board was held, by invitation, in the rooms of the superintendent of public instruction in the State Capitol, on April 3, 1877.[42] Dr. J. D. Plunkett, Dr. T. A. Atchison, Dr. James M. Safford, Dr. E. M. Wight, and Dr. R. B. Maury were present, each of whom took the oath of office prescribed for the state officers. At this meeting, Dr. Lindsley was appointed secretary of the State Board of Health. "From the time of the organization of this board until his death, with one short intermission, he was its efficient secretary and in effect its executive officer."[43]

The legislature having failed to make an appropriation for the expenses of the board, Dr. Lindsley served for two years without salary. He had to pay his own traveling and office expenses. The other members of the board had also to pay their own expenses, and the printing press of Messrs. Tavel, Eastman, and Howell furnished the board with blanks, books, and stationery without compensation.

It will be recalled that Dr. Lindsley was at this time health officer of the city of Nashville. He was, therefore, serving the city and the state concurrently in his efforts to improve the public health.

The State Board found in the beginning that it had no place in which to meet. It therefore accepted the invitation of the Nashville Board of Health to use its office until quarters could be provided.

At the first adjourned meeting of the State Board of Health, Dr. Lindsley filed the following bond:

---

[41] *First Report of the Tennessee State Board of Health*, 1880.
[42] *Daily American* (Nashville), April 4, 1877: "Newly appointed State Board of Health met for the first time yesterday, April 3. Dr. J. D. Plunkett was unanimously elected president. Dr. J. Berrien Lindsley was appointed secretary."
[43] *Centennial History of the Tennessee Medical Association*, p. 172.

CHAMPION FOR PUBLIC HEALTH 143

This instrument witnesses that we, John Berrien Lindsley and bondsmen, are hereby held and firmly bound unto the State of Tennessee in the sum of ten thousand dollars, as provided in Section No. 4, Chapter 98, Acts of Tennessee, 1877.

The condition of this obligation is such that, whereas the above named John Berrien Lindsley has been elected by the State Board of Health secretary of the said Board for the term of five years from the fourth of April, 1877.

Now, if the said John Berrien Lindsley shall faithfully keep and preserve the records of said Board and discharge the duties of said office faithfully and impartially, then the above obligation shall be null and void; otherwise to be and remain in full force and virtue.

(Signed) JOHN BERRIEN LINDSLEY

At the second meeting of the board, on June 30, 1877, Dr. Lindsley was instructed to communicate with local authorities in the towns of the state and urge them to organize local boards of health.[44]

A meeting of the board was called on November 1, 1878, and a resolution was adopted to send representatives to the meeting of the American Public Health Association which was to be held in Richmond, Virginia, on November 19 of that year. Dr. Lindsley was sent as one of the delegates, who were instructed to invite the convention to hold its next meeting in Nashville. They succeeded in securing the convention for the following year.[45] With reference to this meeting, Dr. W. M. Clark said:

It brought a large number of eminent, sensible, and influential gentlemen in close and intimate relation with the South, paving a way for the renewal of the old fraternal feeling that joined the profession together in one common bond in antebellum days, so rudely severed by the war. I have good reason to believe that this meeting contributed more to this happy end than all previous assemblies although many attempts had been made by both political and religious bodies.[46]

[44] *First Report of the Tennessee State Board of Health*, 1880.
[45] *Daily American* (Nashville), November 18, 1879: "American Public Health Association met in Nashville. One of the main topics was how to prevent the spread of epidemics."
[46] *First Report of the Tennessee State Board of Health*, 1880; also *Centennial History of the Tennessee Medical Association*, pp. 415-416.

The yellow-fever epidemic of 1878 was one of the most violent that the state, and perhaps the South, had ever known. This epidemic occurred after the organization of the Tennessee State Board of Health but at a time when the Board was impotent and had no power to stay the ravages of the plague. The legislature had organized a state board of health in name only. "It had no power to enforce its advice nor money to pay its agents; hence it could only look on and take counsel of despair during its entire course. But it taught the people the great necessity of amending the law by which it was created."[47]

As a result of the ravages of this epidemic, public sentiment was ripened for a more effective organization. An amendment was prepared by the legislature, after consultation with members of the board, and was adopted at the session of 1878-79. This amendment increased the authority of the board and provided for an appropriation. Now that funds were made available for a broader program of activity, Dr. Lindsley felt it to be fitting that he should offer his resignation. "Dr. Lindsley was elected secretary but resigned because his duties as health officer were so exacting."[48] On March 31, 1879, he addressed the following letter to the president of the board:

J. D. PLUNKETT, M.D.
PRESIDENT OF THE STATE BOARD OF HEALTH

DEAR SIR:

In view of the recent action of the General Assembly of the State of Tennessee, increasing the membership of the Board and greatly enlarging its ability and powers, I deem it proper to resign the office I have had the high honor of filling during the past two years.

With heartfelt thanks for the confidence reposed in me by the Board, I remain, with high respect,

JOHN BERRIEN LINDSLEY
Secretary, State Board of Health

[47] *First Report of the Tennessee State Board of Health*, 1880.
[48] *Daily American* (Nashville), January 16, 1879: "On Wednesday, January 15, a bill was introduced into the House by a Mr. Smith to amend the act to create a State Board of Health." *Ibid.*, January 24, 1879: "Bill passed in legislature on January 23 favoring the passing of a national quarantine law."

CHAMPION FOR PUBLIC HEALTH 145

Dr. Lindsley's resignation was accepted after an expression of appreciation for his faithful service had been given by the board. Dr. W. M. Clark was elected to succeed him on salary. Dr. Clark, in making his report later, said, "The fact that so much was accomplished by the board without money should excite the admiration of all the people of Tennessee."[49]

When the State Board of Health met on April 2, 1884, Dr. T. A. Atchison, a member of the board, resigned and Dr. Lindsley was nominated by Dr. Plunkett to fill the vacancy. He was unanimously elected. At this same meeting, an election was held for president and vice-president. Dr. Lindsley's name was presented for president of the board and Dr. J. M. Safford's for vice-president.[50] Both were elected.[51]

On January 1, 1883, Dr. Clark submitted his resignation, which was reluctantly accepted by the board.[52] Dr. Clark seems to have been an able executive officer and left with the esteem and kind wishes of the board. On the same day, Dr. C. C. Fite, of Shelbyville, Tennessee, was elected executive secretary of the board. On May 29, 1884, Dr. Fite presented his resignation, to take effect July 1.[53] He, too, had rendered good service and was urged to continue in office. Regret was expressed by the entire board at his leaving.[54]

At the meeting of the board on July 1, 1884, Dr. J. M. Safford nominated Dr. Lindsley and he was unanimously elected to fill out the unexpired term of Dr. Fite as executive health officer of the state of Tennessee. Dr. Daniel F. Wight, of Clarksville, was

---

[49] *First Report of the Tennessee State Board of Health*, 1880.

[50] *Daily American* (Nashville), April 3, 1884: "Dr. T. A. Hadden, at the regular meeting of the State Board of Health on April 3, asked to be released from the presidency. His wish was granted and Dr. J. Berrien Lindsley was unanimously elected to succeed him."

[51] *Second Report of the Tennessee State Board of Health*, 1884.

[52] *Daily American* (Nashville), January 3, 1883: "The Tennessee State Board of Health met on January 2. At this meeting the Secretary, Dr. W. M. Clark, retired and turned his job over to Dr. C. C. Fite."

[53] *Ibid.*, May 30, 1884: "On Thursday, May 29, at a special meeting of the State Board of Health, Dr. C. C. Fite resigned as Secretary and executive officer because it took too much time away from his practice."

[54] *Second Report of the Tennessee State Board of Health*, 1884.

elected to fill the vacancy caused by Dr. Lindsley's acceptance of the secretaryship.[55]

As executive secretary of the State Board of Health, it became Dr. Lindsley's duty to compile the second quadrennial report of this board. "In entering upon a record of the past four years' work of the Tennessee State Board of Health," he said, "two embarrassments confront me: (1) a want of acquaintance with the work, owing to the fact that three and one-half years of that period were filled by other executive officers; (2) the difficulty in selecting from a voluminous mass of minutes, reports, and correspondence such material as will fairly represent the board in its daily functions." In this second report, an octavo of six hundred pages, Dr. Lindsley begins with a tribute to Dr. J. D. Plunkett, who, he said, "is due the honor of having initiated and carried to successful conclusion the measures which have resulted in giving Tennessee a high rank among those communities which have caught the inspiration of true democracy and scientific progress in health education."[56]

This volume was the first of a large number which followed in the interest of public health in Tennessee, and should remain an enduring monument to Dr. Lindsley's able and earnest service in behalf of public health work in the state.

In the spring of 1884, the need for intensive educational work in public health was evidently apparent to Dr. Lindsley, who was at that time president of the board. In his efforts to eradicate yellow fever and malaria in Tennessee, his procedure was remarkably scientific (though the causes of these diseases were not at that time clearly understood). He appears to have been working far in advance of exact knowledge concerning the causes of these epidemics. He reorganized the health department and appointed committees on (1) vital statistics, (2) prisons, (3) geological and topographical features in Tennessee in reference

---

[55] *Daily American* (Nashville), July 2, 1884: "The State Board of Health met on July 1. Dr. Lindsley was elected secretary. Dr. J. D. Plunkett took Dr. Lindsley's place as President, and Dr. D. F. Wight, of Clarksville, filled the vacancy on the board resulting from Dr. Fite's resignation."

[56] *Second Report of the Tennessee State Board of Health*, 1884.

CHAMPION FOR PUBLIC HEALTH 147

to sanitary relations, (4) transmission of tuberculosis from milk and meat of infected animals, (5) inland quarantine, (6) epidemic and contagious diseases. Special committees on the following were created: (1) water supplies of Tennessee; (2) school hygiene; (3) abattoirs; (4) railroad hygiene.[57]

Dr. Lindsley selected these committees with great care, and was executive enough to see that they functioned. As a result, many interesting reports and articles on health problems of the state were made available for distribution. A number of these reports and articles are included in the reports of the Tennessee State Board of Health. The educational work done by these committees contributed largely to the enlightenment of the public with reference to health problems and no doubt laid the foundation for a permanent health program in Tennessee.

In 1885, the Tennessee State Board of Health issued its first monthly bulletin. The initial number appeared on July 31, 1885, and carried the following announcements:

In taking charge of the State Weather Service, which has recently been turned over to the State Board of Health, the consideration of the question as to what form for the future these reports should go to the public in resulted in the determination to begin the issuance of a monthly State Board of Health bulletin in which the meteorological report should appear, together with the report and extracts from official correspondence of county, municipal, and town boards of health in the State, noting sanitation undertaken and progress made.

In order to finance this bulletin, it was necessary to admit to its columns advertisements of a select nature. It was thought at that time that meteorological conditions had a very important bearing on public health. As a result, much of the valuable space in this publication was devoted to the condition of the weather at various points in the state. In this volume, as well as in the previous reports of the State Board of Health, there is a great deal of discussion concerning "the wonderful effect of

[57] This and the following statements are from *Centennial History of the Tennessee Medical Association*, p. 421.

ozone on public health." The following paragraph will serve to show the prevalent idea on the importance of "ozone":

> Ozone, as you know, is nature's great deodorizing and purifying principle that oxidizes emanations from decomposing animal and vegetable substances, with which the air is unceasingly being contaminated, thus rendering them innocuous, and fitting the air for the further subsistence of animal life.

The theory was that ozone was found in concentrated form at certain points of high elevation, and at "lower altitudes it was in diminutive quantities." There is today a small village on the Cumberland Plateau named Ozone. The distinguished Dr. W. K. Bowling, Dr. Lindsley's colleague in the founding of the medical school of the University of Nashville, agreed that consumption did not exist among the native population of the tablelands of the Cumberland Plateau where ozone was abundant. He wrote:

> In answer to the question, "How many cases of pulmonary tuberculosis have you known to occur on Walden's Ridge among people native to the mountains?" eleven physicians say, not one—all of them have been engaged in the practice there more than three years.

Dr. Lindsley, as executive health officer of the state and editor of the monthly *Bulletin,* used the columns of this publication to report the health conditions over the state. These reports were submitted to him by the local health officers of the counties where health units were established. Although published in abbreviated form, they served to show the general conditions over the state. A typical report follows:

LAKE COUNTY, TENNESSEE, DR. M. DONALDSON, COUNTY HEALTH OFFICER.—Have only one or two new cases of typho-malarial fever to report. All reports point to a lull, or present abatement, in the prevalence of this disease, so common in the month of May, as reported. From inquiry among my brother physicians I find dysentery, remittent and intermittent fever somewhat in the ascendency and prevailing to some extent.[58]

[58] *Bulletin of the Tennessee State Board of Health,* Vol. II (July 31, 1886), No. 1, p. 3.

CHAMPION FOR PUBLIC HEALTH 149

Each number of the *Bulletin* carried editorials, news items, and current discussions relating to health work. At regular intervals Dr. Lindsley made his quarterly reports to the board. The following pages will give an abstract of the more important of these reports for the purpose of showing his contribution.

In submitting his report to the board on July 6, 1886, Dr. Lindsley confined his remarks to the organization and administration of the health service in the counties and towns of the state.

Since my last report, county boards of health have been organized in the counties of Humphreys, Lake, Lawrence, Loudon, Montgomery, and Rhea, leaving the following counties still without organized boards of health: Anderson, Cheatham, Claiborne, Clay, Cumberland, Dickson, Fentress, Grundy, Henderson, Hickman, Lewis, Meigs, Monroe, Van Buren, Trousdale, Union, Warren, and White.

He emphasized the fact that there were still twelve counties in the state without sanitary organizations, notwithstanding the law which specifically required that each county organize a board of health. The attention of the county authorities, he stated, had been called to this important obligation, and assurance had been given him that the matter would be brought before the county courts at their next quarterly meeting. The organization of these local boards was encouraged for the purpose of serving the people in the various counties and also for perfecting the machinery of the state health organization that it might serve more effectively in times of epidemic.

Appreciating this as do the executive committee, they have not, nor will they for the future, abate their efforts a single iota, until a live, practical-working health organization exists in every county; at least in those counties in which it is required by law.[59]

Dr. Lindsley closed this report with a reference to a bill pending before the councils of a number of the larger towns which would require burial permits before interment. He was much gratified over the fact that Clarksville and Pulaski, Tennessee,

[59] *Ibid.*

had just reported the passage of this regulation. He felt that every incorporated town in the state should be enabled to give information concerning its health condition. Such a regulation would furnish accurate data for a monthly mortality report. Nothing, he said, gave the town's condition of health so unequivocally as a carefully kept death register.

His next report to the Board of Health was submitted at the quarterly meeting on January 4, 1887.[60] In this report, he reviewed the communications submitted during the year from health officers. All of these communications indicated clearly that Tennessee, during the year 1886, "was remarkably free from widespread virulent epidemics."[61]

The mortality statistics are as yet too meager and have been kept for too short a period to enable any true comparison to be reached. Indeed, without a complete system of vital statistics, all statements as to the relative health of different years must be mere guesses.

He outlined the program of the State Board of Health in its efforts to carry into effect a law passed by the previous state legislature which was designed to establish health boards in all the counties. Upon the efficiency of these local health organizations depended the effectiveness of the program of the State Board of Health. As a result of unceasing effort, Dr. Lindsley was able at this meeting to report local health organizations in eighty-two counties. Concerning the remaining counties, he says:

Doubtless the few remaining counties will soon fall into line, more especially as now the appearance of cholera in South America and the outbreak of yellow fever in Mississippi last October has aroused the entire public to the need of being ready for any and all contingencies.

It might be said here that Dr. Lindsley had many years' experience in working with Tennessee legislatures. His work with the University of Nashville, the Tennessee State Teachers' Association, the State Board of Health, and other organizations had

---

[60] *Daily American* (Nashville), January 5, 1887.

[61] This and the following statements are from the *Bulletin of the Tennessee State Board of Health*, Vol. II (January 31, 1887), No. 7, p. 83.

brought him in frequent contact with the legislative body of the state. He had been disappointed in the early days in dealing with this body, particularly with reference to the University of Nashville. Later, he learned to approach them in a rather practical way, and we find him in his later years much more successful in getting legislative support for his public welfare measures. In submitting to the board this particular report, he was greatly interested in securing the passage of an effective law for the registration of births, marriages, and deaths. The Tennessee legislature was due to meet in a few days. In order to secure support for his bill, he had sent out several thousand more copies of the monthly *Bulletin* than were usually printed, and had made a special effort to get the support of the professional men and other prominent citizens "in every corner of the state."

The next quarterly meeting of the board was held on April 12, 1887. Dr. Lindsley's report was rather brief, but emphatic. He reviewed the history of the health department, which had been operating exactly ten years, and referred to the niggardliness of the legislature during those years. In this report, he shifted his point of view somewhat when he said, "the warding off or diminishing of the terrors of epidemic diseases, while of so great importance in the public estimation, is really the minor work in a true board of health."[62] Emphasis was now laid on the "ever present" diseases which destroy so many lives and cause such widespread suffering and loss of time and money. This was the field which would demand the eternal vigilance of those engaged in public health work. He predicted that "through applications of steam and electricity to the daily use of the human family" length of days would be added, not only to individuals but to entire nations as well.

The State Board of Health was called to a special meeting on August 16, 1888. A yellow-fever epidemic was raging in Florida and measures had to be taken to protect Tennessee citizens from an influx of Florida residents.[63] After some discussion, a motion

[62] *Ibid.*, Vol. II (April 30, 1887), No. 10, p. 131.
[63] *Daily American* (Nashville), August 16, 1888.

was made to confer with the Governor concerning the amount of funds to be placed at the disposal of the board. A recess was voted to permit a committee to wait on His Excellency. Governor Taylor, then at Gainesboro, received the following communication from the committee:

The state board of health is now in session to take cognizance of the dangers of yellow fever infection from Florida. It deems it necessary to establish quarantine stations at threatened points on our southern frontier with officers there located for its enforcement. The comptroller and treasurer have agreed to furnish funds for the purpose on order from Your Excellency. Please inform the board whether you will issue such order. Immediate action is necessary. Possibly not more than $2,000 will be called for under present circumstances.[64]

After some discussion, an order was issued by the board declaring a quarantine against the principal Tennessee towns having communication with the stricken areas in Florida.[65] Inspectors were assigned to duty at Memphis, Chattanooga, Cleveland, Milan, and Grand Junction. During the weeks following, Dr. Lindsley devoted all of his time to this problem.

In making his next report at the quarterly meeting on October 16, he said:

The work of the board during the past quarter has been the stamping out of an incipient smallpox epidemic in July, and the isolating of the entire State of Tennessee from a threatened invasion of yellow fever. In each instance the greatest success has ensued, proving most satisfactorily the perfection of the machinery now in the sanitary service of the State. . . .

The yellow fever, originating in Florida and breaking out in Alabama and Mississippi, has caused an alarm without precedent and an interruption to commerce without example. Tennessee, from its long extended frontiers and many great lines of transit, was peculiarly liable to invasion; yet such has been the prompt and energetic action of the executive committee in the work of inspection and isolation as thoroughly to preserve the entire State intact. It may be truthfully said

---

[64] *Bulletin of the Tennessee State Board of Health*, Vol. IV (September 15, 1888), No. 2, p. 17.
[65] *Daily American* (Nashville), August 17, 1888.

CHAMPION FOR PUBLIC HEALTH 153

that this board has thus gained a national reputation for efficiency and foresight.[66]

As early as 1883, Dr. Lindsley's board had recommended certain definite improvements in order to make the State Capitol more comfortable for those who must occupy it. As a result, the General Assembly passed a resolution requesting the State Board of Health to recommend improvements, with particular reference to ventilation, heating, and water closets. The recommendations were evidently made and ignored, for when Dr. Lindsley submitted his quarterly report on January 8, 1889, he approached this question again with emphatic language.

> The Capitol, architecturally a noble copy of the classic Greek, is for living purposes worse than a barn. . . .
> There can be no doubt that the lives of individual members of the Supreme Court, of executive functionaries, and of the general assembly have been shortened by exposure to the dangers of the Capitol, resulting from bad ventilation and defective heating.
> Five minutes' exposure to damp walls or to searching drafts have, in a multitude of recorded cases, resulted in long continued illness or in death.[67]

The sanitary condition of the old capitol building must have been very bad at that time. We find the State Board of Health unremitting in its insistence for "radical improvements in the State House." A second resolution was passed by the board and transmitted by Dr. Lindsley to J. B. Lea, speaker of the Senate. This agitation resulted in the passage of a bill by both the Senate and the House which led to a thorough examination, followed by the usual elaborate and comprehensive report of an investigating committee. Three conditions were given which needed attention. First, the water closets were so situated and constructed as to draw up "foul sewer gases from the drain pipes between the building and Lick Branch." At times the atmosphere of the whole lower corridors was permeated with gases.

---

[66] *Bulletin of the Tennessee State Board of Health*, Vol. IV (October 15, 1888), No. 3, p. 41.
[67] *Ibid.*, Vol. IV (January 15, 1889), No. 6, p. 105.

Second, the building was heated with stoves and fireplaces, a makeshift arrangement which even in 1889 was outmoded in public buildings. Third, Dr. Lindsley said that as to ventilation "during that portion of the year when the building is most used, there is simply none."[68]

He called attention to the fact that the year 1888 had been marked by the occurrence of smallpox in the state for the first time in three years. He warned the board that the reports which his office received from other state boards of health showed emphatically that smallpox was prevalent in many localities—hence the necessity for constant alertness with reference to this disease and the importance of the only recognized prophylactic, vaccination. As to yellow fever, he still felt that the outlook was not optimistic. His view was shared, he said, by all the sanitary authorities in the southern states familiar with this disease. There was but one way open; namely, to look the situation squarely in the face and be ready for any emergency. He recommended that four cities, Memphis, Nashville, Chattanooga, and Knoxville, should without delay build hospitals to accommodate persons suffering from communicable diseases. He stressed the fact that these cities were centers of travel and were visited annually by thousands, not only from Tennessee, but from other states far and near.[69]

The frequent epidemics which afflicted the South from 1830 until near the end of the nineteenth century had been of vital concern to Dr. Lindsley and the group of medical men around him. The average citizen accepted them as a matter of course and lived in a constant state of dread from one outbreak to another. To many, they were sent by God as a visitation upon a sinful world. The Asiatic cholera epidemic which visited the South and Tennessee in 1849, taking the lives of many of her best citizens, among them former President James K. Polk, received a great deal of thoughtful attention by Dr. Lindsley, who had graduated just a few years before from the medical school

[68] *Ibid.*, Vol. IV (April 15, 1889), No. 9, p. 155.
[69] *Daily American* (Nashville), January 10, 1889.

CHAMPION FOR PUBLIC HEALTH 155

of the University of Pennsylvania. Even at that time, Dr. Lindsley had strong convictions that certain precautionary methods in sanitary science could to a large extent prevent these epidemics, although the causes of the diseases and the media of their transmittal were then unknown. "The grand lesson" that "epidemics do not move with irresistible fury" had been learned many years before he and his colleagues were able to teach this lesson to the citizens of the state. It has been mentioned elsewhere in this chapter that Dr. Lindsley was given credit for preventing, through his well-organized program of sanitation, the spread of the yellow-fever epidemic of 1878 to Nashville.

In propagandizing the discovery that through preventive medicine and scientific sanitation epidemics could, in a large measure, be avoided, Dr. Lindsley and his colleagues brought to a distressed people hope and peace and a feeling of security. The following brief abstract of his report to the quarterly meeting of the State Board of Health on July 2, 1889, suggests something of the progress made:

Just five years ago your board did me the honor to elect me to the position of secretary. At that very meeting the first telegraphic news was read announcing the unexpected and violent outbreak of cholera in its most virulent form in a Mediterranean port of France.

This announcement caused great alarm throughout Europe, and no small amount of uneasiness in America, especially in our own interior valley from the Dominion to the Gulf of Mexico.

During 1885 and 1886 portions of Italy and Spain were scourged, and also a few points in South America.

However, contrary to all previous history, the plague did not spread over Europe, nor did it visit the United States.

This fact attracted, of course, very wide notice, and everywhere an explanation was demanded.

Only one solution could be found. Whereas in 1832, 1849, 1866, 1873, this disease was allowed to take its own course, no effort in most cases whatever being made to prevent its entrance, on this occasion exactly the opposite plan was pursued.

A few years back the entire machinery of state preventive medicine was unknown. In 1884 most European and American governments maintained national, state, and city boards of health, more or less effi-

ciently. Hence and hence alone the difference. Those portions of Southern Europe were ravaged where scientific sanitation was not only neglected but really unknown. Its spread from these regions, where it caused untold misery, terror and mortality during three years, into the rest of Europe was prevented by prompt, scientific and humane quarantine measures relating to communities, and by rigid isolation and disinfection of individual cases occurring outside of infected districts.

It got into Brazil and Chile because of gross violation of sanitary axioms. It avoided the United States because of the strict observance of those axioms.

As a consequence the value and merit of boards of health, and of sanitary regulations faithfully carried out, have been greatly enhanced in public estimation. *The grand lesson has been learned that epidemics do not move with irresistible fury. This is a great gain, of inestimable value to the public peace, comfort and safety.* I know that this is so in Tennessee, for previously to this last splendid demonstration of sanitary progress the words "Asiatic cholera" have always evoked images of desolation and dismay in the minds of the thousands who had gone through the experience of the four previous epidemics.

Since 1884 the experience with smallpox and yellow fever has also taught our people the great lesson that epidemic diseases need not prevail; and that their very prevalence is proof conclusive of gross and culpable neglect on the part of rulers somewhere.

This lesson will not be lost. Typhoid fever, diphtheria and scarlet fever will soon be in the category of diseases which should be prevented. Each case will be minutely studied, its origin ascertained, and its causation of other cases obstructed by thorough isolation and disinfection.

Just four years ago, the board, after mature deliberation, decided to devote about one-third of its small annual appropriation to the publication and distribution of a monthly bulletin so as to reach every locality of and every interest in the State. . . .

Thus far the value of this publication is demonstrated. At least seven other States have followed our example. Exchanges from every part of Tennessee and from all portions of the Union give us valuable sources of information, and enable us to make Tennessee well and favorably known as a State eminently adapted to the best class of immigrants from the malarial South or the arctic North.

The bulletin has awakened much interest in many localities for better sanitation. Thus a foundation for rapid and enduring practical

CHAMPION FOR PUBLIC HEALTH 157

work has been laid by you, which will enable the board to make great progress in its highest and most enduring lines right away. And here much is to be done. Nashville and Memphis, through their municipal authorities, do not sufficiently back their health officers, Chattanooga is asleep, Knoxville is away behind the times, our smaller cities and towns all need more efficient sanitation.

The cheering fact, however, prevails that the people are ahead of their rulers and will soon replace them by more faithful servants.[70]

Dr. Lindsley served as secretary and executive officer of the Tennessee State Board of Health until the time of his death, in 1897. Although his duties increased with the years, there is little evidence that his efficiency declined with approaching age. The minutes of the board, which he kept in his own handwriting, were copious and adequate to the last. The monthly *Bulletin*, which he edited, increased in quality and in service. His last quarterly report, submitted only a few weeks prior to his death, gives evidence of sustained vigor and mental alertness. And finally, after an investigation by the legislature and a consequent reorganization of the State Board of Health in 1897, Dr. Lindsley was highly commended for the efficiency of his office and received the unanimous vote for re-election for the ensuing term of five years, which was to end April 6, 1902.

Let us now briefly review Dr. Lindsley's life as a pioneer in medical and health education in the South.

In 1850 Dr. Lindsley, himself a graduate of the school of medicine of the University of Pennsylvania, gathered around him a distinguished group of physicians and founded the medical school of the University of Nashville. This institution was a success from the beginning and was soon to rival the older and wealthier schools of the East.[71] Three members of its faculty were subsequently chosen president of the American Medical Association: Dr. Paul F. Eve in 1858, Dr. W. K. Bowling in 1875, and Dr. William T. Briggs in 1891. By 1880 this institution had furnished to the American Medical Association five vice-

---
[70] *Bulletin of the Tennessee State Board of Health,* Vol. IV (July 12, 1889), No. 12, p. 207.
[71] *Southern Practitioner,* XIX (1897), 221.

presidents, "an honor up to that time conferred upon no other college in America."[72] From 1851 to 1880, the institution had matriculated 6,991 students, 2,200 of whom had received degrees in medical science.

In 1861 every Southern state was represented in the student body, in addition to several states of the North and East. Alumni of this institution went out over the South and West to carry the gospel of organized medicine. They contributed to the establishment of other medical schools. In 1909 there were in the South fifty-six medical schools, with an annual enrollment of over 8,600 students and approximately 1,800 graduates annually. We find records of eighteen attempts to establish medical schools within the borders of Tennessee.[73] Eleven of these institutions were in operation at one time. Measured in terms of present-day standards, these schools were unquestionably inadequate. They did, however, represent an expression of the interest in and need for medical education. It was inevitable that refining processes should reduce the number, and we later find only two of these schools in operation.

The University of Nashville medical school no doubt maintained the highest standards possible at the time and popularized the use of medical service until the Civil War placed its devastating blight upon the institution. The story of how Dr. Lindsley cared for the buildings, grounds, and equipment of the university during the war period has been told. From the fall of Fort Donelson, in February, 1862, until 1866, the military authorities of the Federal government were in possession of the campus, using it for hospitals and barracks. Although the institution was in the hands of strangers, the actual work of the college did not cease during the entire period of the Civil War. When the Federal troops entered Nashville, they found Dr. Lindsley and three professors teaching about forty students. This instruction con-

[72] Otis S. Warr, "The History of Medical Education in Tennessee," *Centennial History of the Tennessee Medical Association, 1830-1930*, p. 367.
[73] *Ibid.*, p. 356.

CHAMPION FOR PUBLIC HEALTH 159

tinued while the buildings were being used for hospital purposes. Merriam says:

> Literally surrounded by the dead and the dying, professors still lectured and students still listened. While the battle of Nashville was raging around the city and cannon were booming from Fort Negley nearby, young men were being trained to go forth and heal the wounded and minister to the dying. The medical faculty could afford to indulge in a burst of exultation over the past and of hope for the future.[74]

During the years of the war hundreds of physicians from all parts of the country visited the university and found "the museum of the medical department splendid, copious, and unique."[75] Although the institution did not cease to function during the war, it never recovered its ante-bellum prosperity.

In May, 1870, Dr. Lindsley resigned as chancellor, but he retained his chair on the medical faculty until 1873, when he retired as professor emeritus.

Dr. Lindsley rendered other services to medical education not related to the University of Nashville. The *Nashville Journal of Medicine and Surgery,* a publication edited in the early fifties by the distinguished Dr. W. K. Bowling, had a long and honorable record of service. Dr. Lindsley contributed his own salary to the support of this magazine in its early years.[76] Dr. Lindsley was one of the active members of the American Public Health Association and was treasurer of this organization from 1879 to 1891.[77]

In 1880, the *Sixth Annual Announcement of the Medical Department of the University of Tennessee* stated:

> It is with pleasure the faculty announce that Drs. W. K. Bowling and J. Berrien Lindsley, whose names are familiar to every medical man in America, have accepted positions respectively in the depart-

[74] *Op. cit.,* p. 49.   [75] *Ibid.*
[76] Charles S. Briggs, editorial, *Nashville Journal of Medicine and Surgery,* LXXXIII (January, 1898), 50.
[77] *Southern Practitioner,* XX (January, 1898), 38.

ments of theory and practice of medicine, and state preventive medicine.[78]

In this bulletin we find the course in state preventive medicine, as outlined by Dr. Lindsley:

> The great prominence which the branch of medical science and practice has assumed within a period of two to twenty years leaves the medical student of the present day no option for ignorance. The repeated epidemics of recent years have stimulated the whole country, more especially the South and West, to great activity in sanitary reforms. Boards of health are everywhere the order of the day. Aware of the heavy pressure upon the student's time and energies, nothing will be attempted by the lecturer beyond an outline of the great principles of public hygiene and such special instruction as will enable the pupil to at least comprehend the duties of the health officers and of health boards.[79]

The outline of this course, taught by Dr. Lindsley while at the University of Tennessee, is significant because it indicates his consuming interest in public health education and sanitary reform.

In 1912, following the location of the medical school of the University of Tennessee in Memphis, one of the buildings was named "Lindsley Hall," commemorating the name of Dr. J. Berrien Lindsley, "the organizer and first dean of the University of Nashville Medical School and a towering figure in the annals of medical education in Tennessee."[80] Lindsley Hall is the home of the administrative department of the College of Medicine and School of Pharmacy.

There was perhaps no individual more active in the Tennessee Medical Association than Dr. Lindsley. After the Civil War, when an attempt was made to vitalize the activities of this association, Dr. Lindsley and three of his colleagues were appointed to examine the constitution and proceedings of the organizations of other states and report such amendments to the

---

[78] September 6, 1880.   [79] P. 9.   [80] Warr, *op. cit.*, p. 387.

constitution and by-laws as would improve the Tennessee Medical Society. The committee recommended a new constitution in 1875. It was adopted and put into effect in 1876. "The new constitution was largely the work of Dr. J. Berrien Lindsley, chairman of the committee, who had submitted it with the report that argued at length the necessity for a more thorough organization of the physicians of the state."[81]

In 1871, Dr. Lindsley was appointed a committee of one on the history of the Tennessee Medical Society. Within a few years he had developed plans for a large volume to be known as "The Medical Annals of Tennessee." The society approved his plans. He proposed to publish this volume if the society would guarantee him $1,000 and would agree to receive 200 copies of the published work for its files. This the organization pledged itself to do. The book was planned as an octavo volume of about 600 pages and was to be sold to subscribers at $5.00 each. The prospectus of the book contained the following outline:

Part I. The history of the Tennessee Medical Society, including an abstract of its annual proceedings, analysis of the more important papers, and sketches of its prominent members.

Part II. A similar history of the East Tennessee Medical Society.

Part III. Biographical sketches and reminiscences of eminent deceased physicians throughout the state.

Part IV. The epidemics and medical topography of Tennessee.

Part V. Historical topics of the medical institutions of Tennessee, as schools, hospitals, etc.

Part VI. Origin of Tennessee Medicine, being reminiscences of the schools which have molded the profession of the state, written by Tennessee students.

Part VII. The medical literature of Tennessee under two heads, (a) Index of writers, (b) Index of subjects. It is hoped to make this division of the work exhaustive, giving the name of the writer of every article furnished to any medical periodical by any Tennessee physician, if only half a dozen lines.

Part VIII. List of surgeons furnished by Tennessee to the army and navy.

[81] *Ibid.*

Part IX. Tennessee in the American Medical Association.

Part X. A general index, minute and copious, followed by lists of contributors and subscribers.[82]

The proposed "Medical Annals of Tennessee" apparently did not arouse great enthusiasm among the physicians of the state. Compilation of the material was never completed because of several conditions. First, there was not sufficient money available to guarantee the publication of such a volume had it been compiled. And second, about the time this work was to be seriously undertaken, Dr. Lindsley became secretary and executive health officer of the city of Nashville, and later of the Tennessee State Board of Health. Thereafter, his time and energy were largely consumed in executive and routine duties.[83]

Dr. Lindsley died on December 7, 1897. The regular meeting of the Nashville Academy of Medicine, on December 16, following, was observed as a memorial to him. There was a large attendance of the members and other physicians and friends of Dr. Lindsley. Dr. Deering J. Roberts, editor of the *Southern Practitioner,* read a paper on Dr. Lindsley's contribution to the development of medical and health education, after which the following appropriate resolutions were adopted:

WHEREAS, The Nashville Academy of Medicine has assembled on this occasion to pay tribute to the memory of the distinguished Dr. J. Berrien Lindsley, therefore be it

Resolved, That the official organization of the medical profession of Nashville take cognizance of the death of the founder of medical education in this city with peculiar and profound sorrow.

Resolved, That, as many of us honor him as his students, we feel an individual and personal loss as well as a collective and associated bereavement.

Resolved, That his long and worthy life as a scholar, teacher, medical journalist, historian, hygienist, minister and philanthropist, has been unusually blessed and unselfishly useful.

Resolved, That as the executive officer of our State Board of Health, his timely and efficient services have wrought incalculable good that we, as physicians, can most fittingly appreciate and revere.

[82] The Lindsley Papers. [83] *Ibid.*

CHAMPION FOR PUBLIC HEALTH

Resolved, That his wide and scholarly attainments, consistent Christian character, gentle and lovable personality, dignified and noble bearing, earnest and righteous living, will be an inspiration to his juniors and a criterion for his peers most worthy of emulation.[84]

Teacher, physician, medical journalist, historian, hygienist, minister and philanthropist—what achievement might not have been his had he devoted his life and fine intellect to any one of these several fields!

[84] *Southern Practitioner,* XX (1898), 40.

APPENDIX A

CHRONOLOGICAL OUTLINE OF THE LIFE OF JOHN BERRIEN LINDSLEY

1822   Born October 24, 1822, at Princeton, New Jersey.
1823   Baptized May 18, 1823.
1836   Entered freshman class, University of Nashville.
1838   Became private pupil of Dr. Gerard Troost.
1839   Graduated with A.B. degree from the University of Nashville.
1840   Admitted into the First Presbyterian Church, Nashville, Tennessee; Dr. Edgar, pastor.
1841   June 4, entered W. G. Dickinson's office as medical student after having received the A.M. degree from the University of Nashville. October 26, left Nashville to attend medical lectures in Louisville.
1842   Arrived at home on March 1 from Louisville.
October 18, left for Philadelphia to attend medical school.
1843   Received M.D. degree, medical school, University of Pennsylvania. Elected member of the Tennessee Medical Society.
1844   At home through summer and fall.
September 10, death of his youngest brother, Philip.
1845   June 8, 6:00 P.M., at the bedside of Andrew Jackson, who died at the Hermitage.
December 5, 6:00 P.M., his mother died after an illness of three months.
1846   June 6, began pastorate at Smyrna Church, Rutherford County; served six months.
October 13, ordained as an evangelist in the First Presbyterian Church, Nashville, Tennessee.
1847   April 18, began preaching as domestic missionary; served twelve months.
1848   June 7, set out on a tour with Dr. Troost and others through the northern and middle states.
Charter member of the American Association for the Advancement of Science.
1849   Rendered able service through the cholera epidemic in Tennessee. Began keeping a diary.
Charter member of the Tennessee Historical Society.
1850   Discussed with Dr. Meigs for the first time his medical project and later organized medical school.
September 14, Dr. Troost, his friend and teacher, died.
October 11, appointed professor of chemistry and pharmacy in the medical school of the University of Nashville.
October 14, elected dean of the faculty.

APPENDICES

1851 Became a trustee for the common schools of South Nashville; acted as chairman of first meeting.
Elected a member of the American Medical Association.

1852 Delivered fifth and final lecture before thirty-three candidates for graduation in the medical school.
Began teaching geology in Dr. Lapsley's Seminar.
Went abroad for instruction in European countries. Left Nashville in February and returned September 28.
Called on George Peabody while in London.

1853 Projected plans for building program on university campus.

1854 Projected plans for consolidation of the Western Military Institute with University of Nashville.
Addressed the alumni in memorable lecture.

1855 Elected chancellor of the University of Nashville.
Completed union of Western Military Academy and University of Nashville.
May 25, Philip Lindsley, his father, died.

1856 Published study on Dr. Porter. Became a member of Board of Education.
The degree of Doctor of Divinity was conferred upon him by the College of New Jersey (Princeton).

1857 February 9, married Sarah McGavock, daughter of Jacob McGavock, granddaughter of Felix Grundy.

1858 Left Nashville April 16 for extended trip through the East. Returned to Nashville June 29. On this trip he visited Belvue Hospital, attended meeting of American Scientific Association in Baltimore and Tract Society meeting in Philadelphia.

1859 Made geological tour through Illinois. Trip to New Orleans.
Sent L. J. Halsey manuscript on Philip Lindsley.
Left Nashville on July 1 with Mrs. Lindsley and Mary L. McGavock for Ireland, England, France, Switzerland, and a return trip through Canada.
Returned to Nashville in October.

1860 Accompanied Tennessee and Kentucky legislatures to Columbus, Ohio, in one of the greatest Union demonstrations of the year.
Left Nashville June 7 for extended trip east. On this trip he arranged for publication of manuscript on life and works of his father (Philip Lindsley) through L. J. Halsey and Lippincott. Trip included Quebec, Canada, where he ascended Mt. Washington on July 17 to witness the great eclipse. Packed and shipped to Nashville large collection of minerals.

1861 Went to Richmond to see if volunteer surgeons were wanted.

1862 February 17, appointed post surgeon of Nashville hospitals. Held this office until March 4 following.

APPENDICES

Engaged in operation of medical school and teaching duties.

May 12, preached installation sermon of the Reverend Mr. Bardwell, First Presbyterian Church, Nashville, Tennessee.

1863 May 16, received news of the death of brother-in-law, Randall McGavock, killed at Raymond, Mississippi.

Time spent in protecting university property and teaching duties.

1864 Perfected with Dr. Bowling a plan for a free medical school, something after the fashion of the University of Michigan.

June 26, preached in First Presbyterian Church—accepted the Reverend Mr. Bardwell's resignation.

1865 June 26, elected a member of the Board of Education of Nashville by the City Council.

July 20 and 21, attended State Teachers' Convention in Knoxville "where the most villainous sort of politics were in evidence."

September 30, wrote address on popular education which was later published.

1866 Entered upon duties of superintendent of Nashville Public Schools.

1867 Organized Montgomery Bell Academy and petitioned the Peabody Education Fund to appropriate money for a normal school.

1868 Published notable editorial, *Our Ruin, Its Cause and Cure,* which contributed to the overthrow of the Nashville city government.

1870 Resigned as chancellor of the University of Nashville. Helped organize the Tennessee College of Pharmacy, in which he was professor of materia medica during its existence.

1873 Retired from the medical school as professor emeritus.

1874 Published *On Prison Discipline and Penal Legislation.*

1875 President of the Tennessee State Teachers' Association.

1876 Elected health officer of the city of Nashville.

Published *History of the Law School of Cumberland University at Lebanon,* 1876.

1877 Elected executive secretary of the Tennessee State Board of Health. Edited second and third reports of the Nashville Board of Health.

1878 Was in charge of the health work of Tennessee during the yellow-fever plague.

1879 Edited *Second Quadrennial Report of the Tennessee State Board of Health.*

1880 Elected professor of sanitary science and state preventive medicine in the medical department of the University of Tennessee.

1886 Published *Confederate Military Annals,* a splendid volume of 1,000 pages.

1887 Published *Practitioners of Medicine as Men of Science* and *Public Health Movement.*

1889 Published *On the Cremation of Garbage* and *Popular Progress in State Medicines.*

1897 Died, December 7, at his home in Nashville.

APPENDIX B

WRITINGS OF JOHN BERRIEN LINDSLEY

A. PUBLICATIONS OF JOHN BERRIEN LINDSLEY

1. Address Before the Alumni Society of the University of Nashville delivered on the 3d of October, 1854. Published by request of the Board of Trustees, Nashville. Cameron & Fall, Book and Job Printers, Corner of College and Union Streets, 1854.[1]

    8vo, pp. 25.
    Edition, 1,000 copies.
    Contains a history of the University.

2. A Brochure on the Life and Character of Robert M. Porter, Late Professor of Anatomy in the University of Nashville. Address delivered at Nashville, Nov. 8, 1856. Published by the class. Nashville, Tenn.: Printed by E. Valette, 1856.

    8vo, pp. 47.
    Edition, 7,000 copies.

3. On Medical Colleges. An Introductory Lecture to the course of 1858-'59 in the Medical Department of the University of Nashville. Published by the class. Nashville: Printed by James T. Bell & Co., *Daily Gazette* Office, 1858.

    8vo, pp. 22.
    Edition, 2,000 copies.
    A brief sketch of American medical education, with suggestions for improvements, most of which have been adopted by the great schools.

4. Our Ruin: Its Cause and Cure. By a Poor Rich Man. Nashville, Tennessee, November 14, 1868.

    8vo, pp. 16.
    Edition, 2,000 copies.
    A "reconstruction" pamphlet. Led to the ousting of the city government of Nashville and the appointment of a receiver, an event unprecedented in American municipal annals.

5. The Present Conditions and Prospects of the University of Nashville. Important Report by Chancellor Lindsley.

    8vo, pp. 8.
    Edition, 500 copies.
    Reprint from *Nashville Union and American,* May, 1870.

---

[1] Publications No. 1 through No. 13 are listed in the *Annual Report of the American Historical Association for the Year 1889,* pp. 304-306.

APPENDICES

6. Report of Prof. J. B. Lindsley, M.D., Chairman of the Committee on Education, to the Nashville Board of Trade, October 28, 1871. Nashville, Tenn.: Printed at *Union and American* Book and Jobs Rooms, 1871.

    8vo, pp. 14.
    Edition, 500 copies.
    Reprint from *Nashville Union and American*.
    Showing the early and continued eminence of Nashville in educational work.

7. African Colonization and Christian Missions. *Theological Medium*, Vol. IX, October, 1873, 8vo, pp. 24.

    Edition, nearly 1,000 copies; reprint, 300 copies. Widely circulated.
    Favorably noticed with copious extracts in *African Repository*, 1874. It solves the African problem, as time is now demonstrating, by Christian civilization.

8. On Prison Discipline and Penal Legislation; with Special Reference to the State of Tennessee. Written for the July number of the *Theological Medium*. In substance preached at the First Cumberland Presbyterian Church of Nashville, August 9 and 16, 1874. Nashville, Tenn.: Printed at the Southern Methodist Publishing House for the Robertson Association, 1874.

    8vo, pp. 64.
    Reprint from *Theological Medium*, a Cumberland Presbyterian quarterly.
    Edition, 3,000 copies.
    Abounds in historical and bibliographical data.

9. Sources and Sketches of Cumberland Presbyterian History. *Theological Medium*, April, 1875, ended in October number, 1879, 8vo, pp. 639.
    Mainly a compilation from newspapers and church records, with much assistance from eminent Cumberland Presbyterian ministers, especially Richard Beard, D.D., and A. B. Miller, D.D.

10. The History of the Law School of Cumberland University at Lebanon, Tenn.

    8vo, pp. 25.
    Reprinted from *Theological Medium*, October, 1876, 3,000 copies.

11. The Confederate Military Annals of Tennessee. First Series. Embracing a Review of Military Operations, with Regimental Histories and Memorial Rolls, compiled from original and official sources, and edited by John Berrien Lindsley, M.D., D.D. Printed for subscribers. Nashville: J. M. Lindsley & Co., Publishers, 25 South Eighth Street, 1886. Electrotyped and printed at the Southern Methodist Publishing House.

APPENDICES

Royal 8vo, pp. 910.
Illustrated by 35 steel plates, containing 116 likenesses.
Reviewed in *New York Evening Post*, March 19, 1887; also in *The Nation*.

12. Cholera in Tennessee, 1833. *Transactions of the Medical Society of the State of Tennessee* at its Fifty-fifth Annual Session, April, 1888, pp. 112.

    8vo, pp. 7.
    Edition, 1,000 copies.
    Purely historical data. Reprinted in *Southern Practitioner*, April, 1888.

13. Popular Progress in State Medicine. By J. Berrien Lindsley, M.D., of Nashville, Tenn., Chairman of the Section. Delivered in Section on State Medicine at the Fortieth Annual Meeting,
    American Medical Association, June 25, 1889. Reprinted from the *Journal of the American Medical Association*, July 13, 1889. Chicago: Printed at the office of the Association, 1889.

    16mo, pp. 12.
    Edition, 500 copies.
    Reprinted from the *Southern Practitioner*, Nashville, August, 1889; also, in the *Texas Health Journal*, Dallas, November, 1889.

14. On the Cremation of Garbage. Read in the Section of State Medicine at the Thirty-ninth Annual Meeting of the American Medical Association, Cincinnati, Ohio, May 8, 1888.[2]

    Reprinted from the *Journal of the American Medical Association*, October 13, 1888.
    12mo, pp. 12. Reprints, 100 copies.

15. Articles on Gerard Troost and William Walker, in *Appleton's Cyclopedia of American Biography*.

16. Edited eight volumes of the *Monthly Bulletin of the Tennessee State Board of Health*, 1886-'93. [This number had been increased to thirteen at the time of Dr. Lindsley's death in 1897.]

    8vo, pp. 8. 1,000 copies.

17. Appeal to the Citizens of Davidson County in behalf of their University. Nashville, June 12, 1856. Cameron & Fall, printers, 1856.

    8vo, pp. 8. 1,000 copies.

18. Editorials in *Nashville Dispatch*, January and July, 1866. Literary and Political Topics. The only Southern paper then published in Nashville.

---

[2] Publications No. 14 through No. 29 are listed in the *Annual Report of the American Historical Association for the Year 1892*, pp. 265-266.

APPENDICES

19. Hints Respecting a Complete University for Nashville, Tenn. Presented to the board of trustees June 28, 1867. By J. Berrien Lindsley, chancellor.

    8vo, pp. 4.
    100 copies for private distribution.

20. Nashville and the University. An address by J. Berrien Lindsley, chancellor of the university, delivered in the Masonic Hall at the opening of the sixteenth session of the medical department, November 6, 1865. Published July 14, 1869. Nashville, Tenn.: W. H. F. Ligon, printer, 1869.

    8vo, pp. 16. 1,000 copies.

21. Address to the People of Tennessee on Popular Education. Submitted to the State Teachers' Association at Nashville, October 12, 1869, by J. Berrien Lindsley, R. P. Wells, S. R. Rodgers, committee, and adopted by the Convention.

    In *First Report of the Superintendent of Public Instruction of the State of Tennessee*, 1869.

    8vo, pp. 5. Small print. 7,000 copies.

    "This able and well-timed address, prepared by Rev. J. B. Lindsley, M.D., D.D., Chancellor of the University of Nashville, an earnest and constant friend of the system of free universal education in Tennessee, I insert not only for its intrinsic merit, but as essential to a correct idea of the opinions and efforts which led to the establishment of the system in the State."

    —John Eaton, Jr., *Superintendent of Public Instruction*.

22. The Jesuits. In the *Theological Medium* (a Cumberland Presbyterian quarterly), July, 1872.

    8vo, pp. 20.

23. Epidemics and Sanitary Reform. In the *Theological Medium* (a Cumberland Presbyterian quarterly), January, 1874.

    8vo, pp. 26.

24. A Review of McFerrin's Methodism in Tennessee. In the *Theological Medium* (a Cumberland Presbyterian quarterly), January, 1875.

    8vo, pp. 36.

25. A Plea for Normal Schools in Tennessee—The part they play in the Intellectual Progress of the Age. Address of J. Berrien Lindsley, M.D., D.D., president of the State Teachers' Association, delivered before that body January 21, 1875, and the Tennessee State Grange, at Knoxville, February 18, 1875.

    Published in the Knoxville and Nashville papers.
    Reprinted from the *Nashville Union and American*. Nashville, May, 1875.

    8vo, pp. 8. Small type, double columns. 1,000 copies.

This address unfolded the plan for a great normal college at Nashville under the joint patronage and control of the State, the University of Nashville, and the trustees of the Peabody Education Fund. This plan has been very successfully carried out.

26. Report as secretary of the Tennessee State Board of Health, in second report to that board, 1885. Sanitary Wants and Progress in Tennessee.
    8vo, pp. 200. 3,000 copies.
27. Practitioners of Medicine as Students of Science.
    Reprint from the *Transactions of the Medical Society of the State of Tennessee,* April, 1887.
    8vo, pp. 3. 100 copies.
28. The Medical Profession and the Public Health Movement. Read before the Tri-State Medical Association of Mississippi, Arkansas, and Tennessee, November 7, 1887.
    Reprint from the *Mississippi Valley Medical Monthly.*
    8vo, pp. 8. Reprints, 100 copies.
29. Address on State Medicine; the People and the Public Health Movement. Delivered at the forty-third annual meeting of the American Medical Association, at Detroit, Mich., June 7, 1892.
    Journal of the American Medical Association, July 2, 1892. Reprints, 100 copies.
    8vo, pp. 16.
    Reprinted in the *Southern Practitioner* for August, 1892. Nashville, Tenn.
30. Second Report of the Board of Health of the City of Nashville for the Year Ending July 4, 1877.
    230 pages printed by Tavel Eastman and Howell, Nashville, Tenn.
31. Third Report of the Board of Health of the City of Nashville for the Two Years Ending December 31, 1878.
    384 pages printed by Tavel Eastman and Howell, Nashville, Tennessee.

B. UNPUBLISHED EDITORIALS OF JOHN BERRIEN LINDSLEY

IN

I. PRIVATE JOURNAL ENTITLED "THOUGHTS AND HINTS,"[3] VOL. I

1860

Separate Secession	Nov. 9, pp. 1-2
The Great North-West	Nov. 9, p. 2
The Union Strengthened by Enlargement	Nov. 9, pp. 2-3
Political Bigotry	Nov. 13, p. 3
American Slavery Peculiar	Nov. 14, p. 3

[3] The Lindsley Papers.

172 APPENDICES

American Slavery Permanent	Nov. 14, p. 4
Preparatory Medical Education	Nov. 22, pp. 4-5
Slavery a Protective System for the African Race	Dec. 9, p. 5
The American Union a Protection to Slavery	Dec. 11, p. 5
Disunion the Destruction of Slavery and of the Negroes	Dec. 11, p. 6
Disunion Brings War	Dec. 11, pp. 6-7

1861

Industrial Museum—Geological Survey of Tennessee	Jan. 20, pp. 7-8
Judicial Blindness of the Lincoln Cabinet	June 15, p. 8
The Southern Conspiracy	June 15, pp. 8-9
A Sectional Government Ruinous to Empire Nationality	June 16, p. 9
The North-West Making Its Mark	June 16, p. 10
Is the Unity of the Country Gone?	June 18, p. 10
Southern Independence—Slave Holding Republic	June 18, pp. 10-11
Great Empires are Civilizers	June 30, p. 11
The Civilized World	June 30, pp. 11-12
Self-defensive Spirit of Conquest	June 30, p. 12
Cause of Disunion Twofold	June 30, pp. 12-13
Natural Science—a Comparison	June 30, p. 13
Secession and War	July 8, p. 14
Introduction to Bible Lessons	Oct. 6, p. 15
Slavery is a Political, not Religious Institution	Oct. 27, pp. 15-16
Roman Dominion, Peace and not War	Nov. 3, p. 16
Palestine as the Seat of a Witnessing People	Nov. 10, pp. 16-17
The African in America	Nov. 10, p. 17
The Americans a Homogeneous People	Nov. 10, pp. 17-18
Overseers. Factors	Nov. 28, p. 18
The Study of Medicine a Liberal Education	Dec. 7, p. 19
National Sins	Dec. 10, p. 20
The Southern Movement Against the Three Great Tendencies of Modern Times	Dec. 10, pp. 20-21
Democratic Party and Disunion	Dec. 22, p. 21
Slavery Protects the Africans	Dec. 22, pp. 21-22

1862

European Sympathy	April 2, pp. 22-23
Despotism of Revolutionary Periods	April 6, p. 23
Trust in God	April 6, p. 24
Prayer for Governments	April 6, p. 24
Key to the Great American Civil War	April 6, p. 25
National Glory Mis-credited	April 8, p. 26
Abolitionists and Secessionists Truly for Peace	April 8, pp. 26-27
Benjamin Franklin	April 9, pp. 27-28

APPENDICES 173

The Seven Years' War	April 9, pp. 28-29
Southerners and History	April 18, p. 29
Statesism Northwards	April 25, p. 30
Colonizing Nations	April 27, pp. 30-31
America's Mission	May 4, p. 31
Fame and Wretchedness	May 4, p. 32
Mouth of the Mississippi	May 4, pp. 32-33
Hospitals	May 4, pp. 33-34
Happiness in Midst of Unsettled Government	May 5, p. 34
The Life Interior and Exterior of Peoples	May 5, pp. 34-35
North Versus the South	May 6, p. 36
The Divine Judgments in the Present War	May 6, p. 36
Goodness of the African Race	May 6, p. 37
Subjugation	May 7, p. 37
Union	May 7, p. 38
The Origin and Destiny of the Negro Race in North America	May 8, p. 39
DeFoe the Father of Historical Novelists	May 8, pp. 39-40
Laboring People in France	May 8, p. 40
South Carolina and Massachusetts	May 8, pp. 40-41
Treason a Common Crime in 1643, 1776, and 1861	May 18, pp. 41-43
Liberty and Union, Now and Forever, One and Inseparable	May 10, p. 43
Moderate or Wise Men Lonely in Civil Commotions. Bigots Have Company	May 10, pp. 43-44
The European Commonwealth Threatened by the Two Great Powers East and West	May 10, p. 45
Deprivation of Political Privileges not Ruinous	May 10, p. 46
Physicians and Clergymen Belong to Humanity and not to a Nation	May 10, p. 47
DeFoe's History of the Plague	May 11, pp. 47-48
DeFoe as an Educator	May 15, p. 48
Peace Always	May 16, pp. 48-49
Consolidated States of America	May 18, p. 49
The Clergy with the People	May 18, p. 50
A Drive Through Virginia, Pennsylvania, New Jersey, New York, Ohio and Kentucky	May 25, p. 51
A Day Among the Strawberries	May 25, pp. 51-53
War and Philosophy	May 31, p. 53
The Restorations of 1660 and 1848	June 2, p. 54
Education. Government—Religion	June 2, pp. 54-55
Equally Extreme and Radical	June 6, p. 55
The Slavery Rebellion	June 6, p. 56
Conquest. Subjugation	June 6, pp. 56-57

APPENDICES

Brigandism	June 8, p. 57
The Institution North and South	June 10, pp. 57-58
Speedy Restoration of the Union the Salvation of Slavery	June 10, p. 58
Reconstruction the Only Basis of Permanent Peace	June 12, pp. 59-60
Independence and not Rebellion	June 12, p. 60
Anglo-Saxon Contests for Liberty	June 12, pp. 60-61
New England Will Erect Monuments to the Southern Heroes	June 12, p. 62
New England Should be Tolerant of Southern Patriotism	June 12, pp. 62-67
Southern Conspiracy. A Huge Mistake	June 16, pp. 67-71
We Can't Live Together. An Absurdity	June 17, pp. 71-73
Commercial and Social Intercourse Will Heal the Wound	June 17, pp. 73-74
Reconstruction Is the Word	June 18, pp. 74-77
Penance Needed by Ascetics: Not by Men in Active Life	July 13, p. 77
A False Diagnosis	July 13, pp. 77-78
Must the Mississippi Be in One Government?	July 20, p. 78
Abstractions. Nonsense	July 20, p. 78
The Root of the Disease. Northern Fanaticism	July 20, p. 79
The American Government of To-day a Paradox	July 20, pp. 79-80
Barbarism of War	July 22, p. 80
True Cause of the War	July 26, pp. 80-81
Reorganization of the Union	July 28, pp. 81-82
Probable Result of European Intervention	July 29, p. 82
Fanaticism	Aug. 1, pp. 82-83
Great Features of Spanish History	Aug. 2, p. 83
Book of National Songs	Aug. 16, p. 84
Manual Labor and Intellectual Work	Aug. 24, p. 85
Paternal Affection	Aug. 21, p. 85
Mysticism	Aug. 24, pp. 85-86
Faith	Aug. 25, p. 86
Robinson Crusoe	Aug. 27, p. 87
Church and State	Aug. 29, pp. 87-88
New England's Nationality	Aug. 29, pp. 88-89
Constitutions	Aug. 31, p. 89

II. "Thoughts and Hints," Vol. II

1862

Hope	Oct. 5, p. 1
Calvin and France	Oct. 6, pp. 1-2
Gen. A. S. Johnston	Oct. 7, pp. 2-4
Wm. Jas. Bass	Oct. 5, pp. 4-6

APPENDICES

Spirit of Northern People	Oct. 8, pp. 7-8
Spirit of Southern People	Oct. 8, pp. 8-10
All Northern People Not Fanatic	Oct. 9, pp. 10-12
Liberty Dormant Not Dead	Oct. 9, pp. 12-13
The Black Stone	Oct. 10, pp. 13-14
American Principles	Oct. 10, pp. 15-18
New England Born of Rebels	Oct. 11, pp. 18-19
American Principles Not Anarchical	Oct. 11, pp. 20-21
White and Black	Oct. 11, p. 22
Black Aided by White	Oct. 11, pp. 22-23
Selfishness the American Sin	Oct. 12, pp. 23-26
Depopulation	Oct. 12, pp. 26-27
Sanity of the United States Government	Oct. 12, p. 27
English Self-Conceit	Oct. 12, p. 28
Divine Sovereignty	Oct. 12, p. 28
War	Oct. 12, p. 29
The Question at Issue	Oct. 12, pp. 29-30
The Emancipation Edict—Futile or Devilish	Oct. 13, pp. 30-33
Napoleon a Giant	Oct. 13, p. 33
True Causes of the Revolution	Oct. 14, pp. 34-36
The Constitution Dead	Oct. 14, p. 36
Negro Policy of the Union Government Infamous	Oct. 14, p. 37
Status of Non-Combatant Rebel	Oct. 14, pp. 37-39
Social Results	Oct. 15, pp. 39-40
Slavery in Tennessee	Oct. 15, pp. 40-41
Foreign Intervention	Oct. 16, p. 41
Volunteering	Oct. 16, p. 41
Vindictiveness	Oct. 18, p. 42
Secession and Slavery	Oct. 18, p. 42
Emancipation of the South	Oct. 18, pp. 42-43
Anglo-Saxon Revolutions Conservative	Oct. 19, p. 43
How May the War End?	Oct. 19, p. 44
Hamilton	Oct. 19, pp. 44-45
Washington and Hamilton	Oct. 19, pp. 45-46
Enemies to a Government Fatal Administrators	Oct. 19, pp. 46-47
Adams and Jay	Aug. (1863) p. 47
Constitution Framers	Oct. 23, p. 48
All for a Letter	Oct. 23, p. 48
National and Individual	Oct. 24, pp. 48-49
Thoughts on Study of Medicine	Nov. 8, pp. 49-50
Stockjobbing, Speculating, Etc.	Nov. 10, pp. 50-51
Calamities and Habit	Nov. 10, p. 51
John Adams	Nov. 10, p. 52
My Present Reading	Nov. 10, pp. 52-53

APPENDICES

Governments and Force	Nov. 17, p. 53
The Negro	Nov. 17, p. 54
Conservative Revolutions	Mar. 28 (1863), p. 54
Course of Reading (as Chancellor)	pp. 54-55
Oaths	Nov. 17, p. 56
Southern Genius Witnessed by:—	pp. 56-57
Kindliness to the African Race	Dec. 5, pp. 57-58
Complicate Science—Empiric Art	Dec. 7, pp. 58-59
Foreign Intrusion	Dec. 7, p. 60
A Five Year Course of Medicine	p. 60
The American Democrat	Jan. (1863), pp. 61-62
Female Genius	p. 62
Free Thinking	Dec. 20, p. 63
A Little Learning	Dec. 20, p. 63
Limited Government	Dec. 20, p. 64
Causes of the Civil War	Dec. 22, pp. 64-66
Hemming Slavery In and Thus Choking It	Dec. 25, pp. 66-69

1863

Anarchy Strong Government	Jan. 4, pp. 70-72
Invading Army—Invaded Country	Jan. 4, p. 73
Schemes, Plans, Purposes, Hopes, Projects, Visions, Dreams	pp. 73-74
Iniquitous Treatment of the People in the Invaded States	Jan. 10, pp. 76-77
Commonwealth of Nations	Jan. 11, pp. 78-79
State of the Question	Jan. 13, pp. 79-80
American Figure of Anticipation	Jan. 14, p. 80
Vastness of British Empire	Jan. 14, pp. 80-81
Burke	Jan. 14, pp. 81-82
British Wealth and Sin	Jan. 18, p. 82
The North Revolutionary	Jan. 27, p. 82
Does God Reign?	Mar. 3, p. 83
Professional Arrogance	Mar. 3, pp. 83-84
Professional Confidence	Mar. 4, pp. 84-85
Professional Hypocrisy	Mar. 5, pp. 86-87
East Indians and Fraud Modern Diplomacy	Mar. 9, pp. 87-88
The Three Mighty Empires	Mar. 9, pp. 88-89
Napoleon Overworked	Mar. 10, pp. 90-91
American Institutions Vital	Mar. 10, p. 91
The Golden Mean	Mar. 13, pp. 91-92
The Polish Imbroglio	Mar. 12, pp. 92-93
Evil Days Not Peculiar to America	Mar. 13, pp. 93-94
Europe and America	Mar. 13, p. 95
Massachusetts Gratitude	Mar. 14, pp. 96-97

APPENDICES

Mexico and France.................................Mar. 14, p. 97
A Peculiarity in the Revolution of 1776..............Mar. 15, pp. 97-99
Peace or War—The North Had the Option...........Mar. 15, pp. 99-100
Anarchy and Military Despotism...................Mar. 16, pp. 100-101
In War the Innocent Suffer Most..................Mar. 16, pp. 101-102
Who Brought the War Upon the Country?..........Mar. 16, pp. 102-103
The Reign of Factions............................Mar. 17, pp. 103-104
Party..Mar. 17, pp. 104-105
The South Too Haughty.........................Mar. 17, pp. 105-106
Fanatism of Slavery.............................Mar. 18, p. 106
Destructiveness of War..........................Mar. 20, p. 107
Reconstruction.................................Mar. 20, pp. 107-108
German Talent for Governing.....................Mar. 22, p. 108
Empire and Diversity............................Mar. 25, pp. 108-109
Perversion of Truth.............................Mar. 25, p. 109
Russia and America.............................Mar. 25, pp. 109-110
Submission to Disliked Rule......................Mar. 25, p. 111
No More Denunciation of Britain..................Mar. 26, p. 112
1861—The Antidote for 1776.....................Mar. 26, p. 112
Democracy and Slavery..........................Mar. 26, p. 113
American Political Dictionary.....................Dec. 27, p. 113

APPENDIX C
LETTERS FROM WILLIAM WALKER[1]

PHILADELPHIA, PENN.
Nov. 6, 1841

MR. J. B. LINDSLEY

My Dear Friend,

According to your request, I asked Mr. Phillips whether he had yet received the box of shells which you sent him. He said he had not. The last time I spoke with him was two weeks ago. Whether he has since received them I know not. The Academy is very much in want of such shells and is very anxious to procure them. Their collection of marine shells is the most complete and best arranged part of their cabinet. The collection of minerals and fossils also is good. To the anatomical student the Wistar Museum attached to the University is the most interesting in the city. The foundation for it was laid by presentation to the University of Dr. Wistar's Museum by Mrs. Wistar. Afterwards additions were made to it by the presidents of the Pennsylvania Hospitals. It has been fostered by Horner, and the body of the collection now consists of his contributions. The most important preparations by Wistar were those of the lymphatics, made by Mascagni, and imported from Italy by Dr. W. — Horner has made many vast preparations—chiefly illustrative of general anatomy. There are some preparations in comparative anatomy—but these are few. One is the injection of the lacteals of a rhinoceros with mercury by Mascagni; this is beautiful. An interesting specimen for its physiological bearings is a foetal pig colored red by feeding the mother with madder during pregnancy.

Write me soon; remember me during life, and may we finally meet in that 'rest which remaineth for the people of God' is the prayer of your friend

WM. WALKER

PARIS July 15th 1843

My Dear Friend,

What an age since I parted from you! How often have I recalled the words which you last uttered! "God bless you!"—had this been said, as it is too often repeated, it would not have affected me; but the trembling voice and the filling eye plainly indicated that these words had, in your mouth, their full signification. Alas! I was too light-hearted to know the

[1] William Walker to John Berrien Lindsley, The Lindsley Papers.

APPENDICES

value of the treasure with which I parted. We can not, indeed, estimate the value of a true, a loving friend; we can only approximate to it when we mix much with the world, and discover the emptiness of pretended friendship, the hollowness of the ten thousand professions which ceremony makes. But I must not entertain you with such melancholy reflections.

For two months and a half I have been in the *centre* of France, from which radiate all the influences, social, moral, literary, political, scientific, and religious that move the whole nation. What a field is here opened for the observation of man! No matter what be your tastes or pursuits, here they can be gratified and indulged. The social, moral and religious state of the French people is highly interesting—to the man, but more particularly to the Christian. You know I have a great *penchant* for this sort of observation; and I try to see the French character in all its Protean phases. For the sake of studying the students, I have made the acquaintance of several of them—students in law—they may suffice as a specimen, for here all students are of the same description. Some of them are a curious *mélange;* they will live on six sous per day, and in the evening expend their money at the coffee-house or the theatre. Most of them have mistresses, and nobody thinks them any the worse for it. Indeed, the relations of the two sexes among all classes of society are horrible. You find many married couples, between whom there exists a tacit agreement that the husband may have as many mistresses and the wife as many lovers as each may choose. Such is the case not only in the higher classes of society, but also in the lower; among the old and feeble as well as the young and vigorous. The poison is found in every vein; the effects of it may be seen on the whole body. What a striking lesson may the moralist learn here! Where are moral obligations unless Christianity confirms them? John, I wish you were here for a few days, in order to observe the state of society; you may read these things in books, but when you observe them, you feel them in all their force, you can enter into their full signification. When will France rise from her moral prostration? The signs of the times are not discouraging.

One of my first visits in the capital was to the French Institute; and though I could understand very little of what was said during the *séance*, it was interesting to see the members, and their manner of transacting business. Dumas was in the chair; he is one of the most conspicuous scientific men in Paris. He is yet young, not being, I should judge from his appearance, more than 45 years old. He was the son of a baker, was apprenticed to an apothecary in Geneva, attracted the notice of Prevost while yet very young, and was associated with the latter in his experimental researches in physiology. Coming to Paris, he obtained his degree of Doctor of Medicine, and launched into chemistry. I have been several times to the École de Médecin in order to hear him lecture. He had an audience of 7 or 800. Indeed his *cours* is *plus suivi* than (pardon these Gallicisms—but they are very convenient) that of any professor whom I have heard. Not only the medical students, but persons advanced in science, go to hear him, because he has not yet published the views which he delivers orally. His course is organic chemistry. Of course, his views are pretty generally adopted to the exclusion of those of . . . in regard to some points of physiological chemistry or chemical physiology, whichever you may choose to style it. Speaking the other day with a physiologist and naturalist engaged chiefly in microscopical researches, I asked him some questions about the formation of fat; he gave the ideas of Dumas, and when I spoke of . . . he very slightingly remarked that . . . physiological opinions were adopted by no one but his students. But where am I? We commenced with the Institute, and have got into the midst of chemical physiology. Let us return to the learned body. Arago and Floriens, the perpetual secretaries, were sitting to the right of Dumas. Arago is of gigantic proportions, but he has the air of a reflecting man. He is very popular among the multitude. His political opinions, and his course in the Chamber of Deputies, are very much admired by the liberal party. He has always been consistent—always spurning the advancement which ministers have offered him as the price of political probity. When he lectures on astronomy, *tout le monde,* as the French say, tries to hear him. A French medical student (upwards of 40 years old) told me that he had gone to the Observatory this year to hear Arago's introductory lecture, and that his coat was literally torn to pieces by the crowd which waited before the door, several hours in advance of the commencement of the lecture. But again I wander. The academicians are not very polite in their sessions. Most of them read or write during the whole time. A lively discussion arose during the evening between Cordier and another member; a good deal of disorder prevailed and Dumas was frequently obliged to ring his silver bell. A few months ago, there was a severe struggle for the place in the medical and surgical section rendered vacant by the death of Sarrey. There were numerous candidates: Lisfrane, Bourgery, Velpeau & several others, among whom was the tendon-cutter, M. Jules Guerin. To the honor of the Academy the section didn't nominate the latter as one of the candidates for the place. Velpeau & Lisfrane were the principal ones named: the former got the place. Velpeau was present the evening that I attended and was gliding among the members conversing with them, and appearing to me very like a snake. To me, there is something very repulsive in his countenance; and I would much rather that the surgeon of La Pitie (Lisfrane) had got the place.

I am living in the *Quartier Latin,* at some distance from fashionable Paris. The Jardin des Plantes is not ten minutes' walk from my *pension.* La Pitie is also near, being about 100 yds. distant. I have heard many of the professors at the Jardin, and at the Sorbonne (Biot, Blainville, Milne,

Edwards, Valenciennes, etc.) but there is not enough room for me to tell you about them all. At present, I have a private teacher in anatomy and physiology—Laurent, the *suppléant* of de Blainville at the Sorbonne. With him I am studying microscopical observation. Besides the practical lesson which lasts for 1½ hours every other day, he generally converses with me for an hour after the termination of the lesson. Yesterday we had a very lively discussion in regard to the method of studying the natural sciences, and physiology in particular. He avows to me that he is deeply imbued with *spiritualism*. He thinks that I will gain much by contact with the French in as much as I have been educated in a too matter-of-fact school—a school too cautious in making deductions from facts. The *spiritual* school of anatomists and physiologists is somewhat in the ascendant here. Dr. Blainville, who exercises a vast influence over the French anatomists and naturalists, as well as Geoffrey St. Hilaire are deeply tinged with *a priori* notions. My teacher is constantly deprecating the old hypotheses of the German school, and yet, he is continually following a series of . . . [page torn] matter-of-fact man would call) phantoms. The philosophical anatomists (as they style themselves) are examining only the form; the motto is "La forme est le fond de l'organisation." As the physiognomist pretends to read the character in the features, so they search the function in the form. As Liebig says, they study too little the movements (molecular) of the animal economy.

During the autumn and winter I shall remain in Paris to study anatomy, physiology and the German language. In the spring, I hope to go to Germany—first to Göttingen to study physiology, and chemistry, perhaps afterwards to Giessen. You must let me know what your views are when you write; in order to know how to direct your letters to me, it will be best, perhaps, to ask my father always. Until February, however, you can direct to the care of Hector Bossange, 11 Quai Voltaire. If you leave Nashville, you will let me know it beforehand.

Remember me to your father's family, as also to Dr. Troost & Family; to Stout, Farquharson—especially Gower; let me know where the latter is. That we may meet once more, in health and love, is the ardent prayer of
Your devoted friend & fellow student,
WM. WALKER

When you write let me hear of Edgar & Wm. Litton; remember me, if you see them, to both.—There are a thousand things which I want to say to you; but, as often happens when we have much to say, I know not where to commence. When we meet again, if it please the Almighty to permit this, we shall have much to say. In the mean time, may you be blessed in all your efforts to arrive at "the stature of the perfect man in Christ Jesus." Do not forget to visit my father and mother as often as you can.

APPENDICES

PARIS, November 14th 1843

MY DEAR FRIEND,

Yesterday I received your letter of the 6th ultimo, which afforded me much satisfaction; not only gave me pleasure, but also conferred a benefit. You say in the first paragraph that you were gratified to learn that I possessed less *philosophy* but more *humanity* than you expected. I am sorry, my dear John, that you ever thought my *philosophy* was opposed to *humanity*. With me, the highest philosophy is humanity; the greatest benefactor, the best philosopher. The cold systems of the mere intelligence are but the statue; true—a Phidias can sometimes make it appear animated; but, the moral emotions and affections only can breathe into it the breath of life. Last winter, it was you who were more of the Stoic than I. For some years I have been convinced that the key of wisdom lay in the words of the apostle: "Charity never faileth: but whether there be prophecies they shall fail; whether there be tongues, they shall cease; whether there be knowledge, it shall vanish away." And charity is not that vague something of which, like the spirit in Job's dream, you cannot discern the form and that indefined feeling which embraces everything. This general emotion is often the mist which hides real love. In science, you know that we can never reach the generalities, but through the individual facts, neither in the divine science, can we attain universal benevolence, but with the moistened eye and touched heart of individual friendship.

You need not be afraid of wearying me by an account of yourself; it is precisely the subject on which I wish you to dilate. In regard to your theological studies, I have not understood whether you would pursue them in Nashville or at some Seminary.—You say that I will probably find you here (at home?) when I return; may we be so happy as to embrace each other once more! And Jesse Hume is settled at Gallatin! I wish him all the *personal* success possible. When we last parted, it was after a long discussion on the Trinity; no doubt he thinks me an archheretic, but I am sure that if he thinks thus, he also pities me. Be sure and remember me to Rev. Washington, and ask him if he thinks that I can forget him? I am almost ashamed to ask him to write to me, without first writing to him; however, you may tell him that I should be delighted to hear from him. I hardly write to any one but my parents. Remember me also to Edgar and all other friends—particularly to Dr. Troost. I hope to see the dear old man alive and well when I return.

The present position and the prospects of France are extremely interesting. The ministry Guizot has been in power for three years—longer than any other ministry since the accession of Louis Philippe. Nevertheless, it is far from being popular. M. Guizot has the opinion that a limited monarchy such as that of Great Britain is the best form of government; whereas a very large portion of the French people lean toward a republic. Many of the journals (opposition, of course) predict the fall of the ministry after the meeting of the Chambre de Députés. One of the subjects which has, of late, most engaged attention is the fortifications of Paris. Against this measure, many of the journals were furious; because, as they said, the real object of this work was not to defend the capital, but to hold it in subjection. As soon as there might break out a revolution, the government would turn the cannons towards the city. Many were in favor of going immediately to work in order to tear down the fortifications. Perhaps the question will engage the attention of the Chambre during the winter. There is also pending another important discussion—viz. "La Liberté de l'enseignement." Many complain of the monopoly of the University. Among the most violent opponents of the monopoly are the priests—a strong proof that they will advocate any cause which advances their order. To hear a Catholic priest talking of liberty, is like a monster talking of beauty. But they oppose the University for good reasons—they wish to get the reins of education into their own hands. These priests look not beyond the moment; they see not that the principles which they advocate will prove the destruction of their existence. I become more and more convinced each day that the spirit of freedom and of Romanism are enemies. Certain it is that Romanism admits not religious liberty; can civil liberty exist without religious? Popery places a chain around the mind in regard to many subjects of inquiry; and this cannot but hamper the thought in the investigation of all other points. It is to be feared that Catholicism will get a hold in our country, and that there will be some trouble in dislodging it.

Nov. 20

I had intended to send this letter by the packet of the 16th, but various circumstances having prevented me from finishing it, I was obliged to detain it a week.

More than six months have elapsed since I landed in Europe; and my visit has already had a great influence on many of my opinions. It has made me more of an American than ever—more fond of my country's institutions, and prouder of her history and her resources. Let scribbling tourists ridicule as much as they please our customs and our opinions (particularly the high opinion which we have of our republic)—there is no patriot who can be more justly proud of his country than the American. When I see in two of the august states in Europe (England and France) the existence of powerful shackles on the tongue, if not on the thought (for who can fetter thought?), I rejoice that there is a "land of the free." In England, a man must be of the Anglican church in order to hold many public stations; in France, every newspaper must receive the royal *timbre*. But there seems to be a time approaching when many of the abuses of monarchy will fall to the ground. The recent revolution in

Greece, the attempted insurrection in Italy, the state of affairs in Ireland seem to announce better times.

True, that in respect to the actual amount of literature and science, we may be in the rear of several European nations; but I doubt if such will be the case for the course of twenty years. It is better to have the capability of making rapid acquisitions in knowledge, than to have already a huge mass of knowledge without any extra-ordinary capacity. Our institutions, our modes of thinking and acting, the character of the people, render our position favorable for the pursuit of knowledge and truth—no matter what may be the description, or rather department of science; let monarchy bestow as much encouragement as she pleases on the devotees of science; let her load them with gold and titles, republicanism holds out a far more glittering prize in the honor and esteem yielded by the citizens of the state. In the ancient world, when was philosophy or science at a higher point than when its protectors were Athenian citizens?

The information contained in your letter in regard to yourself was different from what I expected. From what you said last winter I thought it very probable that you would fix yourself near Lebanon and practice medicine during the last summer. You seem, however, to have given up all idea of practicing "the healing art." What you say in regard to the number of physicians, is very true; there is no famine as to that variety of wheat—or perhaps of tares. I think, however, that there will be soon a revulsion in the trade. As our political wiseacres said in regard to the late money derangements of our country, every exaltation is followed by a depression. The market is beginning to be overstocked; a lowering in the price will necessarily follow; the venders will consequently diminish; and the equilibrium of trade be established. Or let us take a more professional analogy. Suppose the medical profession to be represented by some vital part—with all due respect to the cook, let us take the stomach. If some irritation (in this case, the desire of living without working is the irritant) exist in the organ, an inflammation generally ensues; but the *vis medicatrix naturae* (what would become of a doctor if he hadn't the right to talk his nonsense in Latin, so that nobody can understand his folly?) intervenes, and establishes the synergy—*caten invisibilis*—between various parts of the body:—for according to Jackson's definitions, health is the synergy (derived, permit me to say, from two *Greek* words . . . with, εsγos working,—i.e. working together) of the organs: disease, the want of *synergy* or harmony. I might entertain you with a long dissertation on the danger of these irritations and inflammations in the body social, literary, moral, scientific, religious and political as well as in the body material; but I am satisfied that one who has sustained a Thesis on the very grave and difficult subject, "Inflammation," fully appreciates their importance. To become more serious—I really think that there is more need of preachers than of physicians in the western country. Besides, the turn of your mind, the education which you have received, the principles which you have imbibed, the circumstances which surround you—all tend to lead you into the theological, rather than the medical profession. You speak of your early impressions; early impressions are hard to erase. They are like the figures which we make on caoutchouc; by an exertion of force you may stretch the *gum elastic* until the figures disappear; but when you relax your efforts, they resume their original character. It is said that no idea which enters our mind is ever entirely removed; often, we see the spectre, as it were, of our departed notions or opinions. By experience, I know how firm is the hold of these early and long-cherished ideas. With me, whilst a child and a boy, I had determined on a political career; there have been times when I thought that the last vestige of such an idea had disappeared, but often it re-appears to me, in my waking dreams, leaving me uncertain whether it be an angel of light or an angel of darkness.

Perhaps it will be agreeable to you to receive a French journal now and then; I shall send you some, in order that you may judge personally of the spirit of the press in this country. It may also serve to inform you that I am well and do not forget my old friend. Were I certain that Rev. Washington would remain in Nashville, I would also forward him some newspapers. Be sure and write me as often as possible, and let me know how you advance in your studies. With regard to the opinions of Mrs. Shelley in regard to the French females, I think that what she says is true; it is also true that religious ideas are more prevalent among the middle classes, than among the higher and the lower orders.

Remember me to your father and family.

The French paper is so thin that I will have to put my letter in an envelope. It is to be hoped that *Uncle Sam* will not make you pay *double*.

With the warmest feelings of friendship, and the most ardent prayer for your welfare and happiness, I am,

Yours,
WM. WALKER

Jan. 9, 1844, from W. Walker

LONDON 27th March 1844

MY DEAR JOHN,

I have delayed answering your letter of the 9th Jan. until my arrival in England; and I now snatch some moments from the most disagreeable of all occupations—sightseeing and "lionizing"—in order to devote them to the most agreeable—correspondence with an old friend. Perhaps you will not assent to the epithet of "disagreeable" as applied to "sight-seeing," but I think that even your patience and *legs* would be tired out if you were in London for a few days. The pavements are as hard as an anvil and much more inelastic, so that walking on a turnpike road is bliss in comparison with walking on London pavements. And then the distances! Oh! it is horrible to relate, and with a heavy heart, I must say. . . .

When I write to you, John, I don't feel in the *Descriptive* fit; buildings and scenes and all the other themes of guide-books are too cold and inanimate for the letters of friendship. Even society, with its many-sided faces, disappears when I think of writing to you. After all, what are these but phantasmagoria! . . . 'tis delightful to view the fleeting shadows as they pass; they are beautiful like the rainbow, but like it they are momentary and nourish not. But the beams of friendship—they give us light and they nourish. And Love is abiding—he flees not in sorrow or in joy, in time or in eternity. Let us have but the loving heart—and the kindly eye and the affectionate tongue, and what care we for gilded palaces or crumbling ruins or lofty arches! There is no delight but one like the pouring out of the heart to a friend who can listen and sympathize and counsel. What a time it will be, John, when our lips "touched with celestial fire" can tell what words of earth can ne'er convey! Then will it be truly the speech of heart to heart; then shall we see each other "face to face"—now "we see through a glass darkly"—we see but the reflection of each other's souls. Meanwhile, we can lean upon each other in this journey through the world; sometimes as we scramble through the briars we can pull the thorns from each others hands, and apply salves to the wounds, and midst the meadows we can together pluck the flowers.

I almost envy you the life you lead at Nashville; and though we do not walk bodily together, my mind figuratively wanders with you over the green grass and midst the high trees. And how plainly every thing comes before me! Now we are on the cliffs of the Cumberland, just below the reservoir; you have a long tin mustard box in your hand, and every now and then a luckless snail is thrown into it; and with converse sweet we while away the hour. Sometimes it is a subject of taste which we discuss—favorite passages of a favorite author—(yes, John, every time I read Milton's *L'Allegro* and *Il Penseroso*, I think of you, and of your fondness for them)—or the higher and more interesting subjects which relate to God and eternity engage our attention. When will these happy hours come back again! When shall we again walk

> On the dry smooth-shaven green
> To behold the wandering moon,
> Riding near her highest noon,
> Like one that had been led astray
> Through the heaven's wide pathless way;
> And oft, as if her head she bowed
> Stooping through a fleecy cloud.

You know that we used frequently to speak of the great characters which have appeared in the world, and attempt to analyze feelings and opinions by the light of biography. The more I think of the "inner self" the more do I feel how much interest there would be in a complete history of all the revolutions in sentiment and principles which occur in a single human mind. When we look within and see the motions of our hearts, how strange do they seem! What an influence may the smallest circumstance have upon our whole being! The reading of a single sentence,—nay, the hearing of a single word may change the whole course of existence. Who can tell what an hour may bring forth? And how vain in man to say "I *will* do."! Yet how great, frequently, is the power of the human will! It is this mixture of greatness and littleness, of strength and weakness, which confounds.

I take the opportunity afforded by the return of Gen. Barrow to write to you; and as my meeting with him was accidental, and as he starts from London today, I hope that you will view with a friendly eye the shortish, rambling style, etc. etc. of this letter. As your father used to advise us never to make apologies, however, just take the latter part of the previous sentence for what it is worth. I do plainly confirm that I am ashamed not to have commenced sooner to write and so making a clean breast—as the newspapers say of the confessing criminal—I rely on your mercy for a pardon.

Remember me kindly to your father and family—also to all our friends. In the bond of friendship

Yours, truly & lovingly,
WM. WALKER

P. S. I gave Dr. Lane of Ohio a letter of introduction to you; he wishes to have Cumberland shells. Will you do what you can to furnish him with them?

VENICE November 19th 1844

MY DEAR JOHN,

I received your very agreeable letter—without a date—yesterday morning. At the beginning of your letter, you seemed to be at a loss what to say; but, at last, you got to the subject most interesting to me—the *Ego*. News from the *backwoods*—which I am fool enough to think as civilized, if not more so, than the old countries of Europe—is always agreeable, whether of a general or purely local nature. But news, as you say, comes to us now-a-days through the papers rather than through letters. Besides, anybody can write the news to me. There is, however, one thing, John, which no one but a friend can write to me—the feelings of a friend's heart. "France's thousand mouths" may shout to me the name of a Presidential candidate; but, with eagerness, I turn from the deafening cry, and listen to the friend who whispers me his hope and his fears, his lofty aspirings and ardent struggles. No matter in what mood I am, anything from you, would never be thrown aside; though my spirit were "dark as Erebus," a word from you might "illuminate" it; though it were joyful as Elysium, a . . . of yours would darken it.

Since leaving England, I have passed through Belgium, Rhenish Prussia, up the Rhine through Switzerland into Italy. But I have not space or time, now, to tell you all the wonderful things that I have seen. The impressions of art "we cannot tell, yet cannot all conceal." When I get you, some of these days, to myself, I will *bore* you thoroughly with a long account of admeasurements, distances, etc. Indeed, I intend to make the guide-books my study in crossing the ocean—as I have not yet studied them—in order to be *au fait* in these matters. I don't think that I have the organ of Distances. I was in such a thrill of awe whilst in Cologne and Milan cathedrals that I did not think of counting, by steps, the width, length, etc.—so I can't tell these things on my own authority. Many people, I know, will say what in the world was the *use* of going to such places, if not to learn their size, etc.—tut—tut—

How beautiful is the old *mythos* of Time devouring his children. A moment is born, devoured,—and where is it? Yet how much may depend upon a moment; the whole history of a man may be centered in an instant. The story is told of the father of Francesco Sforza that while a peasant boy he was desirous of entering upon a military life; and one day taking a hatchet, he said to himself, "If I lodge the axe in yon tree, I will become a soldier; if not, I remain in my present condition." The hatchet was lodged in the tree, and his son, Francesco, became Duke of Milan. Many a man's fate depends upon the cast of a hatchet. This is one side, but look at the other. Is not every moment fraught with consequences of the utmost importance? Were we masters of the science of *soul's* calculations, would it not be a rational problem given any one moment of a man's life, to find his whole past and future? Take any link of a chain and hold it on high; all the links on both sides, hang by the one link. Astrologers seized on one moment—that of birth—as most fit for these calculations of life; the falsity of their prognostications arose from their neglecting altogether the most important element of the problem—the disposition of the infant. They noticed only the external circumstances; but as breathing depends as much upon the lungs as upon the state of the atmosphere, our life depends as much, if not more, upon the *internal* than the *external* conditions. Here lies the difficulty—to know the state of the infant's mind. Then what a number and variety of disturbing causes necessarily enter into the calculation! *Enfin,* it is a most puzzling problem.

Such is the nature of our reflections when arriving at one of the turns in life we cast a backward look on the road over which we have passed. We are too young, however, to have a long road behind us, and we look forward more than behind. At least it is so with me. The future! The future! Something always coming but never here. Some portions of the past too are very interesting; the present, however, is almost always tiresome. When I was in Paris and London, I didn't enjoy them half so much as before I saw them or after I left them. Anticipation and recollection are the great sources of happiness—at least, to the mind. We have, in English, the three poems which exhaust all the Pleasures—Imagination, Hope and Memory. The great pleasure is that of Imagination; the forms of Hope and Memory are beautiful when tinged with the colors of fancy—without the coloring, they are very ordinary things—These are what may be called the purely *mental* pleasures; there are others above and beyond—the moral pleasures—the pleasure of venerating and worshipping Deity—the pleasure of doing good.

I am getting very tired of the wandering life I have led for some time, and look forward, with pleasure, to the time when I shall be again in the active, stirring world of the west. I do not know exactly when I shall be at home; some time, probably, in April or May next. On the 8th of May, I will be twenty-one; and I hope to pass that day at home.

You must be quite learned in Theology by this time; in a year and a half of study a man may do a vast deal. I hope you have given up your idea of becoming a missionary, and purpose taking up your abode in some civilized part of the world where a fellow can have a chance of seeing you every now and then. Ah! John, it is a hard thing to live in the world without our natural friends—those whom birth has given us. So, I hope you have fallen, or will fall, in love with some young lady near Nashville and get married; and I hope, like a true *cara sposa*, she will govern you completely and not let you emigrate into any outlandish region where you will have no companions but gibbering savages or half-civilized pagans.

Au plaisir de vous revoir—as the misses in French boarding-schools are made to say—I am

Your friend, affectionately,
Wm. Walker

Dr. J. B. Lindsley

New Orleans Feby. 25th 1846

Dear John,

I ought to have written to you some time ago; but you know how apt man is to be absorbed in the trifles which are "seen" and to be led away from the things "unseen" which are real. How hard it is for us to abstract our minds from the sensible, and fix them on the spiritual! Rare friendship is, I conceive, one of our most spiritual enjoyments. Love has in it some alloy,—something "of the earth, earthy"; ambition is too often the desire of mere power, without the qualification of power for doing good; but friendship is abused only by being false, hardly ever by being too intense.

The week after I got to the city I commenced the study of the Civil Code; and am now engaged in reading the commentary on it by Toullier in twenty-volumes. Luckily these volumes are not very large, and I hope to finish, on an average, one of them every five or six days. So in this commentary, I have work enough for three or four months. My preceptor's name is Mott—no relation, however, of the surgical Bombastes Furioso. You have no idea of the profaneness of the people of New Orleans. Now there is Mr. Mott; looking at him, I would suppose him almost incapable of saying an oath, but yet I hadn't been in the office long before my ears were saluted with words that I had deemed long before consigned to draymen and porters. They do not think it any violation of politeness to swear in the presence of people for whom you have the least respect imaginable. This common use of oaths appears to be produced by an absurd affectation of energy. Not content with activity and simple power, they must have bustle and swelling words. A man wants to have the appearance of strength although he is conscious of weakness.

Carnival has just ended, and with it a host of fooleries went out. There were maskings and balls, and processions and such like things; at which one knows not whether he ought to laugh or weep. Perhaps it is better and wiser to laugh, as they may be in their nature like the small-pox; let them break out and appear on the surface lest they prey on and destroy the internal organs. The twenty-second was celebrated on Sunday by the military; there was a grand sham-fight in the suburbs of the town. By the way, you must let me know how Dunkellibben succeeded in their celebration.

I am living with Farquharson, and we get on very well together. He has taken a high stand among the medical men here and will no doubt succeed in his profession. F. dines at a restaurant, but I take my meals at a boarding-house in our neighborhood. Since I got to New Orleans I have got one letter from home, of about half-a-dozen lines. I write now a sort of introductory to our correspondence in the hope of provoking you to a long answer. You shall hear from me again in a short time. Farquharson desires to be remembered to you: remember me to all friends in Nashville, particularly to Dr. Troost and your father.

Yours, truly,
Wm. Walker.

Mr. J. Lindsley

Sep 5th 1847

My Dear John,

Owing to the heat of New Orleans I have been spending several weeks on the lake shore and expect to be kept here some time longer. The fever is uncommonly violent in its forms this year, so that every one who can leave town—even those who had thought themselves acclimated, is flying from the infected region. There were no particular reasons for my remaining in the city, and so I came over here. A Frenchman was saying the other day that he thought it a bad excuse for staying that a man couldn't leave his "business"; for, said he, what will a man's business be good for when he is dead?

You said in the letter written in August and which I did not get until yesterday that you had written to me several times without an answer. The letters must have miscarried, inasmuch as I have never received them. So, you see, I am not so much to blame as you thought for. But do not understand me to offer as an excuse for not writing to you that I had got no letters from you. I should not think of standing so much on ceremony. The truth is I had so many little things during the winter and spring to harass and annoy me, that I hardly felt sufficiently good humoured to write to a friend; and an ill-natured letter is not like an ill-natured speech in that one can . . . out at the other. On the contrary, it has an air of malice *prepense* and words which in conversation would be passed unnoticed look quite hostile when staring at you with their darkened faces from the pale and agitated paper. There is a fine piece of mock-heroic for you worthy the pen of an old and experienced newspaper writer! Wouldn't I be a fine fellow to follow after the army and give *magnificent relations* of its incomparable exploits? Then, notice, if you please, how many points of excellence there are in that fine sentence of mine: even the *meagre merit* of alliteration—*pale paper*—may be found in it. 'Twas quite unintentional too, I declare:—an inspiration of genius sudden as "winged words" of the magnetic telegraph!

I shall remain here until the yellow fever abates in New Orleans—possibly until the middle of October. Continue, however, to direct to New Orleans as I will thus get your letters sooner.

Remember me to your father & family; also to Dr. Troost & family.

Truly, Your friend

Wm. Walker

New Orleans, March 18, 1848

Well, my dear fellow, I didn't think you were so much of a politician as your last letter led me to imagine. To be sure, I knew you were a Whig, and that your political opinions were decided; but I hardly thought you would be so violent against the *"unbounded arrogance"* of the Executive and all that. Indeed, the Whigs had better make you one of their electors and get you to take the stump during the ensuing campaign: for from your last letter I think you would make an admirable stump-speech. As to my going over to the democracy, you know it is but a return to old principles; and my faith in the old creed will be so much the stronger, as I have passed through the stage of skepticism, and am now more secure in my opinions than if I had adopted them as a mere matter of course.

As to the Executive arrogance of which you speak, I think that the course pursued by Mr. Ritchie in denouncing all those who oppose the war as moral traitors is about on a par with various other declamations and denunciations given forth by the press—hardly more unreasonable or more censurable than the fierce and uncompromising articles which daily issue from the office of the *New York Tribune*. Not that I am the least disposed to seal up the lips of Mr. Greely or of any who advocate the same views and opinions. On the contrary, I rather admire the fierceness and fearlessness with which the *Tribune* stands up for what it considers right and justice; and regard its course as vastly preferable to that of so many Whigs who in the selection of a candidate for the Presidency seem to look altogether to availability, without at all supposing that a man's declaration of his principles is a pledge which the people ought at all times to require of their servants.

I send you another newspaper article which I have lately published; and although you are a Whig, yet as I know you value your principles and are therefore most likely to be in favor of Mr. Clay as the candidate for the Presidency, you will probably concur with the views I have expressed.

I shall see you, I hope, in the course of the next summer, when we shall have an opportunity of talking over all that has happened to both of us during the last two years. Why don't you say something in your letters about our old Friend Dr. Troost? From your not mentioning him I suppose he must be just as usual. Remember me to him when you see him, and tell him that one of the greatest pleasures I anticipate in going to Nashville this summer is in meeting with him, my friend and instructor. Remember me to your father; and believe me,

Truly, your devoted friend,
WM. WALKER

GRANADA, NICARAGUA Nov. 26th 1855

MY DEAR JOHN,

Have you forgotten your old friend? If you have he has not forgotten you or the many pleasant hours he has spent with you or the fund of ample knowledge he has learned from you.

If you have any memory of our past studies and friendship do not fail to induce someone skilled in geology and botany to come to this country. There is no finer field for a naturalist than here; and as a Scotchman warms to the tartan so does the heart of your humble servant to the students of science.

This government needs scientific men; and I will see that they do not starve if they come here.

Don't forget or fail to comply with this request of

Your faithful friend,
WM. WALKER

DR. JOHN B. LINDSLEY

APPENDIX D

MISCELLANEOUS CORRESPONDENCE

CINCINNATI Sept. 15, 1850

J. BERRIEN LINDSLEY, M.D.

Dear Sir

Your favor of the 7th inst came to hand yesterday and I reply immediately as you desire— As regards the shells you know to be common both to Ohio and Tennessee, a few specimens only of each will be desirable— Generally about 4. or 5. of each will be all that is necessary of such species unless there is a marked difference between the Tennessee specimens and those of the same species found also here— Where there is much difference a few additional specimens would not be amiss—

With regard to those which are peculiar to Tennessee I have already expressed my wish that the specimens should be ad-libitum, or rather ad infinitum if possible— I would not ask for them in this way if I did not feel perfectly satisfied that I could return you a full and fair equivalent—

I hope you may be able to procure for me an ample supply of your species, but if the season is not favorable for that purpose I shall hope that you will be able to get the missing ones hereafter for me— I think I have mentioned to you my great desire to have as many species of Melania and Auculosa as possible— I once got a few of these Melania's from near Columbia in your state, and they were exceedingly interesting— I wish now to get them from every part of your state— You have near Nashville some species of the genus Polygyra of which numerous specimens would be very acceptable to me— You have also some Carocolla's, Such as Carocolla cumberlana dicay Spinosor and Helicoides, it would gratify me exceedingly to get a large number of specimens— Of the Melanias which I know from the Cumberland. I may mention the alveare andexcurara as being great favorites of mine—

Do you also collect the fossils of your neighborhood— They are I presume not much different from our own but Nashville I think stands a little higher in the scale of silurian fossils than Cincinnati— I have a considerable number of species of fossils from this neighborhood to spare and it might not be uninteresting to compare them with yours—

It may be best as you say to wait until you come here before putting up a complete suite of Ohio shells for you. . . .

I will follow your directions strictly with regard to sending a box and intended to do so before receiving your letter in order to avoid not only the additional freight but also the additional risk and delay which would naturally attend a reshipment at Smithland.—

I am much obliged to you for the notice which you sent me containing the proceedings with regard to the death of the late Dr. Troost— Whom will the trustees select to fill the place which was so long and so ably filled by the late incumbent—

I am very respectfully and sincerely y. f.
JOHN G. ANTHONY

P. S. My eyes are improving rapidly, but I do not like to use them much as yet for writing and therefore have one of my boys to write for me—

(John G. Anthony to John Berrien Lindsley, The Lindsley Papers)

CINCINNATI, November 19th, 1850.

J. BERRIEN LINDSLEY, M.D.

My Dear Sir,

As you have probably by this time ascertained whether you will be likely to visit this city or not during the present year, I write to know what you have determined upon and whether I shall send you the specimens I have prepared for that purpose by Nashville Packet at once or still retain them and hand them to you in person.— I would like very much to see you here, but if you have given up all thoughts of visiting us this season the specimens can be sent at once as they are all prepared and packed leaving a very small space in the box which I can fill up if need be at any moment— I have put up in this way about 175 species including specimens of all our Unios excepting one, of all our Anodous excepting! and all the Alasmodous found in this state— I have commenced putting in some from other localities and will fill the box in that way—

I hope you have succeeded in getting a goodly number of species during the summer— We had not much success here in that way our river having been at no time low enough to admit of our collecting any but the most ordinary species— There are many species which we never find unless the river becomes very low indeed and we had no chance with such this summer—

I hope you will be pleased with those which I can send you and find something among them which may be new and interesting to you— If there is anything which you wish more of please advise me as I have in most cases sent you but few specimens of each species because I supposed you intended them for your own cabinet more— If you have any exchanges however in which our species would be useful to you or if you wish any more specimens for your own collection I will furnish them—

Among the species found here and also in the Cumberland river is the Unio Cylindricus. Say but I understand that yours have generally, colored nacres— If this be the case I would like as many as you can spare of this species as ours are uniformly white.

I shall be happy to hear from you as soon as possible after you receive this and give me directions how to procede

Sincerely
I am your frd.
JOHN G. ANTHONY

(John G. Anthony to John Berrien Lindsley, The Lindsley Papers)

NEW ALBANY, July 23, 1852

MY DEAR DAUGHTER,

A letter arrived this morning for Eliza from Berrien, dated Paris, June 25. He writes in good health & spirits. He expected to leave Paris for Geneva the next day—thence to Cologne, Berlin, St. Petersburg, Moscow, Sweden, Denmark, London, etc. to New York about the first of September. Among other things, he says: "Tell Mr. Crockett that I send two boxes of apparatus from Paris, which he must have insured at Walker's —do not forget." This is all he writes about said boxes. I do not know the route pursued by Mr. & Mrs. Hoyt—nor where a letter can reach them. I feel much anxiety about Lawrence. I have heard nothing since the receipt of your letter of the 9th inst. I am greatly obliged to Mr. Crockett for the papers which he sends me. My best regards to him. The weather here is dreadfully hot and oppressive. We may commence our northern journey in the course of a month. I can sit in my study only a part of the morning, on account of the heat.

I resigned my office in the Seminary on the 16th but the Board declined accepting—and begged me most respectfully & unanimously to withdraw the same. I mention this because I had stated to Dr. Lapsley my determination to resign—etc.

Berrien thinks Nashville superior to any & all big cities of Europe.

Your affectionate Father,
PHILIP LINDSLEY

(Philip Lindsley to Margaret Lawrence Lindsley, The Lindsley Papers)

CAMBRIDGE, Oct. 1, 1855.

DEAR SIR,

I do myself the pleasure to forward to you, and ask you to accept a copy of a small Dictionary.

Such a manual may be of little or no use to you, but I hope you may think it not wholly unfit for the uses for which it is designed.

With great respect,

Your most obt. servt.,
J. E. WORCESTER

J. BERRIEN LINDSLEY, M.D.
Chancellor Univ. Nashville

(J. E. Worcester to John Berrien Lindsley, The Lindsley Papers)

APPENDICES

Dear Sir;

Allow me to make an appeal to you to help me in a matter of considerable scientific interest at this moment, in my investigations.

Several species of turtles have been described from specimens collected in the vicinity of Nashville, which it would be important for me to compare with some others found in different parts of the country. Should there be in your University a complete collection of the turtles found in your State, I would feel thankful if you could lend them to me for comparison and forward them at once by express. I shall take good care of them and return them faithfully. If no collection has been made and preserved, would you have the kindness, as soon as the spring opens, to have as complete a series of all the different kinds found with you, collected for me, & forwarded alive, by express, packed up in straw or hay, or if you can add to these full grown specimens some of their eggs & if possible also young just hatched. It would be a great addition to my forthcoming work to be able to make a thorough examination of these turtles.

Very respectfully yours
L. Agassiz

Cambridge 18th Feb. 1856
Prof. J. B. Lindsley
Nashville

(L. Agassiz to John Berrien Lindsley, The Lindsley Papers)

Dear Sir,

Your little note has given me much pleasure & I feel truly grateful for your kind offer. There is one kind of collection you could make for me which would be of the greatest scientific value & I believe give you little trouble in making it. I want particularly the small fishes of all your western brooks & ponds, all the minnows & small fry which nobody thinks of catching & which are therefore very difficult to obtain for scientific purposes. The best way of getting them is to have a small bag of gauze sewed to a wire circle & this attached to a cane or pole with which to sweep the waters. Boys are very fond of such occupations & in a few afternoons could make an invaluable collection. The specimens may best be preserved in alcohol or whiskey, & empty pickle jars may serve for putting them up. I am certain that in a few days you might in this way receive a number of new species.

Next to this I should like very much some of the beautiful new species of freshwater shells described from your waters by Mr. Lea of Philadelphia, within the last few years.

With many thanks   Yours very truly

J. Berrien Lindsley, Esq.   L. Agassiz

I hope we shall soon be able to hold our scientific meetings in renewed harmony.

(L. Agassiz to John Berrien Lindsley, The Lindsley Papers)

APPENDICES

St. Louis, Nov. 4, 1863

Dr. J. B. Lindsley,
Nashville, Tenn.:

My dear Doctor,

Allow me to introduce to your acquaintance and kind attentions, W. Thompson of England. He is on a travelling tour through the country, and I know no one who can give him more information concerning your region than yourself. I therefore trust that you will make his stay in your city as pleasant and profitable as circumstances will allow.

How are you these war times? I hope we may meet before a great while. I see that your school is again in operation. We have just commenced with a class of 120 and increasing. Last session we had 155 students.

With best wishes and regards ever,

Yours sincerely
Charles R. Pope, (M.D.)

(Charles R. Pope to John Berrien Lindsley, The Lindsley Papers)

1622 Locust St., Philadelphia
Mar. 19, 1867

My Dear Sir,

I did myself the pleasure last month to send you a parcel to Care of Gamble & Co containing my XL Vol Oles which I hope you have rec before this—

The plates are remarkably well done & I am sure you will be satisfied with the Vol-

I trust that some of your students are interested in Nat- Hist & that you can induce them to collect particularly from the West of your city into Arkansas.

I am very Re
Yr f
Isaac Lea

Pres. Lindsley

p. s. I do not forget how greatly I am obliged to you for the many fine specimens you have given me at various times— I assure you that they have been made very useful—

(Isaac Lea to John Berrien Lindsley, The Lindsley Papers)

APPENDICES

BEAUVOIR MISS
11th March. 1887

J. BERRIEN LINDSLEY M.D.

My Dear Sir,

I duly received and acknowledged the beautiful and valuable volume of which you are the author. The work is to me rendered doubly dear as another one of the offerings made by woman to the cause of the South, for such it became when the Southern States alone contended for the freedom and independence which the constitution was formed alone to secure & preserve.

Please give my cordial thanks to Mrs. Lindsley, the sister of a hero in the war between the States, and daughter of a comrade in arms of the immortal Jackson. I trust the example you have set will be followed by other states for the commemoration of Patriots who dared all for States Rights and self Government, the priceless heritage which descended to us from our Fathers of the Revolution.

Respectfully & truly
Yours,
JEFFERSON DAVIS

Private

It is a lingual solecism to term the resistance of states to coercion "a rebellion." Subjects, not sovereign, may "rebel" and the states won their sovereignty in the war of 1776. It is politically inaccurate to term ours a "civil war," which properly applies to a war between factions of one body politic, whereas ours was a war between states united by a Federal league for enumerated purposes, & therefore it was a war between States which being united by consent separated in the exercise of their reserved sovereignty.

J. D.

(Jefferson Davis to John Berrien Lindsley, The Lindsley Papers. The above note "Private" was written on a slip of paper enclosed in the letter. The "hero" refers to Randal W. McGavock, Col., 10th Tenn. Regiment. Mrs. Lindsley's father was Jacob McGavock, who fought with Jackson at the battle of Horseshoe Bend.)

689 MADISON AVE
NEW YORK
Mar 12th '88

DR. J. BERRIEN LINDSLEY

DEAR SIR

Your very courteous letter has just arrived. I appreciate it highly, as I need hardly assure you.

Unfortunately, as I have written Judge Lea, I am unable to come in May, as I originally intended; and therefore expect to make my appearance about the 24th or 25th of this month, unless it is inconvenient for you.

APPENDICES 199

I shall let you know the exact date some days in advance, and shall have the honor of calling on you immediately after my arrival.

I have heard of the interesting work on which you are engaged through General Wheeler of Alabama.

Thanking you for your courtesy

I am

Very truly yours

THEODORE ROOSEVELT

(Theodore Roosevelt to John Berrien Lindsley, The Lindsley Papers. The letter was written in answer to one by Dr. Lindsley promising Roosevelt access to the state archives for material on the latter's work, *The Winning of the West*.)

SEWANEE Nov. 5 88

MY DEAR DOCTOR

I expect to leave here Sunday morning on my way to the land of the Montezumas & will dine with you and as I expect to stay over, one day, in Nashville if you can stow me away in some corner I shall invite myself to partake of your hospitality the Monday of leaving.

With kind regards to all the family I am   Sincerely yours,

E. KIRBY SMITH

DR. BERRIEN LINDSLEY

(E. Kirby Smith to John Berrien Lindsley, The Lindsley Papers)

UNIVERSITY OF THE SOUTH,
SEWANEE, TENN.
Nov. 8th, 1891

DR. J. BERRIEN LINDSLEY:

DEAR SIR:

When I began my work this autumn as Professor of Modern Languages at this University I was at once surprised and delighted to find a rich collection of modern continental literature and my pleasure was still further enhanced by the discovery made some time later when I had time to explore the library that there were a very large number of very valuable and curious books from the older literatures of these languages, books that the scanty means of the University would hardly have enabled them to procure and some of which I had long coveted in vain.

Eager examination soon showed me that I was indebted for my pleasure to you, but I could not believe that one would willingly part with some of these treasures and allowed myself to suppose that I must forego the pleasure of expressing my thanks to the donor. It was but a few hours ago, in a conversation with Mr. Wiggins, that I learned that like Cyrus you were eager that your friends should profit now by what you

APPENDICES

had enjoyed and I hasten to thank you most heartily in the name of the department of Modern Languages and of all its students. I had already made arrangements to draw up myself a careful catalogue of the books in this department to be alphabetically arranged on cards, and all books that can be identified as yours shall be so designated there. I assure you the books will be of permanent service to the department that I represent. These are highly appreciated and will be carefully preserved, while every effort will be made to extend their usefulness. Such works among them not adapted to general perusal are by no means of the least value to the student of medieval manners and literature. It is in this field that I have been working for the greater part of my life in Germany and France and I have found books here that may have been sent with a feeling that perhaps none would soon be found to care for them that have been of help in my private studies that I could not have otherwise procured.

I hope I shall not seem to intrude upon you in writing these few words of thanks. Every student has a little of Dominie Sampson's feelings when he finds himself seated at an unexpected literary feast.

I remain, Dear Sir,

Yours very respectfully,
B. W. WELLS, PH.D.

(B. W. Wells to John Berrien Lindsley, The Lindsley Papers)

TREASURY DEPARTMENT
U. S. MARINE-HOSPITAL SERVICE
OFFICE OF THE SUPERVISING SURGEON-GENERAL,

Jan. 24 1892

MY DEAR DOCTOR,

Your note of congratulation is received and greatly appreciated—.

The Med Record has never been friendly to this Service but I shall try to bring about a change—

I hope you are well & happy & making preparations for that Mexican trip which we all expect to enjoy so much—

Cordially yours
WALTER WYMAN

DR. J. BERRIEN LINDSLEY
NASHVILLE, TENN.

(Walter Wyman to John Berrien Lindsley, The Lindsley Papers)

May 10, 1926

MY DEAR MISS LOUISE:

I have just heard of the fine thing that the Woman's Association of the University of Nashville has done. They could not have done anything better than to have placed Dr. Philip Lindsley's portrait where present and coming generations may know, and knowing appreciate the work of that illustrious man, a pioneer in the educational work of the South.

Many famous men went out from Dr. Lindsley's training to help make our country what it is. I am so glad that it was the Woman's Association of the University of Nashville that made the gift instead of any other organization.

Dr. Lindsley's work for a quarter of a century succeeded by the fine work of your father was a firm foundation for the George Peabody College for Teachers. Dr. J. Berrien Lindsley and Governor Porter were wise in advocating its location upon such a foundation as the University of Nashville. I hope that the Woman's Association of the George Peabody College for Teachers will place the portrait of its benefactor beside that of Dr. Philip Lindsley.

The memory of my thirty-two years in Nashville comes back to me every day. Having chosen the life of a teacher I am sure I could not have enjoyed the work any where else as I did in Peabody College. The students were so courteous, so enthusiastic, so appreciative. Your father and mother must have believed in the saying "the first impressions are the most lasting," and acting upon it they took us, two strangers [Miss Sears and Miss Cutter], into their home and made us thrice welcome. Everything was done for our comfort and pleasure—it was truly an ideal home for us. We were introduced to the best people of the city, including Governor James D. Porter, who was my firm friend through all the years at Peabody.

Those early impressions grown quickly into realizations will always remain with me.

Remember me to the family. With ever so much love,

Ever-remembered,

JULIA A. SEARS

29 UNION ST.
FAIRHAVEN, MASS.

(Julia A. Sears to Louise Grundy Lindsley, The Lindsley Papers. Mrs. Percy Warner, Dr. Lindsley's daughter, was the first president of the Woman's Association of the University of Nashville, and Miss Sears was one of the charter members.)

October 1932

DR. W. D. HAGGARD
NASHVILLE, TENN.

DR. HAGGARD,

When you were in my father, J. Berrien Lindsley's, medical class, he predicted for you a brilliant future if you would work. His prediction has come true.

I see the American College of Surgeons has conferred its highest honor upon you and you deserve it. He would be pleased, so let me congratulate you.

With best wishes, most cordially yours,

LOUISE G. LINDSLEY

DR. W. D. HAGGARD
   NASHVILLE, TENN.

November 1, 1932

DEAR MISS LOUISE:

I appreciate your lovely note very much indeed.

Your dear father was a great inspiration to me. He chose me as his assistant in chemistry and I am frank to tell you that the honor and thrill of that was greater than the honor which you refer to at this time although I am not unmindful and unappreciative of the great courtesy and compliment my profession has bestowed upon me.

Thanking you and with kind regards, I am

Very truly yours,
W. D. HAGGARD

MISS LOUISE G. LINDSLEY
   1806 E. BELMONT CIRCLE
   NASHVILLE, TENN.

(W. D. Haggard to Louise Grundy Lindsley, The Lindsley Papers)

APPENDIX E

RESOLUTIONS AND LETTERS OF CONDOLENCE ON THE DEATH OF JOHN BERRIEN LINDSLEY

RESOLUTIONS
ON THE DEATH OF
DR. JOHN BERRIEN LINDSLEY

The history of the University of Nashville includes the names of men who have been illustrious in every walk of life. Foremost among them is the honored name of Lindsley, borne by one who was its first president, himself a prophet, his life a ministry of education; the other, his son, Dr. John Berrien Lindsley, whose sudden death has cast a gloom over this city where he was so well known and respected and with so many of whose interests he was identified. Graduated from the University of Nashville and continuing his studies in the universities of France and Germany, he was fitted and at an early age entered upon the active duties of life. To the college he loved so well, he gave his best efforts; organizing its medical department he brought it to such a degree of efficiency as placed it at the head of medical colleges in the South. Called to occupy the place of his distinguished father as chancellor of the University, ruling its destinies for fifteen years, it became one of the leading institutions in the country. The Montgomery Bell Academy was still another enterprise born and nourished under his fostering care.

Broad and catholic in his views, regarding education as the safeguard of the nation, one of the greatest problems of his life, a life filled with problems, was this, "How shall this section of country be supplied with liberally-educated, broad-minded, patriotic teachers, teachers who will train the youth to become noble men and good citizens as well as scholars?" The solution of the problem is before us to-day.

Those great enterprises, far-reaching in their influence as they have been and increasing in influence year by year, represent but a small part of the life work of this truly remarkable man. . . .

It is Resolved by the Faculties and Students of the University of Nashville,

That in the death of Dr. Lindsley we are conscious that this college has lost a noble benefactor, a wise chancellor, a true friend—one whose loyalty to its interests has never faltered, but who has been, through its years of adversity and decline as well as its years of prosperity and growth, its staunchest supporter.

That we are deeply sensible of the debt of gratitude we owe Dr. Lindsley for his untiring and successful efforts in the establishment of the Peabody Normal College in connection with the University of Nashville.

That regarding him as the highest type of a Christian gentleman, a ripe scholar, an historian, educator and philanthropist as well as our benefactor and unfailing friend, his memory should be ever cherished and held in deepest respect. On this spot where he worked so faithfully and so well he left his monument in stone, but his more enduring monument is a life consecrated to humanity. The influence of such a life will never die.

That to the family of Dr. Lindsley we extend our truest, deepest sympathy in this hour of their crushing sorrow.

A. L. PURINTON
Secretary

Adopted by the University of Nashville Senate
December 21, 1897

(The Lindsley Papers)

RESOLUTIONS
ON THE DEATH OF
DR. JOHN BERRIEN LINDSLEY

At a meeting of the Faculty of the University of Tennessee on December 10th, 1897, the following resolutions were adopted:

Resolved, That the President and Faculty of the University of Tennessee hereby give expression to their sense of their great loss by the death of Dr. J. Berrien Lindsley on Tuesday, December 7th,—the loss of one whose good-will was ever ready to take the form of active help for the University, and whose friendly counsel and words of encouragement will always have a place in our memory.

Resolved, That the Secretary record this action of the Faculty as a testimony of our respect for the memory of one who has given a full half century of continuous labor to the service of the people of his adopted State; and that the Secretary be directed to send a copy of these resolutions to the family of the deceased and to the Dean of the Medical Department of the University at Nashville.

W. W. CARSON,
Secretary

Adopted by the Faculty of the University of Tennessee
December 10, 1897

(The Lindsley Papers)

APPENDICES
RESOLUTIONS
ON THE DEATH OF
DR. JOHN BERRIEN LINDSLEY

Resolved, That the State Board of Health of Tennessee has lost a co-worker in the cause of humanity and science, whose place can be filled by but few:

Be it further resolved, That as knowledge is not hereditary neither can be purchased by money; that but few of our race will ever accumulate in the great store house of wisdom the supply that our associate had gathered together, that we might draw upon him by the simple asking.

Be it further resolved, That the people of Nashville and the State of Tennessee will miss his detective eye and his industrious hand when dread epidemic envades our borders.

Be it further resolved, That these resolutions be spread upon the minutes of this Board, and that a copy of same be sent to the family of Dr. Lindsley.

Signed;
J. A. ALBRIGHT, M.D.,
President

Adopted by the Tennessee State Board of Health
Thursday, December 9, 1897, 10 o'clock A.M.

(These resolutions were prefaced by a review of the achievements of Dr. Lindsley,
The Lindsley Papers)

RESOLUTIONS ON THE DEATH OF JOHN BERRIEN LINDSLEY BY THE BOARD OF HEALTH OF THE CITY OF MEMPHIS, TENNESSEE

MEMPHIS, TENN., Dec. 3, 1897.

At a meeting of the Board of Health, held this day, the following resolutions in regard to the death of the late Doctor J. Berrien Lindsley, Secretary and Executive Officer of the Tennessee State Board of Health, were unanimously adopted.

Resolved:—That in the death of Dr. J. Berrien Lindsley late Secretary and executive officer of the Tennessee State Board of Health, that Board has sustained the loss of a energetic, intelligent and valuable officer. The state has lost a patriotic and scholarly citizen, one who was ever faithful in the discharge of duties devolving upon him.

That this Board of Health tenders its sympathy and expresses its sense of the great loss sustained by the State Board in the death of Dr. Lindsley.

That our sympathy and sense of sorrow are hereby extended to Dr.

Lindsley's family in this sad hour of their bereavement and irreparable loss.

That a copy of these resolutions be forwarded by the Secretary of this Board to Dr. Lindsley's family, to the State Board of Health, and to the Surgeon General Wyman of the United States Marine Hospital Service.

G. B. THORNTON, M.D.
President

MARCUS HOUSE, M.D.
Secretary

(The Lindsley Papers)

IN MEDIAS RES

... When I saw him last August at the National Conference of State Boards of Health, he was hale and vigorous in appearance. As usual he bubbled over with humor, alternated with instructive hygienic "modern instances," which cropped out in conversation, or in the discussion of the important questions under debate in that Body, which he helped to found and maintain. Despite his patriarchal beard and snowy head, he did not look his years, nor seemed to me to be oppressed by them. But then a man is only as old as he feels, and Lindsley always seemed to feel young. He had grown old gracefully, as generally do the brain workers, who sternly rule their own appetites, instead of being ruled by them. He was a man after my own heart, for he was no drone, but a man "in labors more abundant" than many who have achieved distinction by skillful self-advancement, as did not he. His long, busy, and useful life was a shining exemplification of the axiom, "it is better to wear out than to rust out." But he neither wore out nor rusted out. He literally died in the harness.

(*Iowa Health Bulletin;* The Lindsley Papers)

PHILADELPHIA, Dec. 15, 1897

MRS. J. BERRIEN LINDSLEY,

DEAR MADAM,

I note with deep regret by papers kindly sent me from Nashville that my dear friend Dr. Lindsley has ceased to live. He seemed so full of life and energy when I saw him in Nashville last summer that it is difficult to realize that I shall not meet him again from year to year as in the past. He and I were kindred spirits, fond of historical research and reminiscence, and when in Montreal together took many delightful strolls through the historic portion of that city. He had done more than a long life's work, however, and it is pleasant to know that he was spared a long period of

suffering or of decadence before being called home. With the expression of my sincere sympathy both for yourself and your daughter, believe me
Yours sincerely,
BENJAMIN LEE
Executive Secretary, State Board of Health of Pennsylvania

(Benjamin Lee to Mrs. John Berrien Lindsley, The Lindsley Papers)

SPRINGFIELD, ILL.
December 14, '97

MY DEAR MADAM:

I was indeed greatly shocked this morning to learn of the death of Dr. Lindsley. It seems only yesterday since we were together in Philadelphia, talking over the outbreak of the fever in Memphis. I have the most pleasant recollections of your husband and intended to avail myself of his kind invitation to visit him in the spring.

Dr. Lindsley's death occasions a great loss to the literary and scientific world. I beg that you will accept my warmest sympathy.
Sincerely yours,
J. A. EGAN
Secretary, State Board of Health of Illinois

MRS. J. BERRIEN LINDSLEY

(J. A. Egan to Mrs. John Berrien Lindsley, The Lindsley Papers)

LANSING, Dec. 22, 1897.

MRS. J. BERRIEN LINDSLEY,
NASHVILLE, TENN.

DEAR MRS. LINDSLEY:—

Please accept my thanks for your kindness in sending me a copy of the Nashville American for Dec. 8, 1897, containing the notice of the death of Doctor Lindsley, my esteemed old friend. I wish to express to you and the other members of your family my deepest sympathies and regret that Doctor Lindsley was taken from us so suddenly.
Very respectfully,
HENRY B. BAKER
Secretary, State Board of Health of Michigan

(Henry B. Baker to Mrs. John Berrien Lindsley, The Lindsley Papers)

APPENDICES

BRATTLEBORO, VT., Dec. 14, 1897

MY DEAR MRS. LINDSLEY,

It was a great shock to me to learn of the death of your beloved husband. It is to me a personal loss, for my admiration of his personal traits of character was very great. Strong and fearless for the right, untiring and energetic in his pursuit of those things that were for the elevation of his loved profession and the amelioration of his fellow-man, he leaves an example to those who come after him worthy of emulation. To you personally and your children this bereavement must be very great, however you have much to comfort you in the memories of the past and the hope for the future. May our Father in Heaven keep you and comfort you. Accept my sincere sympathy.

Yours truly,
HENRY D. HOLTON
Treasurer, American Public Health Association

(Henry D. Holton to Mrs. Lindsley, The Lindsley Papers)

WASHINGTON, D. C., Jan. 27th, 1898

MRS. DR. J. BERRIEN LINDSLEY.

MY DEAR MADAM:— A rumor had reached me of the death of Dr. J. Berrien Lindsley, your noble husband; and in reply to my inquiry, Dr. Albright informs me that he died December 7th, last. You and all your family have my hearty sympathy in this great bereavement. This is not only a bereavement for you but for the public that he served so efficiently in so many ways. What a multitude sympathize with you! Of noble nature, cultivated by extended observation and study, controlled by a beautiful spirit, his life was consecrated to the highest aims. None knew him but to honor and love him. My association with him on questions of great interest, I shall ever recall with the greatest satisfaction. For the friends left behind, the painful separation is relieved by the assurance that it is well with him. His devout faith in a Crucified and Risen Savior and his faithful discharge of his Christian duty can leave no doubt that he was among those for whom our Lord has prepared mansions above.

Year by year, I am expected to prepare brief obituary notices of those who have died during the year distinguished in science and education and I shall be obliged if you will send me or have your son send me full notices of the Doctor's many services.

Sincerely yours,
JOHN EATON
United States Commissioner of Education, 1870-1886

(John Eaton to Mrs. John Berrien Lindsley, The Lindsley Papers)

APPENDIX F

RECORD OF READINGS 1842-1863 FOUND IN DR. LINDSLEY'S DIARY

1842

Feb.	21.	Rush: Introductory Lectures. 1 vol. 8vo.	
	26.	Liston: Practical Surgery. 1 vol. 8vo.	
	28.	Nevins: Practical Thoughts. 18mo. A.T.S.	
	"	Nelson: On Infidelity. 12mo. 352 pp. A.T.S.	
March	11.	Drake: On Medical Education. 8vo. 104 pp.	
	29.	Mussey & Lindsly: Essays on Temperance. 18mo. 195 pp.	
April	13.	Mason: On Self Knowledge. 18mo. 191 pp.	
May	19.	Bell: On the Nerves. 8vo. 165 pp.	
	25.	Miller: On Presbyterianism. 12mo. 96 pp.	
	26.	Bossuet: Histoire Universelle.	1841. July 1
	27.	Dunglison: Hygiene. 8vo. 492 pp.	May 6
		Miller: On Baptism—Subjects. 12mo. 64 pp.	
June	13.	Miller: Letters on Unitarianism. 12mo. 312 pp.	June 9
	22.	Annon: Difficulties of Arminian Methodism. 18mo. 342 pp.	
	26.	Mather: Essays To Do Good. 18mo. 108 pp. A.T.S.	
	28.	Miller: Letters To a Theological Student. 12mo. 476 pp.	
	29.	Edwards: Anatomy d'Physiology. 8vo. 312 pp.	
	"	Hallock: Memoir of Harlan Page. 18mo. 230 pp. A.T.S.	
		Arnott: Elements of Physic. 8vo.	April 11
July	3.	Foster: Essays. 18mo. 367 pp.	
	6.	James: Anxious Inquirer. 18mo. 199 pp. A.T.S.	
	"	Campbell: On Miracles. 8vo. 100 pp.	
	17.	Wilberforce: Practical View. 18mo. 375 pp. A.T.S.	April 16
Aug.	9.	Of S. Pearce. 18mo. 288 pp. A.T.S.	July 13
Sept.	1.	Eminent Men of France. 12mo. 336 pp.	May 6
	7.	Stokes: Lectures on Theory & Practice. 8vo. 500.	March 26
	"	Howell: On Communion. 12mo. 296.	July 30

	5.	Memoir of S. Kilpin. 18mo. 155. A.T.S.	Aug. 9
	14.	Channing: Reviews, discourses, etc. 8vo. 600 pp.	June 8
	26.	Abercrombie: On the Intellectual Powers. 18mo. 350 pp.	Sept. 17
		Hall: Sermons. 8vo. 225 pp.	Sept. 1
Dec.	30.	Hodge: Way of Life. 18mo. 343 pp.	Nov. 6

1843

April		Memoir of Lymon & Munson. 18mo. 196 pp.	
		Philips: Life of Milne. 18mo. 320 pp.	
May	3.	Liebig: Animal Chemistry. 12mo. 300 pp.	Apr. 1
	28.	Pike: Persuasives To Early Piety. 18mo. 438 pp. A.T.S.	
June	1.	Channing: On Slavery. 18mo. 187 pp.	
	6.	Stokes: Theory & Practice. 8vo. 500 pp. (2nd time).	May 1
	30.	Harris: Mammon. 18mo. 291 pp. A.T.S.	May 20
July	3.	Burne: On Habitual Constipation. 8vo. 164 pp.	June 23
Aug.	14.	Müller: Elements of Physiology. 8vo. 868 pp.	8
Sept.	2.	Whateley: Kingdom of Christ. 12mo. 300 pp.	Aug. 28
	14.	Henry: On Meekness. 18mo. 158 pp. A.T.S.	20
	16.	Abercrombie: On The Stomach. 8vo. 347 pp.	May 4
	22.	Memoir of H. L. Winslow. 18mo. 480. A.T.S.	Aug. 29
Oct.	8.	Dickinson: On The Five Points. P.B.	6
	9.	Clarke: On Pulmonary Consumption. 8vo. 296 pp.	Sept. 14
	16.	Nevins: Thoughts on Popery. 18mo. 216 pp. A.T.S.	22
	24.	Johnson: On Tropical Climates. 2 vols. 12mo. 730 pp.	Aug. 17
	27.	Magendie: Sur le Sang. 18mo. 382 pp.	March 27
	28.	Holland: Medical Notes. 8vo. 383 pp.	Aug. 27
Nov.	7.	Hodge: On Romans. 12mo. 352 pp.	July 2
Dec.	6.	Pereira: On Food & Diet. 8vo. 325 pp.	Oct. 28
	17.	Memoir of J. B. Taylor. 18mo. 441 pp. A.T.S.	Sept. 22
	24.	Todd: The Sabbath School Teacher. 12mo. 432 pp.	Dec. 11
	27.	Whateley: Logic. 12mo. 350 pp.	Nov. 20
		Horne: Introduction. Evidences. Analysis. Antiquities. 640 pp.	June 21
		The Bible.	

APPENDICES

Miscellaneous: Religious &c 1240 pp. 8vo.
Medical 800 pp. 8vo.

1844

Jan.	12.	Baxter: Saint's Rest. 18mo. 445 pp. A.T.S.	Oct. 24
	31.	*New Testament* (aloud).	1
Feb.	7.	Gallaudet: Child's Book on Repentance. 18mo. 147 pp. A.T.S.	June 20
March	5.	Edwards: On the Affections. 18mo. 276 pp. A.T.S.	13
	7.	Pascal: Les Provinciales. 18mo. 530 pp.	July 13
April	6.	Butler: Analogy &c. 8vo. 222 pp.	March 15
	9.	Bogue: Evidences. 18mo. 252. A.T.S.	27
	12.	Sibb: *The Cn's Portion* (aloud). 24mo. 112 pp. P.B.	April 2
	13.	Alexander: Evidences. P.B.	9
	18.	Watts: On Prayer. 12mo. 235 pp.	March 10
		Gibbon's 15th chapter. Hume on Miracles. 62 & 28 pp. 8vo.	
June	6.	*Gallaudet's* Youth's Nat. Theo. 231 pp. 18mo. A.T.S.	March 20
July	17.	Benson: Sermons (20) 434, 8vo.	July 7
	20.	Young: Night Thoughts. *2nd Time*.	July 4
	27.	Greek Testament.	August 1
	30.	Jay: Memoirs of Winter. 12mo. 371 pp.	June 9
	30.	Cecil: Remains. 12mo. 236 pp.	June 3
Aug.	12.	Mosheim: Murdock's Translation. 8vo. 3 vols. 1600 pp.	May 1
	20.	Bunyan: Grace Abounding. 8vo. 90 pp.	Aug. 13
	23.	Bossuet: Oraisons Funèbres. 18mo. 295 pp.	
	24.	Miller: On the Christian Ministry. 12mo. 388 pp. P.B.	Aug. 16
	29.	The Cn. Preacher. 12mo. 263 pp.	April 20
	29.	Miller: On Ruling Elders. 18mo. 324 pp. P.B.	Aug. 26
	25.	Chalmers: Sermons. 8vo. 382 pp.	May 18
Sept.	3.	Memoirs of Legh Richmond. 12mo. 362 pp.	Aug. 21
	11.	Bunyan: Holy War. 8vo. 210 pp.	Sept. 4
	7.	Macaulay: Miscellanies. 12mo. 940 pp.	June 6
	23.	Hodge: Way of Life. 18mo. 343 pp. *2nd time*.	July 10
	23.	Pollok: Course of Time.	
	28.	Wharey: Sketches of C. History. 18mo. 320 pp. P.B.	Sept. 26
Oct.	14.	Baxter: Reformed Pastor. 15mo. 223 pp. P.B.	Sept. 20

APPENDICES

	15.	Milton: Paradise Lost (aloud).	May 14
	22.	Dick: Theology. 8vo. 2 vols. 1089 pp.	Jan. 1
	25.	Campbell & Rice: Debate on Baptism &c. 8vo. 912 pp.	April 27
	27.	Baird: Religion in America. 8vo. 332 pp.	Aug. 14
	30.	Nevins: Antiquities—Jewish—18mo. 540 pp.	June 29
	31.	Milton: Poems.	May 14
Nov.	9.	A. Clarke: Autobiography. 8vo. pp. 172.	Sept. 29
Dec.	3.	Doddridge: Rise & Progress. 18mo. 445 pp. A.T.S.	Oct. 23
	12.	Hodge: On Romans. 12mo. 352 pp. 2"*Time.*	Nov. 8
	16.	Milman: History of the Jews. 18mo. 916 pp.	Nov. 14
	19.	Thomson: Seasons (aloud).	Nov. 12
	19.	Gibbon: Memoirs of himself. 8vo. 83 pp.	Dec. 16
	26.	Montesquieu: Grandeur et Decadence des Romains. 18mo. 227 pp.	Oct. 8
	26.	Cowper: Poems.	Nov. 11
	29.	Apocrypha. Bible. 1 hour daily. 51 Tracts = 450 pp. 12mo. (mostly when travelling). 52 Sermons = 475 pp. 8vo. Miscellaneous. 1625 pp. 8vo.	Dec. 19
April	20.	Liston: Elements of surgery. 8vo. 636 pp.	Jan. 1
July	12.	Wood: Syllabus	July 4
	25.	Pritchard: On Insanity. 8vo. 339 pp.	March 2
Dec.	2.	Eberle: Notes. 12mo. 248 pp.	May 14
	30.	Bell: On the Teeth. 8vo. 330 pp. Anatomy 100. 8vo. Practice 600. 8vo.	Dec. 26

1845

Feb.	21.	Woods: Old & New Theology. 12mo. 243 pp.	Feb. 19
March	24.	Miller: Clerical Manners. 12mo. 476 pp. *2nd Time.*	Feb. 18
April	13.	Young: Night Thoughts (aloud).	Jan. 1
	4.	Whateley: Rhetoric. 12mo. 444 pp.	March 22
July	29.	Pollok: Course of Time (aloud).	March 13
Aug.	9.	Campbell: On Pulpit Eloquence. 8vo. 100 pp.	Aug. 4
	27.	Sprague: On Revivals. 8vo. 285 pp.	Aug. 19
Sept.	3.	Journal of an African Cruiser. 12mo. 180 pp.	Aug. 28
	13.	Cowper: Task. (aloud).	Aug. 20
	25.	Greek Testament.	Aug. 1:44
Oct.	6.	Memoir of St. Martyn. 18mo. 442 pp. A.T.S.	March

APPENDICES

	7.	Dwight: Theology. 4 vols. 8vo. 2225.	Jan. 1
	11.	Wiseman: On Science & Revealed Religion. 8vo. 400 pp.	Sept. 11
	12.	Jones: On the Rel. Ins. of the Negroes. 12mo. 277 pp.	Oct. 8
	15.	Guizot: Histoire Generale de la Civilisation. 12mo. 430 pp.	Oct. 5
	18.	Edwards: On the Will. 8vo. 85 pp.	Sept. 20
	18.	Hodge: History of the Pres. C. 8vo. 760 pp.	Sept. 17
Nov.	12.	Wayland: Moral Science. 8vo. 448 pp.	Oct. 24
	13.	Davies: Sermons (26). 12mo. 497 pp.	Aug. 10
	15.	Pond: Young Pastor's Guide. 12mo. 377 pp.	Oct. 4
Dec.	4.	Milner: Ec. His. 13 centuries. 3 vols. 8vo.	Jan. 1
	2.	Guizot: Civilisation En France. 18mo. Tome Prem. et Sec. 798 pp.	Oct. 21
	10.	Bancroft: United States. vol. 2nd. 8vo. 463 pp.	Dec. 3
	24.	Thomson: Sermons (24). 12mo. 447 pp.	Nov. 30
	1.	Barrow: On the Pope's Supremacy. 8vo. 430 pp.	Nov. 15
	26.	Macaulay: Essays vol. 3rd, 4th, 5th. 8vo.	Sept. 10
	31.	Krummacher: Elijah the Tishbite. 18mo. 4—pp. *A.T.S.*	Oct. 9
	31.	Shakespeare: King John to Troilus & Cressida.	Aug. 21
		Calvin: On Acts in Latin. 8vo.	June 1, 43
		Sermons 56 = 480 pp. 8vo.	
		Miscellaneous. 1300 pp. 8vo.	
		Theological. 600 pp. 8vo.	

1846

Jan.	8.	Longfellow: Poems.	Jan. 7
	18.	Edwards: On Original Sin. 8vo. 90 pp.	Dec. 18
March	6.	Guizot: Histoire de la Civilisation en France. 750 pp. 18mo.	Jan. 1
April	2.	Bancroft: United States. vol. 2nd & 3rd. 936 pp. 8vo.	Jan. 1
May	4.	Helfenstein: Self deception. 72 pp. 15mo. *A.T.S.*	May 3
	8.	Sparks: Washington. 536 pp. 8vo.	April 3
	27.	Wiseman: Lectures on &c of the Catholic church. 480 pp. 12mo.	Feb. 15
June	9.	Edwards: Sabbath Manual. 131. 18mo. *A.T.S.*	May 27
June	12.	Hawes: Normand Smith. 72. 18m. *A.T.S.*	June 9
	26.	T. Scott: Synod of Dort. 143 pp. 12mo.	24
May	27.	Melville: Sermons. 567 pp. 8vo.	Feb. 13

APPENDICES

July	7.	Neander: His. of the Cn. religion during the first 3 cen. 466 pp. 8vo.	March 24
	18.	Sydney Smith: Critical Essays. 115 pp. 8vo.	July 3
	25.	R. G. Armstrong: Hannah Hobbie. 255 pp. 18mo. *A.T.S.*	June 25
		Greek Testament.	Oct. 1
Sept.	7.	Southey: Minor poems. 288. 24mo. (H.)	Aug. 27
	15.	Mrs. Grant: Memoirs of an American Lady. 295. 18mo.	Aug. 1
	17.	C. S. De Beausobre: Discours etc. Nouveau Test. 846 pp. fol. 2 vols.	Jan. 1
Oct.	14.	Baxter: Saints Rest. 540 pp. 8vo. *A.T.S. 3rd time*.	July 1
	23.	Campbell: Philosophy of Rhetoric. 475. 8vo.	July 10
	25.	Anecdotes for the family. 408 pp. 18mo. *A.T.S.*	June
	26.	Pond: Young Pastor's Guide. 377 pp. 12mo. *2nd time*.	Sept. 10
Nov.	4.	Campbell: Poems. 216. 18mo. (H.)	Jan. 9
	4.	Fuller: Backslider. 122 pp. 18mo. (H.) *A.T.S.*	Nov. 4
	6.	Scott: Last Minstrel. 144 pp. 18mo. (H.)	6
	10.	Calvin: On Galatians. 8vo. 83 pp. Latin	Aug.
	12.	Guizot: Civilisation en France. 350 pp. 18mo.	Oct. 1
	20.	Scott: Lady of the Lake. 210 pp. 18mo. (H.)	Nov. 20
	30.	Prescott: Ferdinand & Isabella. 3 vols. 1540 pp. 8vo.	Aug. 6
Dec.	3.	Fisk: Calvinistic Controversy. 273 pp. 18mo. *M.B.C.*	Nov. 26
	3.	Stokes: Theory & Practice. 500 pp. 8vo. *3rd time*.	March 5
	14.	Beecher: Views in Theology. 240 pp. 12mo.	Nov. 19
	14.	Abbott: N. Dickerman. 140 pp. 18mo. *A.T.S.*	Nov. 19
	15.	Spenser. Faerie Queen. Canto I. 210 pp. 18mo. (H.)	Dec. 11
	23.	E. Robinson: Theo. Edu. in Germany. 135 pp. 8vo.	Dec. 19
	30.	Hall: Scripture History. 516 pp. A.T.S.	May 4
	30.	J. M. Mason: Church of God. 259 pp. 8vo.	July 8
		On Episcopacy 261 pp.	
		26 Sermons. 795 pp.	
		Miscellaneous. 500 pp.	
		Miscellaneous. 1475 pp. 8vo. Drawing 90 hours.	

APPENDICES

Theological 450 pp. 8vo. Latin 60 hours.
Bible 1 hour daily.

27. Butler: Hudibras.   Aug.

1847

Jan.	19.	Perry: German University Education. 12mo. 175 pp.	Jan.
Feb.	4.	Anatomy, one subject.	Jan. 27
March	3.	Browne: Religio Medici. 12mo. 148 pp.	Jan. 20
	8.	Lyell: Principles of Geology. 8vo. 2 vols. 1010 pp.	Jan. 21
	8.	Buckland: Bridgewater Treatise. 8vo. 443 pp. (2nd Time).	Jan. 12
	8.	Whewell: Indications of the Creator. 12mo. 171 pp.	Feb. 2
April	10.	Lyell: Elements of Geology. 12mo. 2 vols. 874 pp.	Jan. 1
	21.	Walker: Statesman's Manual (Historical part). 8vo. 400 pp.	April 3
May	15.	Keble: Christian Year. 16mo. 336 pp.	Jan.
	29.	Carpenter: Human Physiology. 8vo. 604 pp.	Mar. 13
June	24.	Jones: On the Rel. Ins. of the Negroes. 12mo. 277 pp. (2nd time).	
May	1.	Fletcher. Checks to Antinomianism. Vol. 1st. 8vo. 593 pp.	Jan. 1
Aug.	18.	Mrs. Lee: Memoir of Cuvier. 18mo. 180 pp.	July
	22.	Edwards: On Revivals. 12mo. 446. *A.T.S.*	July 27
	27.	Cuvier: Eloges. 1st and 2nd vol. 8vo. 914 pp.	Jan.
	27.	Hitchcock: Elements of Geology. 12mo. 338.	July 19
Sept.	6.	Fuller: The Backslider. 18mo. 122 pp. *A.T.S.* (2nd time).	
	23.	Davidson: History of the Pres. Ch. in Kentucky. 8vo. 371 pp.	Aug. 15
	27.	Herschel: Discourse on the Study of Nat. Phi. 12mo. 270. (2nd time).	Sept. 2
Oct.	12.	Babbage: Ninth Bridgewater Treatise. 8vo. 250 pp.	Sept. 28
	14.	Latimer: Sermons. 12mo. 288. (2nd Time).	Oct. 11
	19.	Shells & Their Inmates. 18mo. 214 pp.	Aug.
Nov.	4.	Jer. Taylor: Selections. 12mo. 288 pp. (2nd Time).	Sept. 28
	18.	Mrs. Somerville: Connection of the Physical Sciences. 18mo. 390 pp.	,,
	18.	Fuller: Holy State. 12mo. 293. (2nd Time).	Sept. 26

216   APPENDICES

	16.	R. Hall: Sermons. 8vo. 300 pp. (2nd Time).	Sept. 26
	23.	Derham: Physico-Theology. 12mo. 451 pp.	" "
Nov.		Butler: Hudibras. (2nd Time).	Aug.
	30.	Foote: Sketches of North Carolina. 8vo. 557 pp.	Oct. 19
Dec.	6.	Headley: Washington & his Generals. 2 vols. 12mo. 720 pp.	" "
	12.	Wesley: Sermons. 2 vols. 8vo. 1084 pp.	Jan. 17
	11.	Life of Dr. Belknap. 18mo. 250.	Dec. 5
	28.	Irving: Knickerbocker. 2 vols. 12mo. 510 pp. (2nd Time).	28
		Liebig: Familiar Letters on Chemistry. 18mo. 180 pp. (2 Times).	
		Ruschenberger: 12mo. Botany 160. Mammalogy 150. Geology 235. Conchology 114. (2 Times).	
		Fownes: Chemistry. Nana: Mineralogy.	
		Blainville: Malacologie.	
		Michaux: American Sylva.	
		Greek Testament.	
		Miscellaneous. 550 pp. 8vo.	
		Drawing 30 hours.	
		Latin 52 hours.	
		Bible 1 hour daily.	

1848

Jan.	5.	Virgil: Aeneid (Latin).	Nov. 5, 46
	"	Barber: Historical Collections. New York, 8vo. 608 pp.	Dec. 23
	12.	Selden: Table Talk. 18mo. 257 pp. (2nd Time).	Jan. 1
	15.	Hitchcock: Geology. 12mo. 338 pp. (2nd time).	Jan. 1
	25.	Lyell: Travels in North America. 12mo. 471 pp.	Jan. 14
Feb.	13.	Cavier: Eloges. 3rd Vol. 8vo. 505 pp.	Jan. 14
	24.	Headley: Napoleon & his Marshals. 2 vols. 12mo. 647 pp.	Feb. 10
	25.	Liebig: Agricultural Chemistry. 12mo. 420 pp.	Feb. 17
	26.	Lawrence: Lectures on Man. 12mo. 392 pp.	Jan. 17
March	3.	Liebig: Chemical Letters. 18mo. 180 pp. (3rd time).	Jan. 1
	8.	Hetherington: History of the Church of Scotland. 8vo. 480 pp.	Jan. 1
	13.	Fownes: Actonian Essay. 12mo. 158 pp.	March 6
	13.	Sullivan: Familiar Letters on Public Characters. 8vo. 417 pp.	" 3

APPENDICES

	27.	W. Scott: History of Scotland. 2 vols. 12mo. 730 pp.	Feb. 29
	"	Prescott: Conquest of Peru. 2 vols. 8vo. 1000 pp.	March 17
	26.	Wickliff: Writings. *P.B.* 12mo. 240 pp.	Feb.
April	19.	Draper: Chemistry. 12mo. 400 pp.	March
May	9.	Memoir of Melancthon. *P.B.* 18mo. 198 pp.	May 9
	14.	Memoir of Howard. *P.B.* 18mo. 159 pp.	" 13
Sept.	1.	Moffat: Southern Africa. 12mo. 405 pp.	Aug.
	1.	Mrs. Tonna: Personal Recollections. 12mo. 303 pp.	"
	2.	Mrs. Sigourney: Poems. 12mo. 305.	Aug.
	4.	J. V. Brown: Memoir of Dr. Finley. 8vo. 186 pp.	Sept. 3
	"	A. A. Bonar: Memoir of McCheyne. 8vo. 148 pp.	Aug.
	5.	A. Cunningham: Life & Land of Burns. 12mo. 363 pp.	Aug.
	13.	Thomas Hood: Prose & Verse. 12mo. 400 pp.	Sept.
	14.	Old Humphrey: Walks in London. 18mo. 286 pp.	"
Nov.	1.	Salazar: Sinner's Conversion. 118mo. 225 pp. (Catholic).	Oct.
	7.	G. Kennedy: Father Clement. 12mo. 155 pp.	Nov. 6
Dec.	5.	Hume: England. Vol. 1st, 8vo. 526 pp.	April 5
	5.	Mrs. Tuthill: History of Architecture. 8vo. 426 pp.	"
	6.	Wilberforce: Practical view. 18mo. 325 pp. (2nd time).	June
	17.	Halyburton: Great Concern. *P.B.* 18mo. 176 pp.	April
		Eakin: British Poets. 8vo. 807 pp.	May, 1847
		Burns: Poems.	Aug.
		German: Ollendorf's Grammar. Steiner's reader. 12mo. 104 pp.	Nov.
		Murray: Encyclopaedia of Geography. 8vo. large 800 pp.	March 17
		Miscellaneous 8vo. 1600 pp.	
		Prescott: Miscellanies, Biographical & critical. 8vo. 638 pp.	
		Choules & Smith: History of Missions. 4vo. 622 pp.	Sept. 1847

APPENDICES
1849

Jan.	4.	J. B. Fraser: Persia. 12mo. 472 pp.	Jan. 1
	6.	Scott: Waverley. 2 vols. 12mo. 520 pp. (2nd time).	Dec.
	20.	Fownes: Prize Essay. 12mo. 158 pp. (2nd Time).	Jan. 16
	26.	Agassiz: Lectures on the Animal Kingdom. 8vo. 58 pp.	Jan. 22
	28.	Scott: Antiquary. 2 Vols. 12mo. 448 pp.	Jan. 8
Feb.	3.	Scott: Guy Mannering. 2 vols. 12mo. 490 pp.	Jan. 29
	12.	Prescott: Conquest of Mexico. 3 vols. 8vo. 1393 pp.	Jan. 6
	18.	W. I. Kip: Early Jesuit Missions in N. A. 12mo. 321.	Jan. 7
	23.	Follen: Deutsches Lesebuch. 12mo. 222 pp.	Jan. 7
March	3.	Miss Austen: Mansfield Park. 12mo. 424 pp.	Feb. 6
	9.	Murray: Encyclopaedia of Geography. 8vo. 400 pp.	Jan. 1
	31.	Chambers: Elements of Zoology. 12mo. 530 pp.	Jan.
	31.	Squier & Davis: Ancient Monuments of the Mississippi Valley. 4vo. 306 pp.	March
Apr.	1.	Bp. Wilson: Introduction to Butler's Analogy. 18mo. 235 pp.	Feb. 26
	12.	Hume: History of England. Vols. 2, 3, & 4. 8vo. 1600 pp.	Jan. 1
May	2.	Carlyle: Cromwell's Letters & Speeches. 12mo. 2 vols. 972 pp.	Apr.
	7.	Scott: Rob Roy. 2 vols. 12mo. 550 pp.	Apr. 15
	20.	Pascal: Pensees. 12mo. 474 pp.	Jan. 28
	"	Shakespeare: 13 plays. 3 vols. 8vo. 1500 pp.	Jan. 7
	30.	Hemans: Poems. Vols. 4 & 5. 12mo. 680 pp.	Jan.
June	11.	Edgeworth: Belinda. 12mo. 463 pp.	
	14.	Mrs. Marsh: Mordaunt Hall.	
	14.	Alison: H. of Europe, first 15 chapters. 8vo. 320 pp.	May, 48
	28.	Dickens: Nicholas Nickleby. 8vo. 404 pp. (equal to 3 Waverleys in size)	May 21
	29.	Lucretius: De Rerum Natura 1' & 2nd, & 3'd books. 3388 lines.	March 1
July	1.	Wordsworth: Poems. 8vo. 185 pp.	Jan. 10
	14.	Greek Testament.	Jan. 18, 48
	19.	Corneille: Chefs D'Oeuvre (12 dramas). 4 vols. 18mo. 1150 pp.	Feb. 12

APPENDICES

		Chalmers: Lectures on Romans (43). 8vo. 230 pp.	Apr. 1
	29.	Memoir of Trosse. 18mo. 121 pp. *P.B.*	
Aug.	1.	Memoir of Andrew Melville. 18mo. 104 pp. *P.B.*	
	3.	Memoir of W. T. Buchanan. 18mo. 116 pp. *P.B.*	
	5.	Memoir of Col. Blackader. 18mo. 118 pp. P.B.	July 13
Sept:	1.	Scott: Tales of My Landlord. 1st Series. Black Dwarf. Old Mortality. 2 vols. 12mo. 655 pp.	
	2.	D'Aubigne: History of the Reformation. 4 vols. 12mo. 1180 pp.	Jan. 7
	4.	Humboldt: Cosmos. 2 vols. 12mo. 742 pp.	July 9
	7.	Macaulay: History of England. Vol. 1 and 2. 8vo. 395 pp.	July 5
	22.	Bird: Natural Philosophy. 12mo. 394 pp.	Aug. 27
	27.	Byron: Childe Harold. 12mo. 235 pp.	Sept. 13
Oct.	1.	Scott: Tales of My Landlord. 2nd s. Heart of Mid-Lothian. 2 vols. 12mo. 650 pp.	Aug. 30
	21.	Gieseler: Ecclesiastical History: Vol. 1. 8vo. 396 pp.	
	23.	Gibbon: Rome. Vol. 1, 2, & 3. 8vo. 1428 pp.	Sept. 12
	23.	Dante: By Cary. Hell. 12mo. 215 pp.	" 28
		Carpenter: Physiology. (2nd time). 8vo. 604 pp.	" 24
		Irving: Sketch Book. 2 vols. 12mo. 500 pp.	Jan.
		Kent: Commentaries. Vol. 1. 8vo. 548 pp.	Oct. 12
		Butler: Analogy. 8vo. 207 pp. (2nd Time).	" 7
		De Sacy: LaBible. (Gen. 10p.) 8vo. 600	Nov. 1848
Dec.		Ansted: Ancient World. 12mo. 378.	Dec.
		Sedgwick: Discourse on the Studies of the University. 157 pp. 12mo.	"
		Scientific miscellaneous. 600 pp. 8vo.	
		Eclectic Magazine. 450.	
		Spanish 55 hours. German a good deal of time.	

1850

April	3.	Scott: Kenilworth. 18mo. 396 pp.	Feb. 4
	26.	Warren: Ten Thousand a Year. 8vo. 432 pp.	Apr. 18
	27.	Bulwer: Last days of Pompeii. 8vo. 140 pp.	" 26
	28.	Mrs. Ellis: Hearts & Homes. 8vo. 714 pp.	Nov. 7
		Lyell: Second Visit to the United States. 12mo. 273 pp.	Jan.

APPENDICES

July	1.	Jones: Life of Ashbel Green. 8vo. 628 pp.	May 5
	2.	Agassiz & Gould: Principles of Zoology. 12mo. 216 pp.	June 30
	13.	Burke: Celebrated Trials Connected with the Aristocracy in Private Life. 8vo. 505 pp.	July 8
	23.	Celebrated Trials. 8vo. 596 pp.	July 13
Aug.	1.	Carpenter: On Alcoholic Liquors. 12mo. 209 pp.	June
Oct.		Stanley: Memoir of Arnold.	June
Nov.		Greek Testament.	
	28.	Abbott: Young Christian. 12mo. 395 pp.	Nov. 3
Dec.		Tupper: Proverbial Philosophy. 12mo. 282 pp.	May
		Miscellaneous = 600. 8vo.	

1851

Feb.		Dew: On Slavery. 8vo. 60 pp.	
April	27.	Gems of Sacred Poetry. 18mo. 304.	Jan.
		Hymns. Presbyterian Board.	
Sept.	7.	Carlyle: French Revolution. 12mo. 1125 pp.	Nov. 5
	14.	McCosh: Divine Government. 8vo. 511.	June
	18.	Milton: Poems.	Nov. 49
		Shakspeare: Lear, Hamlet, Romeo & Juliet, Othello.	

1852

Jan.		Bayard Taylor: Views afoot.
March		Cloy: Speeches. 2 vols. 8vo.
”		Galignani: Paris Guide.
”		London Guide.
”		Tourist in Scotland.
”		Tourist in Ireland.
Aug.	2.	Williams: Our Iron Roads.
Sept.	1.	Beecher: Uncle Tom's Cabin. 12mo. 329 pp.
Sept.	1.	Cooper: Wing & Wing.
”		Cooper: Pilot.
”		Sedgwick: Hope Leslie. 296 pp. 12mo.
”		James: Gentleman of the Old School. 12mo. 383.
		Life of Curran. 2 vols. 12mo. 849 pp.
		Collegians: Gerold Griffin. 12mo. 458 pp.
		Hugo: Notre Dame. 12mo. 400 pp.
		Johnston: Notes on North America. 2 vols. 12mo. 925 pp.

APPENDICES

Johnston: Lectures on Practical Agriculture. 12mo. 220 pp.
        Miscellaneous. 850 pp. 8vo.

1853

May		Lyell: Second Visit to U. S. Vol. 2.	
Oct.	27.	Tappan: A Step from the New World to the Old. 2 vols. 12mo.	
Nov.	27.	Arnold: Arnold's Lectures. 608 pp.	
		Com. on Modern History. 12mo. 421. 1852.	

1854

Jan.	7.	Memoirs of Chalmers. 4 vols. 18mo. 2185 pp.	Nov. 52
May	28.	Keble: Lyra Innocentium. 18mo. 353 pp.	Nov. 53
July	28.	Lectures on the Results of the Exhibition. 18mo. 463 pp.	
Aug.	13.	Whitehead: Life of Wesley. 8vo. 230 pp.	1852
Dec.	3.	Alexander: Practical Sermons. 8vo. 571 pp.	Dec. 53
	26.	Thackeray: Men's Wives. 18mo. 274 pp.	
	27.	Cooper: The Spy. 12mo. 463 pp.	

1855

April		Caldwell: Autobiography. 8vo. 459 pp.	
		Memoirs of Burder.	
June		Bage:	Dec. 53
July	1.	Life of A. Alexander. 8vo. 700 pp.	June 23
	"	Silliman: Visit to Europe. 12mo. 2 vols. 886 pp.	April 54
	29.	Wayland: Memoir of Judson. 2 vols. 12mo. 1066 pp.	April 23
Aug.	10.	Faraday: Non-metallic Elements. 18mo. 293 pp.	1859
		Youmans: Chemical Atlas. 4vo. 106.	July 54
		Mrs. Pyatt: Bell Smith Abroad. 12mo. 336 pp.	July
	19.	McCormick: Camp before Sevastopol. 12mo. 212 pp.	July 15
	27.	Irving: Columbus. 3 vols. 12mo. 1420 pp.	July
Sept.	5.	Liebig: Letters on Chemistry. 12mo. 536 pp.	1853
Oct.	13.	Pouchet: Histoire des Sciences Naturelles au Moyen Age. 8vo. 656 pp.	Aug.
	14.	Neander: History of the Church. Vol. 1st. 8vo. 740 pp.	Aug. 52
Nov.	25.	Neander: History of the Church. Vol. 2nd. 8vo. 768.	Oct. 21
Dec.	27.	Thackeray: Pendennis. 8vo. 774 pp.	Dec. 12

APPENDICES

| | 26. | Kingsley: Hypatia. 12mo. 481 pp. | Dec. 18 |

Miscellaneous: 1800 pp. 8vo. Medical. Theological. Literary. Educational.

1856

June 1. Maretzek: Crotchets & Quavers. 12mo. 346. Steamboat.

    22. Neaneler: History of the Church. Vols. 3rd & 4th. 8vo. 1273 pp.   Dec. 2, 55

July 20. Macaulay: History of England. Vols. III, IV. 8vo. 1435 pp.   June 24

Aug.   Goethe: Werter. 18mo. 190 pp.

Patmore: The Angel in the House.

Sept.   Peirce: History of Harvard University. 8vo. 316 pp.

Lady C. Bury: Diary of George IV. 12mo. 560 pp.   cars

Doesticks. 12mo. 330 pp.   "

Jones: Wild Western Scenes. 12mo. 263 pp.   "

Haklander: Clara, or Slave Life in Europe. 12mo. 533 pp.   "

Dec.   Cockburn: Memorials of his Time. 12mo. 442 pp.   Sept.

Guyot: Earth & Man. 12mo. 334 pp.   July

Taylor: Medical Jurisprudence. 8vo. 610 pp.   March 5

Miscellaneous: 8vo. 370.

1857

Jan. 16. Kane: Arctic Explorations. 2 vols. 8vo. 929 pp.   Dec. 25

Aug. 16. Eliot: History of the United States. 12mo. 483.   Aug. 2

    23. Huber: The English Universities. 8vo. 2 vols. 1190 pp.   1856

Sept. 12. Alexander: Moral Science. 12mo. 272 pp.   June 28

Nov. 8. Greek Testament.

Dec. 7. Gibbon: Rome. Vol. IV. 8vo. 44500.   July 5

    9. Sehman: Chemical Physiology. 8vo. 331 pp.   Nov. 57

    31. Webster: Works. Vols. 1-5. 8vo. 2886 pp.   Nov.

Miscellaneous: Education. 8vo. 585 pp.

Political Economy. 8vo. 495 pp.

Chemistry. 8vo. 300 pp.

1858

Jan. 29. Humboldt: Cosmos. Vols. 3, 4. 18mo. 601 pp.   Jan. 20

    30. Johnston: Chemistry of Common Life. 2 vols. 12mo. 610 pp.   Jan. 1

APPENDICES

Feb.	21.	Gibbon: Rome. Vols. V, VI. 8vo.	Jan. 3
	22.	Garland: Life of Randolph. 2 vols. 12mo. 686.	Jan. 1
	23.	Webster: Works. Vol. VI. 8vo. 601 pp.	Feb. 10
March	5.	Sheppard: Constitutional Text Book. 12mo. 293 pp.	" 2
	9.	Madison: The M. Papers. 3 vols. 8vo. 1624 pp.	Feb. 26
	15.	Weber: Outlines of Universal History. 8vo. 530 pp.	" 6
April	6.	Story: Commentaries on the Constitution. 3 vols. 8vo. 1809 pp.	March
May	27.	Halsey: Literary Attractions of the Bible. 12mo. 441.	Apr. 3
July	5.	Thackeray: Newcomes. 412. 8vo.	Aug. 8, 1856
Aug.	15.	Conybeare & Howson: Life of St. Paul. 2 vols. 1015. 8vo.	March 14
"	31.	Richardson: Sir C. Grandison. 8vo. 791.	Dec. 1855
Sept.	5.	Isaac Taylor: The World of Mind. 378. 12mo.	April
	16.	School Days at Rugby. 18mo.	Sept. 14
Nov.	6.	Hildreth: History of the United States. Vol. 1 & 2. 8vo. 1199.	March 15
	7.	Barran: De l'Education dans la Famille &c. 8vo. 269.	Aug. 4
Dec.	2.	Cuvier: Histoire des Sciences Naturelles. Vol. 1. 432 pp. 8vo.	Sept.
		Miscellaneous: Education. 8vo. 1510 pp.	
		Scientific. 8vo. 180 pp.	
		Religious. 8vo. 300 pp.	
		Political. 232 pp.	
		Italian. 16 hours.	

1859

Feb.	13.	Henry: Life of Calvin. 2 vols. 8vo. 973 pp.	Jan. 2
March	8.	Fielding: Tom Jones. 355. 8vo.	Feb. 28
	19.	Galloway: First Step in Chemistry. 18mo. 303.	1855
April	2.	Hildreth: History of the United States. Vol. 3rd. 8vo. 592.	March 21, 1859
	13.	Lehmann: Chemical Physiology. Vol. 1. 8vo. 648.	Jan. 1858
May	13.	D. N. Lord: Geognosy or &c. 12mo. 412.	Apr. 16
	23.	Carlyle: Past & Present Chartism. 12mo. 386.	Apr. 18
	27.	De la Beche: Geological Observer. 8vo. 695.	March 11, 1856
June	5.	Loyard: Nineveh & its Remains. 2 vols. 8vo. 699.	Feb. 20

APPENDICES

12.	Wayland: Intellectual Philosophy. 12mo. 426.	Feb. 28
Sept.21,24.	Scott: The Monastery. 8vo. 154.	
24,26.	The Abbott. 8vo. 162.	
27,29.	Quentin Durward. 8vo. 172.	
Oct. 6, 10.	Freytag: Debit & Credit. 12mo. 564.	
Nov. 6.	Jahn: History of the Hebrew Commonwealth. 8vo. 429.	June 13
6.	Newman: The Soul. 12mo. 162.	" 13
6.	Minturn: New York to Delhi. 12mo. 488.	Apr. 26
24.	Parisian Sights. 18mo. 245.	Nov.
25.	Humboldt: Cosmos. Vol. V. 18mo. 500.	Nov. 7
26.	Whitney: Metallic Wealth of the United States. 8vo. 510.	May 28
Dec. 22.	Cuvier: His. des Scien. Natu. Vols. 2, 3. 894.	Oct. 18
24.	Kugler: The Schools of painting in Italy. 2 vols. 12mo. 539.	Nov. 13
25.	McCrie: Reformation in Italy. 12mo. 412.	Dec. 18
"	J. Foster: Christian Morals. 18mo. 252.	Jan. 2
26.	Voltaire: Philosophical Dictionary. Vol. 1st. 18mo. 436.	Dec. 4
31.	Shakespeare: Valpy's. Vols. 1, 2, 3. 18mo. 912.	" 8
	Miscellaneous: Educational. Religious. 8vo. 552.	
	Scientific. 8vo. 572.	
	Geographical. 8vo. 600.	
	Italian 55 hours.	

1860

Feb. 18.	Cuvier: His. des Sc. Naturelles. Vols. 4, 5. 8vo. 881.	Jan. 1
19.	Prescott: His. of Ferdinand & Isabella. 3 vols. 8vo. 1951.	Jan. 8
8.	Third Nat. Quarantine Conven. 8vo. 728.	Feb. 14
April 8.	Tocqueville: Regne de Louis XV. 2 vols. 8vo. 954.	" 26
25.	Tocqueville: Regne de Louis XVI. 8vo. 403.	Apr. 8
May 5.	Tocqueville: Démocratie en Amérique. 12mo. 988.	March 26
May 14.	Tocqueville: L. Ancien Régime. 8vo. 479.	Apr. 25
19.	Voltaire: Phil. Dictionary. Vol. 2. 18mo. 408.	Jan. 2
19.	Arago: Notices Biographiques. 3 vols. 8vo. 1969.	March 8
27.	Almae Matres. 18mo. 308.	May 20

APPENDICES   225

Aug.		Bronte: Jane Eyre.	Aug. 3
Sept.	24.	Michelet: L. Amour. 12mo. 464.	Jan.
Oct.	14.	J. H. Newman: Lectures on University Subjects. 12mo. 387.	May 27
Oct.	22.	1374 Hymns. Plymouth Collection. 8vo. 507 pp.	July 1859
	24.	Hugh Miller: Old Red Sandstone. 18mo. 320.	Oct. 19
Nov.	9.	Beccaria: Dei Delitti edelle Penne. 12mo. 83.	March 26
	17.	Coleridge: Aids to Reflection &c. 12mo. 484.	Oct. 8
	30.	Mackenzie: Tyll Owl Glass. 12mo. 255.	Oct. 22
Dec.	10.	R.H.S.: Life & Travels of Humboldt. 12mo. 483.	Dec. 1
	12.	Hamilton: Memoires de Grammont. 18mo. 335.	Nov.
	18.	Hugh Miller: Testimony of the Rocks. 12mo. 500.	Dec. 12
	24.	Coleridge: The French. 12mo. 551.	Nov. 30
	25.	Hugh Miller: Cruise of the Betsey-Rambles &c. 12mo. 524.	Dec. 18
		Regnault: Elements of Chemistry. 2 vols. 8vo. 1475 pp.	1852
		Graham: Elements of Inorganic Chemistry. 8vo. 852.	1851
		Shakespeare: Valpy's. Vols. 4, 5, 6, 7, 8, 9, 10, 12. 18mo. pp. 3531.	Jan. 1
		Miscellaneous: Scientific. 8vo. pp. 423.	
		Politico-Historical. 8vo. 1790 pp.	
		Literary. 8vo. 345 pp.	
		Italian—65 hours.	

1861

Jan.	17.	Lyell: Principles of Geology. 8vo. pp. 835.	Dec. 25
	25.	Forbes: Tour of Mont Blanc. 18mo. 320 pp.	Jan. 18
Feb.	12.	Tyndall: Glaciers of the Alps. 12mo. 446 pp.	Jan. 26
Feb.	12.	Shakespeare: Vols. 13, 14. 18mo. pp. 631.	Jan. 1
	22.	Lyell: Elementary Geology. 8vo. 655.	" 18
Mar.	8.	H. Miller: Schools & Schoolmasters. 12mo. 551.	Feb. 25
	7.	Fievee: Lá Dot de Suzette.	Mar. 8
	31.	Robertson: Charles V. (Prescott.) 8vo. 3 vols. pp. 1787.	Mar. 16
Apr.	7.	Motley: His. of the United Netherlands. 2 vols. 8vo. pp. 1095.	Apr. 1
June	7.	Motley: Rise of the Dutch Republic. 8vo. 3 vols. pp. 1824.	May 16

APPENDICES

Aug.	8.	James: Old Dominion. 8vo. 152 pp.	Aug. 7
Aug.	17.	Burney: Evelina. 12mo. 456 pp.	Aug. 10
Sept.	12.	Kaemtz: Meteorology. 12mo. 480.	Feb. 23
	13.	Bronte: Shirley. 12mo. 572 pp.	Aug. 29
Oct.	1.	Tennyson: Poems. 18mo. 524 pp.	June 26
	24.	Anderson: Course of Creation. 12mo. 376 pp.	Sept. 17
Nov.	13.	Byron: Works. 18mo. 8 vols. 2956 pp.	Apr. 11
Dec.	3.	Lockhart: Life of Scott. 10 vols. 18mo. 3919 pp.	Oct. 4
	16.	Burns: Poems. Vol. 1st. 18mo. 342 pp.	Dec. 2
	20.	Comings: Physiology. 12mo. 324 pp.	Sept.
	26.	Stephen: Section His. of France. 8vo. 710 pp.	Dec. 5
	27.	Somerville: Physical Geography. 12mo. 485 pp.	Oct. 25
	28.	Scott: Life of Swift. 18mo. 505 pp.	Dec. 19
		Miscellaneous: Scientific & Literary. 8vo. 600. Politics. History. 8vo. 540.	

1862

Jan.	11.	Scott: Life of Dryden. 18mo. 453 pp.	Dec. 30
	24.	Scott: Biographical Memoirs. 2 vols. 18mo. 888 pp.	Jan. 11
Feb.	6.	Scott: Paul's Letters. 18mo. pp 354.	Feb. 2
	"	Burns: Poems. Vols. 2, 3. 18mo. 647 pp.	Jan. 1
	9.	Scott: Chivalry. Romance. Drama. 18mo. pp. 395.	" 23
Apr.	7.	H. Miller: First Impressions of England. 18mo. 430 pp.	Nov. 17
	24.	Bancroft: His. of the U. States. Vols. 4, 5, 6, 7, 8. pp. 2369. 8vo.	Mar. 30
May	1.	De Foe: Use and Abuse &c. 8vo. pp. 104.	Apr. 27
	3.	Hazlitt: Life of De Foe. 8vo. pp. 158.	Apr. 30
	5.	De Foe: The Plague Year. 8vo. pp. 86.	Apr. 27
	6.	Michelet: La Femme. 48mo. pp. 468.	Jan. 12
	16.	De Foe: Moll Flanders. 8vo. 112 pp.	May 6
	20.	Sterne: Tristram Shandy. 8vo. 215 pp.	Apr. 16
June	9.	De Foe: Memoirs of a Cavalier. 8vo. pp. 96.	May 20
	10.	De Foe: Roxana. 8vo. pp. 130.	June 6
	10.	Clarendon: His. of the Rebellion. 7 vols. 8vo. 4329 pp.	Apr. 24
	20.	De Foe: Col. Jack. 8vo. pp. 103.	June 11
	30.	Rogers: Table Talk. 12mo. pp. 346.	20
July	9.	Hawthorne: Marble Faun. 2 vols. 12mo. 571 pp.	21
	20.	De Foe: Capt. Carleton. 8vo. 71 pp.	July 14
Aug.	23.	De Musset: Confession &c. 18mo. pp. 353.	Nov. 1861

	28.	De Foe: Robinson Crusoe. First part. 8vo. pp. 114.	July 19
	29.	Sterne: Sentimental Journey. 12mo. pp. 112.	Aug. 9
Sept.	4.	Phin: Grape Culture. 12mo. 375 pp.	Aug. 26
	12.	Trollope: North American. 2 vols. 12mo. 669 pp.	Aug. 27
Sept.	23.	Haliburton: Sam Slick. 2 vols. 12mo. 371 pp.	Sept. 61
	29.	Napier: Peninsular War. 4 vols. 8vo. 1933 pp.	July 22
	30.	De Foe: Jure Divino &c. 8vo. pp. 117.	June 16
	30.	Beranger: Oeuvres. Vol. 1st. 8vo. pp. 411.	Nov. 1861
		Lane: Arabian Nights. 8vo. pp. 864.	May 1854
Oct.	24.	Hamilton, A.: Works. 7 vols. 8vo. 4361 pp.	Oct. 1
Nov.	14.	Swift: Poems. 2 vols. 8vo. 1026 pp.	Sept. 27
	23.	Montesquieu: Esprit des Lois. 3 vols. 8vo. 1146 pp.	Oct. 29
	25.	Arbuthnot: John Bull. 8vo. 174 pp.	19
	28.	Swift: The Drapier's Letters. 8vo. 275 pp.	Nov. 25
Dec.	4.	Jefferson: Works. 7 vols. 8vo. 4189 pp.	Oct. 24
	22.	Adams, C. F.: Life of John Adams. 8vo. pp. 684.	Dec. 15
	25.	Gasparin: Les Etats-Unis en 1861. 18mo. pp. 414.	Dec. 21
	31.	Swift: Tale of a Tub &c. &c. 8vo. pp. 508.	Nov. 30
		Miscellaneous: Historical. Literary. 8vo. 810 pp.	

1863

Jan.	18.	Gasparin: L'Amérique devant L'Europe. 8vo. 556 pp.	Jan.
	28.	Burke: Works. Vols. 1, 2, 3, 4. 8vo. 2155 pp.	Jan. 3
Mar.	2.	Brougham: Statesmen. 2 vols. 12mo. pp. 647.	" 21
	7.	Abbot: Napoleon. 2 vols. 8vo. pp. 1277.	" 7
	25.	Alison: Europe to 1815. 8vo. 4 vols. 2426 pp.	" 29
	"	Adams, J.: Diary & Autobiography. 2 vols. 8vo. 941 pp.	Mar. 9
		Greek Testament	
Apr.	4.	Swift: Gulliver. 8vo. pp. 382.	Mar. 9
June	10.	Dickens: Pickwick. 2 vols. 12mo. 882 pp.	Aug. 60
	14.	Unitarian: Hymns. 18mo. 466 pp.	Aug. 62
	17.	Bede: Verdant Green. 12mo. 338 pp.	June 10
July	3.	Miss Murray: United States, Canada &c. 12mo. 402 pp.	" 18
	18.	Cochrane: Siberia. 8vo. 415 pp.	July 3
	28.	Smollett: Roderick Random. 8vo. 194 pp.	" 25

Aug.	1.	Radcliffe: Udolpho. 8vo. 307 pp.	" 30
	8.	Gaskell: Life of C. Bronte. 2 vols. 12mo. 554 pp.	Aug. 5
	16.	Croly: Salathiel. 2 vols. 12mo. 464 pp.	" 10
	17.	Adams, J.: Correspondence. 4 vols. 8vo. 2426 pp.	March 26
	22.	Clarke: Travels. Russia. 8vo. 446 pp.	Aug. 17

BIBLIOGRAPHY

A. PRIMARY SOURCES

I. DIARIES, MANUSCRIPTS, MILITARY ANNALS, MINUTES

Lindsley, John Berrien. MS Diary. In the possession of Miss Louise G. Lindsley of Nashville, Tennessee.
——— MS Journal. In the possession of Miss Louise G. Lindsley.
——— *Confederate Military Annals of Tennessee.* Nashville: J. M. Lindsley and Co., 1886.
——— "Thoughts and Hints," MS, The Lindsley Papers.
Lindsley Papers, in the possession of Miss Louise G. Lindsley. (These papers consist of diaries, journals, private correspondence, unpublished manuscripts, addresses, and newspaper and magazine articles.)
Lindsley, Philip. MS Diary. In the possession of Miss Louise G. Lindsley.
Minutes of the General Assembly of the Cumberland Presbyterian Church, 1874-1897, archives, Montreat, N. C.
Minutes of the General Assembly of the Presbyterian Church, U.S.A., 1846-1869, archives, Montreat, N. C.
Minutes of the Nashville City Board of Education, July 6, 1866.
Minutes of the Nashville City Board of Health, 1876.
Minutes of the Tennessee Historical Society, 1849.
Minutes of the Tennessee State Board of Education, 1875, 1879.
Minutes of the Tennessee State Board of Health, 1897.
Minutes of the University of Nashville, 1844, 1845, 1850, 1851, 1855, 1867, 1869, vault of Peabody College Library.
Minutes of the University of Nashville and Western Military Institute, 1861, vault of Peabody College Library.

II. ADDRESSES, BULLETINS, PROCEEDINGS, ETC.

Bowling, W. K. *Historical Address to the Graduating Class of 1868, University of Nashville.*
Bulletin of the Tennessee State Board of Health, Vol. II, No. 1 (July 31, 1886), No. 7 (January 31, 1887), No. 10 (April 30, 1887); Vol. IV, No. 2 (September 15, 1888), No. 3 (October 15, 1888), No. 6 (January 15, 1889), No. 9 (April 15, 1889), No. 12 (July 12, 1889).
Bulletin of the University of Nashville, 1839.
Catalogue of the Officers and Graduates of the University of Nashville, 1850.
Catalogue of the University of Nashville, 1861, 1870.
First Report of the Tennessee State Board of Health, 1880.

BIBLIOGRAPHY

Laws of the University of Nashville. Nashville: McKennie Whig and Steam Press, 1840.

Lindsley, John Berrien. *A Brochure on the Life and Character of Robert M. Porter,* vault of Peabody College Library.

——— *Address Before the Alumni Society of the University of Nashville,* 1854, vault of Peabody College Library.

——— "Address to the People of Tennessee on Popular Education," in Eaton, John, Jr., *First Report of the Superintendent of Public Instruction of the State of Tennessee,* 1869.

——— "The Present Condition and Prospects of the University," *Bulletin of the University of Nashville,* May 21, 1870.

——— *On Prison Discipline and Penal Legislation;* reprinted from the *Theological Medium,* July, 1874.

Lindsley, Philip. *Address on Public Schools;* reprinted from the *American Presbyterian* of 1835. The Lindsley Papers.

——— *Lecture on Popular Education,* 1837. The Lindsley Papers.

Proceedings of the First Meeting of the American Association for the Advancement of Science, September, 1848.

Proceedings of the Peabody Education Fund, 1888.

Report to the Nashville Board of Trade, October 28, 1871.

Report of the Tennessee State Board of Health, 1890-97.

Rules and Regulations of the Western Military Institute, 1854.

Second Report of the Nashville Board of Health, 1877.

Second Report of the Tennessee State Board of Health, 1884.

Sixth Annual Announcement of the Medical Department of the University of Tennessee, September 6, 1880.

Tennessee House Journal, 1849-50.

Tennessee Senate Journal, 1847-48; 1857-58.

Third Report of the Nashville Board of Health, 1879.

III. Newspapers

Daily American (Nashville), June 8, 1876; January 19, 1877; April 4, 1877; August 29, 1877; December 19, 1877; March 14, 1878; August 30, 1878; January 16, 1879; January 24, 1879; March 12, 1879; April 11, 1879; October 13, 1879; November 18, 1879; January 3, 1883; April 3, 1884; May 30, 1884; July 2, 1884; August 16, 1888; August 17, 1888; January 10, 1889.

Daily Union, December 16, 1864.

Nashville American, December 8, 1897.

Nashville Daily Press and Times, October 13, 1865.

Nashville Dispatch, July 23, 1862; October 8, 1862; September 20, 1863; September 18, 1866; September 23, 1866.

Nashville Gazette, January 26, 1860.

Nashville True Whig, June 14, 1849.

BIBLIOGRAPHY

Nashville Union and American, April 12, 1867; May 27, 1874; May 26, 1875.

B. SECONDARY SOURCES

I. General

Centennial History of the Tennessee Medical Association, ed. Hamer, Philip M. Nashville: Tennessee Medical Association, 1830.
Clayton, W. W. *History of Davidson County, Tennessee.* Philadelphia: J. W. Lewis and Co., 1880.
Drake, Samuel Francis. *The Life of General Robert Hatton.* Lebanon, Tennessee, 1867.
Eaton, John, Jr. *First Report of the Superintendent of Public Instruction of the State of Tennessee,* October 7, 1869.
Freeman, Douglas Southall. *R. E. Lee: A Biography.* 4 vols. New York and London: Charles Scribner's Sons, 1934-35.
Hale, Will T. and Merritt, Dixon L. *A History of Tennessee and Tennesseans.* 8 vols. New York: The Lewis Publishing Co., 1913.
Halsey, Le Roy J. *The Works of Philip Lindsley.* 3 vols. Philadelphia: J. B. Lippincott and Co., 1866.
Hanaford, Phebe A. *The Life of George Peabody.* Boston: B. B. Russell, 1870.
Holmes, Fred L. *George Washington Travelled This Way.* Boston: L. C. Page and Co., 1935.
Merriam, L. S. *Higher Education in Tennessee.* Washington: Bureau of Education Monograph, 1893.
Moore, John Trotwood. *Tennessee, the Volunteer State.* Chicago: S. J. Clarke Publishing Co., 1923.
Parton, James. *Life of Andrew Jackson.* 3 vols. New York: Mason Brothers, 1861.
Warr, Otis S. "The History of Medical Education in Tennessee," *Centennial History of the Tennessee State Medical Association,* 1830-1930.
White, Robert H. *Development of the Tennessee Educational Organization.* Contribution to Education, No. 62, George Peabody College for Teachers, 1929.

II. Magazines

Altstetter, Mabel, and Watson, Gladys. "Western Military Institute, 1847-61," *Filson Club History Quarterly,* Vol. X (1936).
Briggs, Charles S. Editorial, *Nashville Journal of Medicine and Surgery,* Vol. LXXXIII (January, 1898).
Crabb, A. L. "Henry Middleton Rutledge," *Peabody Reflector and Alumni News,* Vol. VI (1933).
——— "Lines to an Alumnus," *Peabody Reflector and Alumni News,* Vol. VII (1934).

——— "Lines to a Teacher," *Peabody Reflector and Alumni News,* Vol. VI (1933).

Dewitt, Dr. M. B. *Biographical Sketch of Dr. John Berrien Lindsley;* reprint from *Physicians and Surgeons of America,* 1894, vault of Peabody College Library.

Garrett, W. R. "The Genesis of Peabody College for Teachers," *American Historical Magazine,* Vol. VIII (1903).

Little, Charles E. "John Berrien Lindsley, A.B., M.D., D.D.," *American Historical Magazine,* Vol. III (1898).

Nashville Journal of Medicine and Surgery, Vol. LXX (1898).

Southern Practitioner, Vol. XIX (1897), Vol. XX (1898).

Windrow, J. E. "Collins D. Elliott and the Nashville Female Academy," *Tennessee Historical Magazine,* Vol. III (1935), No. 2.

INDEX

ADAMS, C. B., letter to J. B. Lindsley, 15-16
Agassiz, L., letter to J. B. Lindsley, 196
A. & I. Normal School for Negroes, 104
Alabama, University of, Philip Lindsley offered presidency of, 23
Albright, J. A., 205
Alembert, Jean le Rond d', 90
Altstetter, Mabel, and Watson, Gladys, cited, 50
Amblyopia, poor lighting cause of, 136
American Academy of Medicine, Dr. Lindsley a member of, 19
American army of the Revolution, Philip Lindsley's account of, 4
American Association for the Advancement of Science, 19
American Historical Association, 20
American Medical Association, 19, 38, 114, 157
American Public Health Association, 20, 143
American Red Cross, 78
Anthony, John G., letter to J. B. Lindsley, 193-95
Arabian Nights' Entertainments, 6
Arago, 180
Aristotle, 91
Ascham, Roger, 90
Asiatic cholera. *See* Cholera, Asiatic
Askew, Colonel Frank, 81
Asthenopia, poor lighting cause of, 136
Atchison, Dr. T. A., and medical society, 142; resigns from health board, 145
Atlanta, Ga., 79

BACON, Francis, 90
Baker, Henry B., letter of condolence, 207
Barlow, Captain J. W., 80, 81
Barrow, General Francis C., 187
Bartholomew's Hospital, in London, Dr. Lindsley's visit to, 40
Bass, John M., and Nashville city government, 115-16
Bass, Dr. Wm. James, and Dr. Lindsley, 74
Battle of Monmouth, John Berrien II wounded at, 2

Battle of Nashville, 80-81, 83
Battle of Raymond, Miss., 78
Bell, Andrew, 90
Bell, Montgomery, donation to University of Nashville by, 53
Benson, Judge Egbert, Nathaniel Lawrence studies law with, 3
Berrien, Elizabeth, 3
Berrien, Judge John, 1-2
Berrien, John II, 2
Berrien, John McPherson, 2
Berrien family, 1-2
Biot, 180
Blackie, Dr. George F., and health report, 118, 125
Blainville, Dr., 180
Book of Revelation, 6
Bossuet, 90
Bourgery, 180
Bowlecock, Dr., and Dr. Lindsley, 68
Bowen, Professor George T., 25
Bowling, Dr. W. K., 33, 35, 43, 79; editor of *Nashville Journal of Medicine and Surgery*, 159; editorial by, 41; *Historical Address to the Graduating Class of 1868*, etc., 23, 28, 32, 33; on consumption, 148; president of American Medical Association, 157
Bowling Green troops, in Nashville, 65
Briggs, Charles S., cited, 159
Briggs, Dr. Wm. T., 36, 79, 157
Bright, John, 97
Bright, John M., 17
Brougham, Henry P., 90
Brownlow, Governor, of Tennessee, 89
Brown's Creek, 126, 127
Buchanan, Dr. A. H., 33, 35, 43
Buell, General Don Carlos, 71, 73
Buist, Dr., on death registrations, 117
Bulwer-Lytton, Edward, 97
Bunyan, John, 6
Burial permits, 149, 150
Burr, Aaron, 3
Burritt College, 28

CALDWELL, S. Y., 98
Capitol, improvements in, 153

[233]

INDEX

Carbondale, normal school at, 100
Carew, 90
Carson, W. W., resolution on death of J. B. Lindsley, 204
Catholic Cemetery, Nashville, 126
Cattles, Captain, in Nashville, 65
Centennial History of the Tennessee Medical Association, quoted, 19, 142, 143, 147, 148, 158
Chadwick, Edwin, *An Inquiry into the Sanitary Conditions of the Laboring Population of Great Britain,* influence of on Dr. Lindsley, 114
Charles II, 5
Childers, Dr., Dr. Lindsley's reference to, 69
Cholera, Asiatic, 19, 29, 113-16 *passim,* 121, 150, 154-56 *passim*
Cincinnati, Ohio, district physicians in, 123
City Cemetery, Nashville, 126; recommendations concerning, 133
Civil War, 60 ff., 158-59, 160
Clark, Dr. W. M., 143, 145
Clarke, 90
Clarksville, Tenn., wounded soldiers of, 70-71
Clayton, W. W., cited, 80, 87, 115, 118, 127
Clinton College, 28
College of Louisiana, Philip Lindsley offered presidency of, 24
College of New Jersey, occurrence of name of Condict in catalogue of, 3
Coltart, James M., tutor, 26
Comenius, 90
Commission on claims, 78
Condict, Colonel Ebenezer, 3
Condict, Dr. John, 4
Condict, Phebe, 3-4
Condict, Silas, 3-4
Condict family, 1, 3-4
Condillac, 90
Condolence, letters of. *See* Letters of condolence
Confederate Military Annals of Tennessee, Dr. Lindsley editor of, 20, 82
Cordier, 180
County health boards, 149
Cowley, 90
Crabb, A. L., 27; cited, 12, 93
Craighead, Thomas, 23
Crockett, Samuel, 31
Cromwell party, Dr. Lindsley's ancestors and, 1

Cross, Professor Nathaniel, 9, 25, 27
Cumberland College, early presidents of, 23
Cumberland River, 126
Cumberland University, 22-23, 29

DAILY AMERICAN (Nashville), quoted, 116 n, 119 n, 120-21 n, 124 n, 129 n, 134 n, 142-46 n *passim*
Daily Union (Nashville), quoted, 80-81 n
D'Alembert, Jean le Rond. *See* Alembert, Jean le Rond d'
Davidson Academy, becomes Cumberland University, 22-23
Davis, Jefferson, letter to J. B. Lindsley, 198
Deaths, registration of. *See* Vital statistics
Degerando, 90
De Witt, M. B., *Biographical Sketch of Dr. John Berrien Lindsley,* 5, 8, 13-14, 19-21, 113
Dickens, Charles, 97
Dickinson, Dr. William G., 8, 10
Dickinson College, Philip Lindsley offered presidency of, 24
Diseases caused by undue dampness, 122
Donaldson, Dr. M., report of Dr. Lindsley to, 148
Douglass, Alfred William, tutor, 26
Drake, Samuel F., cited, 106
Driver, Captain, 77
Dryden, Mr., preaching at home of, 16
Dufief, 90
Dumas, at French Institute, 179-80
Dumarsais, 90

*E*ARL of Shaftesbury, 97
Eaton, John, *First Report of the Superintendent of Public Instruction, etc.,* 87, 96; letter of condolence, 208
Eaton, Professor Joseph A., 42
École de Médecine, Dr. Lindsley at, 40
Edgar, Dr. J. T., 13, 41
Edgeworth, 90
Education, public. *See* Public education
Edwards, 181
Egan, J. A., letter of condolence, 207
Elliott, Dr. C. D., 63, 66
Ely, George, tutor, 26
Eve, Dr. Paul F., 33, 36, 41, 43, 157, 160
Ewing, E. H., 108

*F*ABER, Jules, 90
Farquharson, 181, 190

INDEX

Federal Burying Ground, 126
Fellenberg, Philipp E. von, 90
Fenelon, 90
Fichte, 91
Fisk University, Dr. Lindsley on, 104
Fite, Dr. C. C., 145
Floriens, 180
Floyd, General John B., 67
Ford, Albert C., on Nashville climate, 118
Forrest, General Nathan Bedford, 73
Fort Donelson, 65-66, 68, 72, 158
Fort Negley, 159
Fort Warren, Randall McGavock, imprisoned at, 72
Foster, R. C. III, as member of reorganization committee, 47
Foster, W. F., "The Progress of the Waterworks," 125
Foster, Wilbur S., on topography of Nashville, 117
Foster's Hill, 81
Franklin College, 28
Fredonia, N. Y., State Normal School, Fifth Annual Report, 1874, 101
Freeman, Douglas Southall, cited, 61

GARBAGE, disposal of, 126, 131
Garden of Pentremites. *See* Pentremites, Garden of
Garrett, W. R., cited, 84-85, 105-6
Gattinger, August, as contributor to health report, 125
Gay, Dr., 71
George Peabody College for Teachers, 83, 95, 104-12 *passim*
Gibson, Dr., of Medical College of Virginia, 41
Gibson, Dr. William, 11; address to students, 9-10
Giles College, 28
Gist, General, 4
Gower, 181
Grand Opera House, Nashville, 132
Griffith, J. O., 98-99
Grundy, Felix, 21
Guerin, Jules, 180
Guizot, 182
Gun factories, in Civil War, 64

HADDEN, Dr. T. A., resignation of, 145
Haggard, Dr. W. D., letter to Louise G. Lindsley, 201-2

Hale, Will T., and Merritt, Dixon L., cited, 65
Halsey, Le Roy J., 9, 26, 54; cited, 5, 24, 26, 30, 93
Hamilton, James, 25, 27
Hamilton, William, 90
Hanaford, Phebe A., cited, 22
Harnisch, 90
Harris, W. T., quoted by Dr. Lindsley, 139
Hatton, Robert, Dr. Lindsley on, 106-7; effort to found normal school, 103, 106
Hawkins, Captain, troops of, 69
Health, public. *See* Public health
Hegel, 91
"Hillman," Steamer, 71
Hinds School, 135-36
Holmes, Fred L., cited, 2
Holton, Henry D., letter of condolence, 208
Hood, General John B., 81
Horner, Dr., 10
Hosack, Dr., cited, 4
Houston, Major, Dr. Lindsley at home of, 16
Houston, Russell, 43, 78
Howard School, 135
Hoyt, Dr., 80
Hume, Dr. Alfred, and his school for boys, 93
Hume, Jesse, 182
Hume, William, reputation of, 23
Hume School, 135

INQUIRY into the Sanitary Condition of the Laboring Population of Great Britain, Dr. Lindsley influenced by, 114
Irving College, 28

JACKSON, Andrew, 2, 198; Dr. Lindsley at deathbed of, 12-13; trustee of Davidson Academy, 22
Jackson College, 28
Jacotot, Jean, J., 90
Jardin des Plantes, 180
Jardine, 90
Jennings, Dr. Thomas R., 36, 43
Johnes, Rev. Timothy, 4
Johnson, Dr., 71
Johnson, Colonel Bushrod R., 50, 52, 54, 57-58, 60, 95
Johnson, Cave, letters received from, 71
Johnson, Colonel Thornton F., as founder of Western Military Institute, 49

Johnston, General Albert S., 66-67, 70, 83
Jones, Dr. Joseph, 115
Jones, Dr. William P., 85, 103, 107, 112

KANT, 91
Kent, Mrs. Robert C., 21
Knight, the publisher, 97

LANCASTER, Joseph, 90
Lane, Dr., 187
Lapsley, Joseph W., tutor, 26
Lapsley, Dr. R. L., 13
Lasteyrie, 90
Laurent, 181
La Vergne, Tennessee, 75
Lawrence, Margaret, 3
Lawrence, Nathaniel, 2-3
Lawrence College, 28
Lawrences, the, 1, 2-3
Lea, Isaac, letter to J. B. Lindsley, 197
Lea, J. B., 153
Lea, J. M., 47
Lee, Benjamin, letter of condolence, 206-7
Lee, Robert E., letter to his son Custis, 60-61; surrender of, 81
Letters of condolence on death of J. B. Lindsley, 206-8
Lick Branch, 126, 153
Lincoln, Abraham, effect of assassination of, on Nashville, 81; election of, 62
Lindsay, Captain A. J., and Dr. Lindsley, 65
Lindsley, Adrian Van Sinderen, 5-6, 10, 31, 68
Lindsley, Annie Dickinson, 21
Lindsley, Eliza Berrien, 6
Lindsley, Colonel Francis, 5
Lindsley, Harvey, tutor, 25
Lindsley, Isaac, 3-4
Lindsley, Jacob McGavock, 21
Lindsley, John Berrien, account of "a little missionary and geological excursion," 16-18; *Address Before the Alumni Society of the University of Nashville, 1854,* 47-49; *Address on Popular Education Before the Tennessee State Teachers' Association,* 85, 98; quoted, 89; "Address to the People of Tennessee on Popular Education," quoted, 96; *African Colonization and Christian Missions,* 21; appreciations from Stearns and Payne, 112; associate editor, *National Encyclopedia of American Biography,* 21; at bedside at Jackson's death, 12-13; bond posted by Lindsley, 142-43; *Brochure on the Life of Robert M. Porter,* 21; candidate for ministry, 12; childhood, 6-8; children of, 21; chronological outline of life, 164-66; committees appointed for public health work, 146-47; contributions and public service, 21; correspondence, with William Walker, 178-92; correspondence, miscellaneous, 193-202; courses of study, 14; death, 157; diary, MS, 8, 15, 20, 33, 40, 64-65, 67-69, 71, 73-74, 77-81, 104; edited *Confederate Military Annals of Tennessee,* 20, 82; edited Nashville Board of Health reports, 1877-79, 21; edited *Second Quadrennial Report of the Tennessee State Board of Health,* 21; edited *State Board of Health Bulletin,* 21; editorial on secession, 63-64; education, 7-12; elected chancellor University of Nashville, 19, 43; elected city health officer, 19, 116; elected dean of medical school, 35; elected member of societies, 19-20; elected president of State Board of Health, 116, 145; elected Prof. of sanitary science and state preventive medicine, 19; elected secretary and executive officer of Tenn. State Board of Health, 19, 142; elected secretary State Board of Education, 108; extracts from diary, 36-37, 50; first appearance of name as minister, 13; geological tour with Dr. Troost, 14-15; *History of the Law School of Cumberland University at Lebanon,* 21; honorary D. D. degree conferred by Princeton, 20; in charge of Confederate hospitals in Nashville, 20; journal, 91; licensed to preach, 12; marriage, 21; material for encyclopedia of Tennessee history, 20, 82; medical club organized, 33; M.D. degree, 8; member City Board of Education, 20, 88; memorial meeting of Nashville Academy of Medicine, 162-63; "Memorial to the State Legislature," 96-97; miscellaneous correspondence, 193-202; Nashville Board of Health, *Second Report,* 1877, 117-24 *passim; On Medical Colleges,* 21; *On Municipal University,* 94-95; *On Prison Discipline and Penal Legislation,* 21, 123, quoted, 83, 97 n-98 n; on Robert Hatton, 106-7; ordained as evangelist, 13; organized medical department of University of Nashville, 18; organized Montgomery Bell Academy,

INDEX

19; *Our Ruin: Its Cause and Cure,* 21; philosophy of education, 89-90, 91, 92-93; plan for "Medical Annals of Tennessee," 161-62; plan for reorganizing University of Nashville, 44-46; plan resulting in establishment of Peabody Normal College, 85; "Present Conditions and Prospects of the University," 54-58; president of Tennessee State Teachers' Association, 20; recommendations to Nashville Board of Health, 120-23; record of readings found in diaries, 209-28; remarks on slavery, 48-49; report to Nashville Board of Trade, 1871, 93, 95; resolutions on death of, 162-63, 203-6; resolutions presented to Tennessee State Board of Education, 110-11; review of development of normal school movement, 99-103; superintendent of Nashville public schools, 20-84; "Thoughts and Hints," 6, 61-64, 72, 171-77; Troost geological collection committed to care of, 15; work for public education, 84-112; work for public health education, 113-63; writings, bibliography of, 167-71

Lindsley, Louise Grundy, 8, 21; letter to, 201-2

Lindsley, Margaret Lawrence (Mrs. Percy Warner), 21

Lindsley, Margaret Lawrence (Mrs. Samuel Crockett), 6, 31

Lindsley, Mary McGavock, 21

Lindsley, Nathaniel Lawrence, 6, 9, 26, 31; Robert Hatton a student of, 106

Lindsley Papers, The, 2-3, 9, 16, 37, 51, 70, 75-77, 84-85, 161-62, 171, 178, 181-208

Lindsley, Philip, 3, 5, 89, 90; accepted chair in New Albany Seminary, 29; *Address on Public Schools,* 91-92; address to citizens of Nashville, 1837, 26; appraisals of merit of, 29-30; diary, MS, 1-5, 7; inaugural address, 24; *Lecture on Popular Education,* 90-91; letter to daughter, 195; letters to J. B. Lindsley, 37, 51; plan for medical school, 50; president of Cumberland College, 23

Lindsley, Randall McGavock, 21

"Lindsley Hall," 160

Lindsleys, the, 5-6, 77

Linsley, President, of Marietta College, 51

Lisfrane, 180

Little, Chas. E., cited, 11-12, 14, 86

Litton, Abram, 9, 25

Litton, Edgar, 181
Litton, Wm., 181
Locke, John, 90
London, England, William Walker on, 185-86
Lookout Mountain, Dr. Lindsley at meeting on, 96
Louis Philippe, 182
Louisiana, College of, Philip Lindsley offered presidency of, 24
Love's Hill, 81
Lowe, 90
Lupton, Nathaniel T., 118, 125, 135

McALLISTER, 120
McCulloch, Dr. J. W., 42
McEwen, John A., tutor, 26
McGavock, Grundy, 78
McGavock, Jacob, 41, 70, 81, 198
McGavock, Randall, 72, 198; death of, 78
McGavock, Sarah, 21, 41
McGavocks, the, 77
McGehee, Professor George W., 25
McKendree Methodist Church, 66
McMasters, Dr., chaplain, 74
Madden, T. L., 114, 125
Mann, Horace, 98
Martin, George, tutor, 25
Mascagni, 178
Masonic Theatre, Nashville, 132
Masonic University, 29
Massachusetts, 96, 97, 98, 116
Massachusetts State Reports, 98
Massey, George P., tutor, 26
Maury, Dr. R. B., 142
Maxwell House, catastrophe at, 78
"Medical Annals of Tennessee," 161-62
Medical Club, letter to trustees of University of Nashville, 34-35; organized, 33
Medical College of Virginia, Dr. Lindsley's visit to, 41
Medical schools, southern, 158
Meigs, R. J., 33
Merriam, L. S., *Higher Education in Tennessee,* quoted, 27, 30, 95, 105, 159
Merritt, Dixon L. See Hale, Will T.
Michigan, 96
Michigan, University of, 53, 79
Middleton, Arthur, 8
Military Academy at Lexington, Va., 51
Miller, Dr. Samuel, Dr. Lindsley baptized by, 6
Milne, 180
Milnes, Monckton, 97

Milton, John, 90
Minutes of General Assembly of Cumberland Presbyterian Church, 1874-97, Dr. Lindsley listed as minister in, 13, 14
Minutes of General Assembly of Presbyterian Church, U.S.A., 1846-69, Dr. Lindsley's name first appears as that of minister in, 13
Minutes of the Nashville City Board of Education, 1866, quoted, 84
Minutes of the Tennessee State Board of Education, 1879, quoted, 111
Minutes of the University of Nashville, 1845, 13; quoted, 1844, 32; 1850, 35; 1855, 43; 1869, 95
Montaigne, 90
Montgomery Bell Academy, 19, 59, 86
Moore, John Trotwood, *Tennessee, the Volunteer State*, 15
Moore, Surgeon General, Dr. Lindsley's interview with, 64
Morehead, Colonel, 70
Morgan, L. D., 43
Mortality statistics. *See* Vital statistics
Morton, Dr. J. W., 116
Mt. Olivet Cemetery, 126
Municipal university, Dr. Lindsley's plans for, 94-95
Myopia, poor lighting cause of, 136

NASHVILLE, University of, 5, 8, 83, 150; closed temporarily, 29; enrollment during Philip Lindsley's administration, 26-27; enrollment in medical school, 39; faculty during Philip Lindsley's administration, 25; founded by legislature, 25; literary department, 42-45; medical faculty's recommendation of J. B. Lindsley for chancellor, 42-43; requirements for graduation from medical school, 38-39; resolution to establish medical school, 35; table showing students during each session, 1824-49, 27; Western Military Institute, articles of union with, 51-52
Nashville, vital statistics of. *See* Vital statistics
Nashville Academy of Medicine, resolutions of, 162
Nashville American, article on Dr. Lindsley in, 140
Nashville Board of Health, 134-35; *Second Report*, 1877, 21, 118, 119, 122-24; *Third Report*, 1879, 21, 120, 128, 130-31, 134, 135, 141

Nashville Daily Press and Times, quoted, 88
Nashville Dispatch, quoted, 73 n, 74 n-75 n, 78 n-79 n, 113 n
Nashville Female Academy, 63, 66
Nashville Gazette, on Dr. Lindsley's trip to Ohio, 61
Nashville Journal of Medicine and Surgery, 35, 41, 159
Nashville Republican, lecture of Philip Lindsley in, 90-91
Nashville True Whig, on cholera, 113
Nashville Union and American, quoted, 93, 99
National Conference of Charities and Corrections, Dr. Lindsley a member of, 20
National Encyclopedia of American Biography, Dr. Lindsley associate editor of, 21
National Prison Association, Dr. Lindsley a member of, 20
Nelaton, Dr. Lindsley hears, 40
Nelson (Dr. Lindsley's servant), 68
Nelson, Anson, on annals of Nashville, 118
Nelson's brigade, in Nashville, 71
New Albany Theological Seminary, Philip Lindsley president of, 29
Newman, J. C., as president of Board of Health, 114
Nichol, Mrs. Josiah, 75
Normal school movement, 99-104; Dr. Lindsley's announcement to the public, 108-9
Normal schools, influence of, 102
Numismatic and Antiquarian Society of Philadelphia, 19-20

OGDEN, Dr., Dr. Lindsley's trip with, 16-17
Ohio University, Philip Lindsley offered presidency of, 23
Olympic Theatre, Nashville, 132
O'Neill, Peggy, and Mrs. Lindsley, 2
Owen, Lieutenant Colonel Richard, 50, 52, 60
Ozone, effect of on public health, 147-48

PARISH, Professor Consider, 25
Parmantier, Professor Nicholas S., 25
Parton, James, *Life of Andrew Jackson*, 2
Patton, Jacob H., tutor, 26
Payne, Dr. W. H., on Dr. Lindsley, 112
Peabody, George, 40, 103, 104, 111

INDEX 239

Peabody College. See George Peabody College for Teachers
Peabody Education Fund, 59, 83, 85, 95, 99, 103, 105, 108, 111
Peabody Normal College, 19, 85, 86, 112
Pearl, Elbridge G., tutor, 26
Pennsylvania, University of, 8, 10; Philip Lindsley offered presidency of, 23, 157
Pentremites, Garden of, 17-18
Pepper, Dr. Wm., letter of concerning Dr. Lindsley, 8
Pestalozzi, 90; Dr. Lindsley on methods of, 137
Philipps, J. T., 90
Pillans, 90
Pim, Dr., 65, 67
Plato, 91
Plunkett, J. D., 114, 116, 142, 144, 146
Polk, James K., death of during epidemic, 154
Pope, Charles R., letter to J. B. Lindsley, 197
Porter, Governor James D., 107, 109
Porter, Dr. Robert M., 27, 33, 35, 43
Priestly, Dr. James, 23
Princeton University, 2-3; Philip Lindsley offered presidency of, 23, 24
Proceedings of the Peabody Education Fund, 104 n, 105, 110, 111-12
Prussia, public instruction in, 96
Public education, 84 ff.
Public health, 113 ff.
Public hygiene, 122, 134
Purinton, A. L., resolution on death of J. B. Lindsley, 203-4

RAVENSCROFT College, 28
Record of readings found in J. B. Lindsley's diary, 1842-63, 209-28
Report to the Nashville Board of Trade, 1871, Dr. Lindsley on education in, 93
Resolutions on death of J. B. Lindsley, 203-6
Roberts, Dr. Deering J., on Dr. Lindsley's contribution to education, 162; *Southern Practitioner*, 84
Robertson, James, 22
Robertson Association, purpose of, 78
Robinson, Dr., Dr. Lindsley's visit to, 17
Robinson Crusoe, 6
Roosevelt, Theodore, letter to J. B. Lindsley, 198-99
Root, Captain J. W., 80
Rothrock, William, tutor, 26

Royal Botanical Gardens, Dr. Lindsley's visit to, 40, 104
Royal Historical Society, England, Dr. Lindsley a member of, 19
Rutledge, Mrs. Henry M., as tutor of Dr. Lindsley, 8

SAFFORD, Dr. James M., 117, 142, 145
St. Hilaire, Geoffrey, 181
St. John's Hospital, 39
Sampson, Dominie, 200
Sarrey, 180
Saxony, 96
"Scavenger boss," in Nashville, 130
Schelling, 91
Scott, Dr., 41
Sears, Barnas, 85, 96, 105-6, 107, 109, 111, 112
Sears, Julia A., letter to Louise G. Lindsley, 200-1
Secession, attitude of Dr. Lindsley towards, 60, 63-64; Robert E. Lee on, 61
Sewage disposal problem, 126-32 *passim*
Sforza, Francesco, 188
Shelley, Mrs., 185
Sheridan, Philip, 75
Sherman, General William Tecumseh, 79
"Sidewalk Issue," attitude of Dr. Lindsley towards, 129
Smallpox, 132; Dr. Lindsley on, 132-33, 154, 156
Smith, 144
Smith, Carlos G., tutor, 26
Smith, General E. Kirby, 54, 95; Dr. Lindsley on, 57
Socrates, 91
Sorbonne, 180
South Carolina, and secession, 61
Southern Practitioner, 1, 42, 113, 157, 159
Sowers, Alfred A., tutor, 25
State preventive medicine, 155-56, 160
State Teachers' Association, organized, 89
Stearns, Dr. Eben S., 111; on Dr. Lindsley, 112
Stephens, Professor Abednego, 9, 26
Stevens, Sir James, 97
Stevens, Moses B., Dr. Lindsley on, 77
Stewart, Professor Alexander P., 25, 42
Stout, M., 181
Straight, Colonel, at Nashville, 81
Swift, Jonathan, quoted, 74

TANAQUIL, 90
Tarbox, L. G., 108

INDEX

Taylor, Dr., Dr. Lindsley on, 71
Taylor, Governor, and health board, 152
Tennessee, University of, medical department, *Sixth Annual Announcement*, 159-60
Tennessee College of Pharmacy, Dr. Lindsley one of organizers of, 86
Tennessee Historical Society, Dr. Lindsley a member of, 20
Tennessee State Board of Health, resolution on death of J. B. Lindsley, 205
Tennessee State Board of Health, *Bulletin*, 21, 148-57 *passim; First Report*, 1880, 142-45; *Second Report*, 1884, 145-46
Tennessee State Medical Association, Dr. Lindsley active in, 160
Tennessee State Medical Society, 134, 141
Tennessee State Penitentiary, 126
Tennessee State Teachers' Association, 84, 87-88, 96; organization meeting, 87-89
Tennessee, University of, *Sixth Annual Announcement of the Medical Department, etc.*, quoted, 159-60
Thackeray, Wm. M., 97
Thirty Years' War, attitude of Dr. Lindsley towards, 76
Thomas, Dr., 70
Thomas, General, Dr. Lindsley's interview with, 73-74
Thomson, Professor John, 25
"Thoughts and Hints." *See* Lindsley, John Berrien
Thornton, G. B., 206
Toullier, 190
Transylvania University, Philip Lindsley offered presidency of, 23
Trimble School, 135
Troost, Dr. Gerard, 9, 11, 25, 27; Dr. Lindsley's geological tour with, 14-15
Trousdale, Leon, letter of, 98

UNION University, 29
Universities. *See names of states*
University of Nashville. *See* Nashville, University of

VACCINATION, 132; Dr. Lindsley on, 122-23, 154
Valenciennes, 181
Velpeau, 180
Venable, M. C., on birth of Dr. Lindsley, 6
Villeplait, Professor Alexander S., 25

Vital statistics, 150, 151; of Nashville, 117, 118-19, 133, 134

WADSWORTH, Dr. Edward, 42
Walker, William, 68; death of, 8; letters to J. B. Lindsley, of, 11-12, 178-92
Warner, Mrs. Percy (Margaret Lawrence Lindsley), 21
Warr, Otis S., cited, 158, 160-61
Washington, George, at home of Judge Berrien, 1-2; Philip Lindsley on, 4-5; and George Peabody compared, 103
Washington College, Lexington, Va., 51
Watson, Gladys. *See* Altstetter, Mabel
Watson, James A., tutor, 26
Watson, Dr. John M., 33, 35, 43
Watson, S., 108
Wells, B. W., letter to J. B. Lindsley, 199-200
Western Military Institute, 45, 49-53, 56, 85-86
Wheeler, General Joseph, 199
White, Dr. Robert H., cited, 86
Wight, Dr. D. F., 145-46
Wight, Dr. E. M., 142
Wilcox, Captain, Dr. Lindsley on, 79
Wilderspin, Samuel, 90
Wilson Spring Branch, 126
Winchell, Alexander, 125
Windrow, J. E., cited, 66
Winston, Dr. Charles K., 33, 35, 43, 47, 79
Winston, R. W., letter from, 98
Winthrop, Robert C., 105; letter of Dr. Lindsley to, 111-12
Wirt College, 28
Wistar, Dr., 178
Woods, James, 43
Worcester, J. E., letter to J. B. Lindsley, 195
Wurtz, Charles Adolphe, 40
Wyman, Walter, letter to J. B. Lindsley, 200

YANDELL, Dr. D. W., 16, 33, 67, 83; Dr. Lindsley's letter to, 69-70
Yellow fever, 19, 113, 124-25, 140-41, 144, 146, 150-52 *passim*, 154, 155, 156, 191

ZOLLICOFFER, General Felix K., 64

www.ingramcontent.com/pod-product-compliance
Lightning Source LLC
Chambersburg PA
CBHW021122300426
44113CB00006B/246